MW00785127

THE CREEP

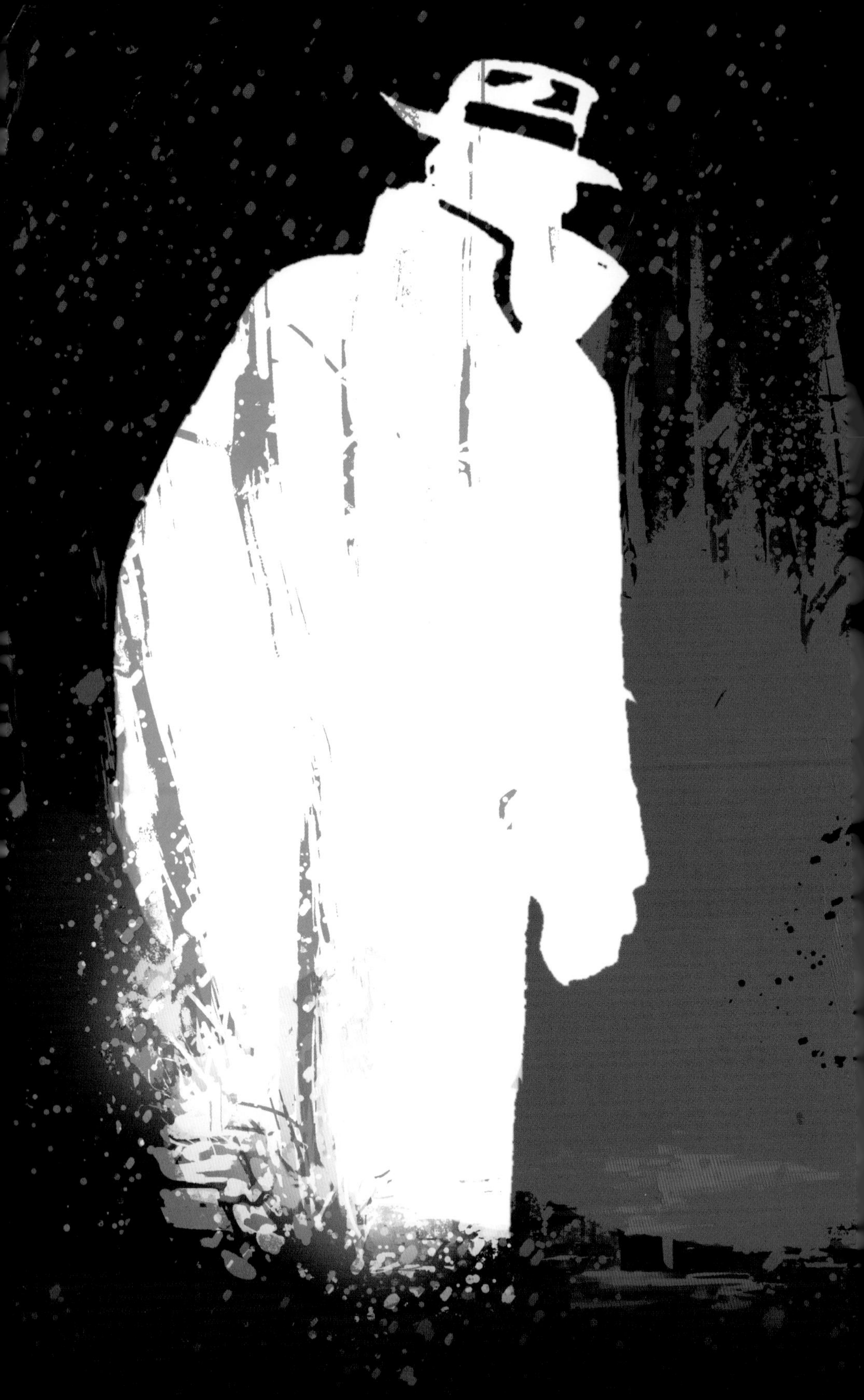

THE CREEP

WRITTEN BY John Arcudi
ILLUSTRATED BY Jonathan Case
LETTERED BY Nate Piekos of Blambot®
COVER BY Tonci Zonjic

CHAPTER ONE TITLE ART BY Frank Miller
CHAPTER TWO TITLE ART BY Mike Mignola with Dave Stewart
CHAPTER THREE TITLE ART BY Ryan Sook
CHAPTER FOUR TITLE ART BY Tonci Zonjic
CHAPTER FIVE TITLE ART BY Jonathan Case

DARK HORSE BOOKS

EDITORS Scott Allie and Daniel Chabon
ASSISTANT EDITOR Shantel LaRocque
DESIGNER Adam Grano
PUBLISHER Mike Richardson

Mike Richardson, President and Publisher | Neil Hankerson, Executive Vice
President | Tom Weddle, Chief Financial Officer | Randy Stradley, Vice President
of Publishing | Michael Martens, Vice President of Book Trade Sales | Anita Nelson,
Vice President of Business Affairs | Scott Allie, Editor in Chief | Matt Parkinson,
Vice President of Marketing | David Scroggy, Vice President of Product Development
| Dale LaFountain, Vice President of Information Technology | Darlene Vogel,
Senior Director of Print, Design, and Production | Ken Lizzi, General Counsel |
Davey Estrada, Editorial Director | Chris Warner, Senior Books Editor | Diana
Schutz, Executive Editor | Cary Grazzini, Director of Print and Development | Lia
Ribacchi, Art Director | Cara Niece, Director of Scheduling | Tim Wiesch, Director
of International Licensing | Mark Bernardi, Director of Digital Publishing

Published by
Dark Horse Books
A division of Dark Horse Comics, Inc.
10956 SE Main Street
Milwaukie, OR 97222

First edition: April 2013
ISBN 978-1-61655-061-5

10 9 8 7 6 5 4 3 2 1
Printed in China

The Creep™ & © 2012, 2013 John Arcudi. All rights reserved. Dark Horse Books®
and the Dark Horse logo are registered trademarks of Dark Horse Comics, Inc. All
rights reserved. No portion of this publication may be reproduced or transmitted,
in any form or by any means, without the express written permission of Dark Horse
Comics, Inc. Names, characters, places, and incidents featured in this publication
either are the product of the author's imagination or are used fictitiously. Any
resemblance to actual persons (living or dead), events, institutions, or locales,
without satiric intent, is coincidental.

This book collects *The Creep* #0–#4, previously published by Dark Horse Comics.

— CHAPTER ONE —

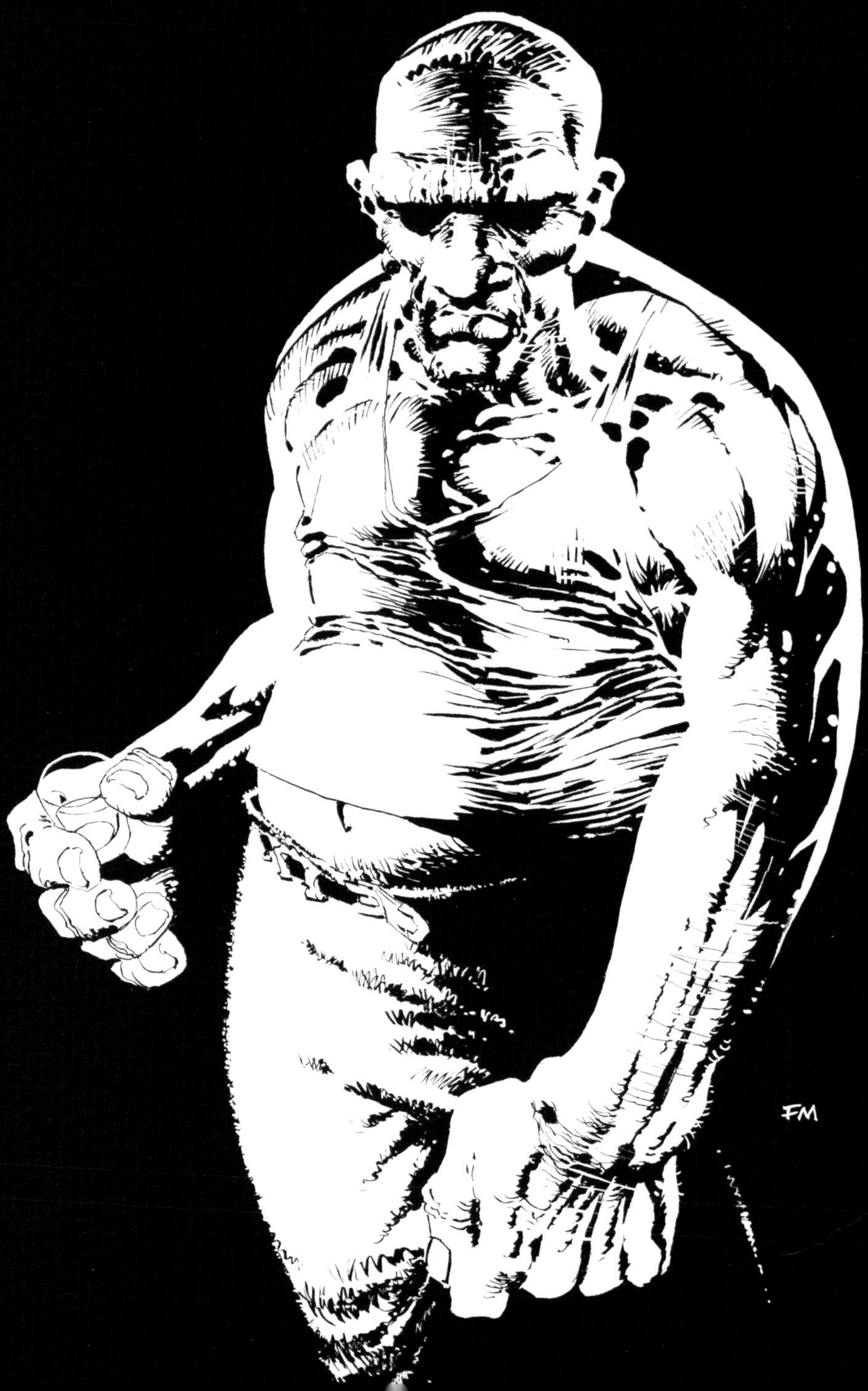
FM

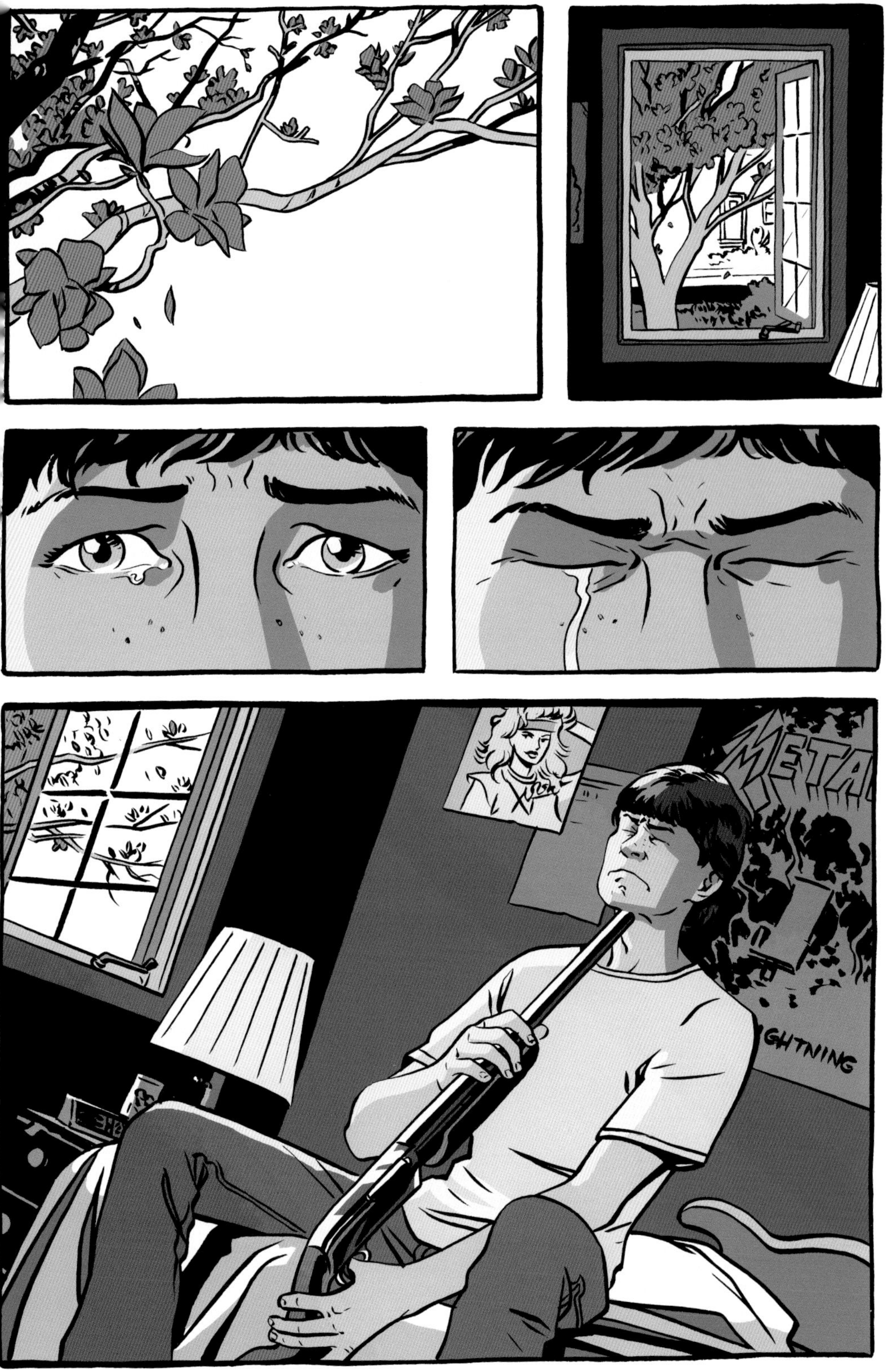
META
GHTNING

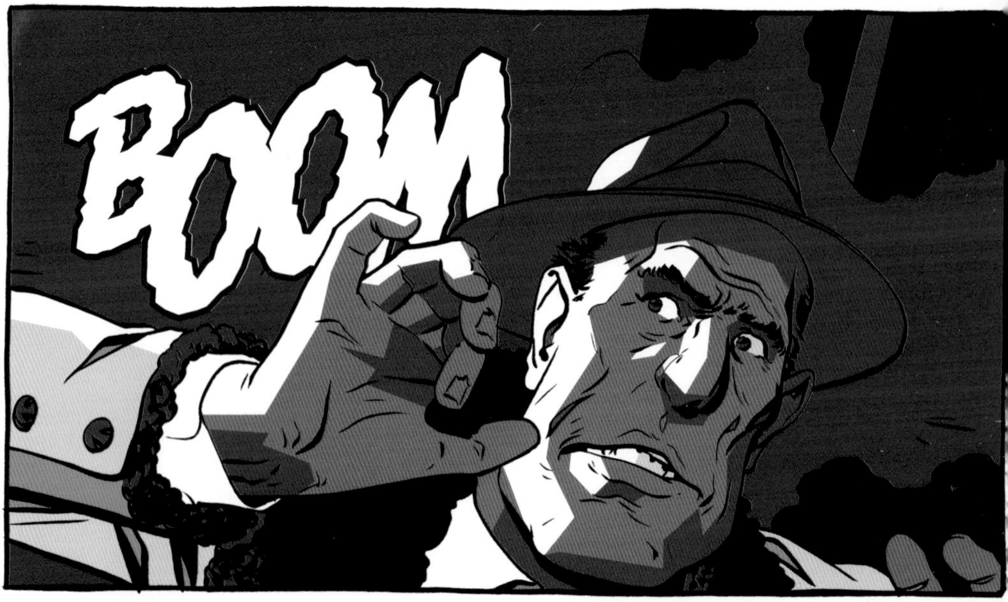
BOOM

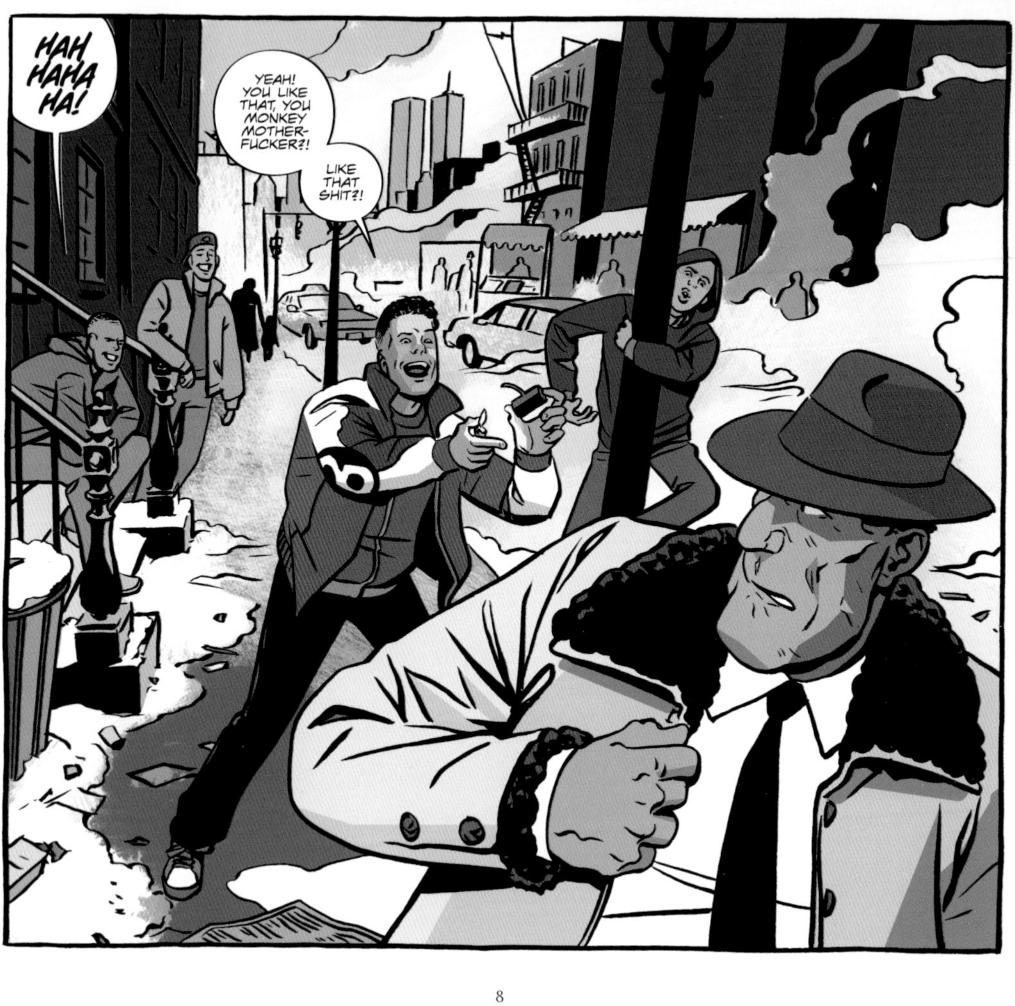
HAH HAHA HA!
YEAH! YOU LIKE THAT, YOU MONKEY MOTHER-FUCKER?!
LIKE THAT SHIT?!

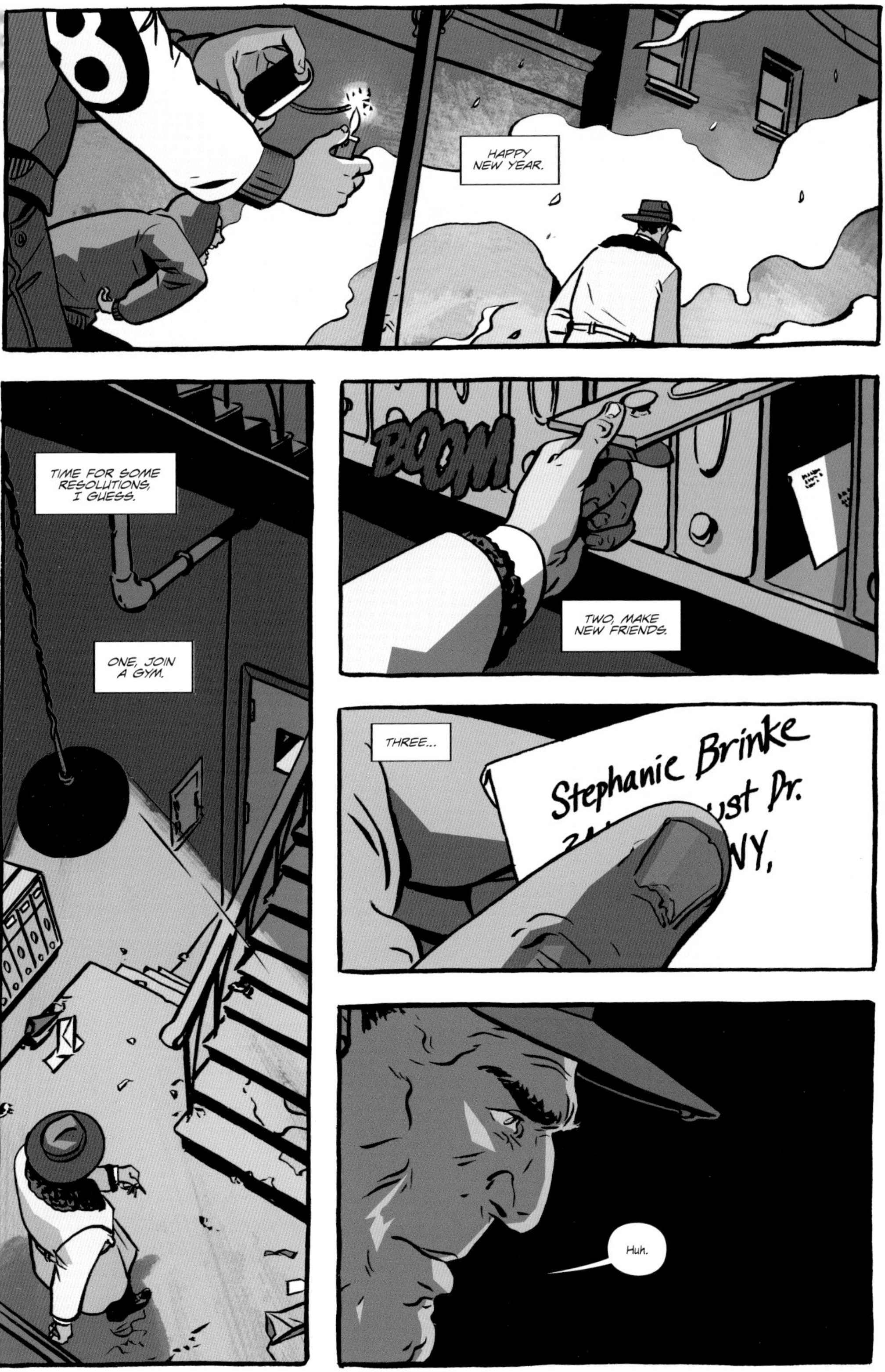
HAPPY NEW YEAR.
TIME FOR SOME RESOLUTIONS, I GUESS.
ONE, JOIN A GYM.
BOOM
TWO, MAKE NEW FRIENDS.
THREE...
Stephanie Brinke
Huh.

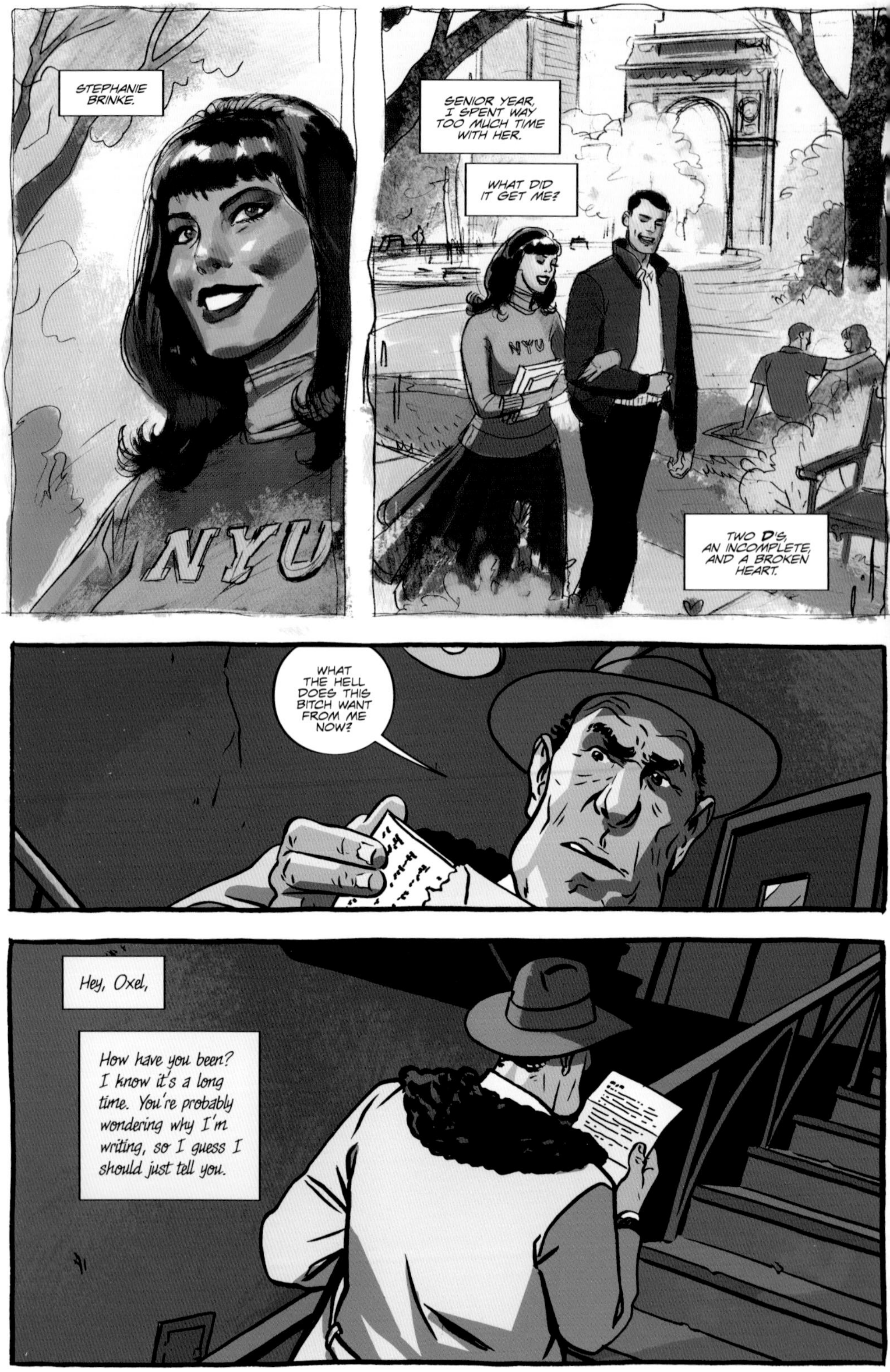
STEPHANIE BRINKE.
SENIOR YEAR, I SPENT WAY TOO MUCH TIME WITH HER.
WHAT DID IT GET ME?
NYU
TWO D'S, AN INCOMPLETE, AND A BROKEN HEART.
WHAT THE HELL DOES THIS BITCH WANT FROM ME NOW?
Hey, Oxel,
How have you been? I know it's a long time. You're probably wondering why I'm writing, so I guess I should just tell you.

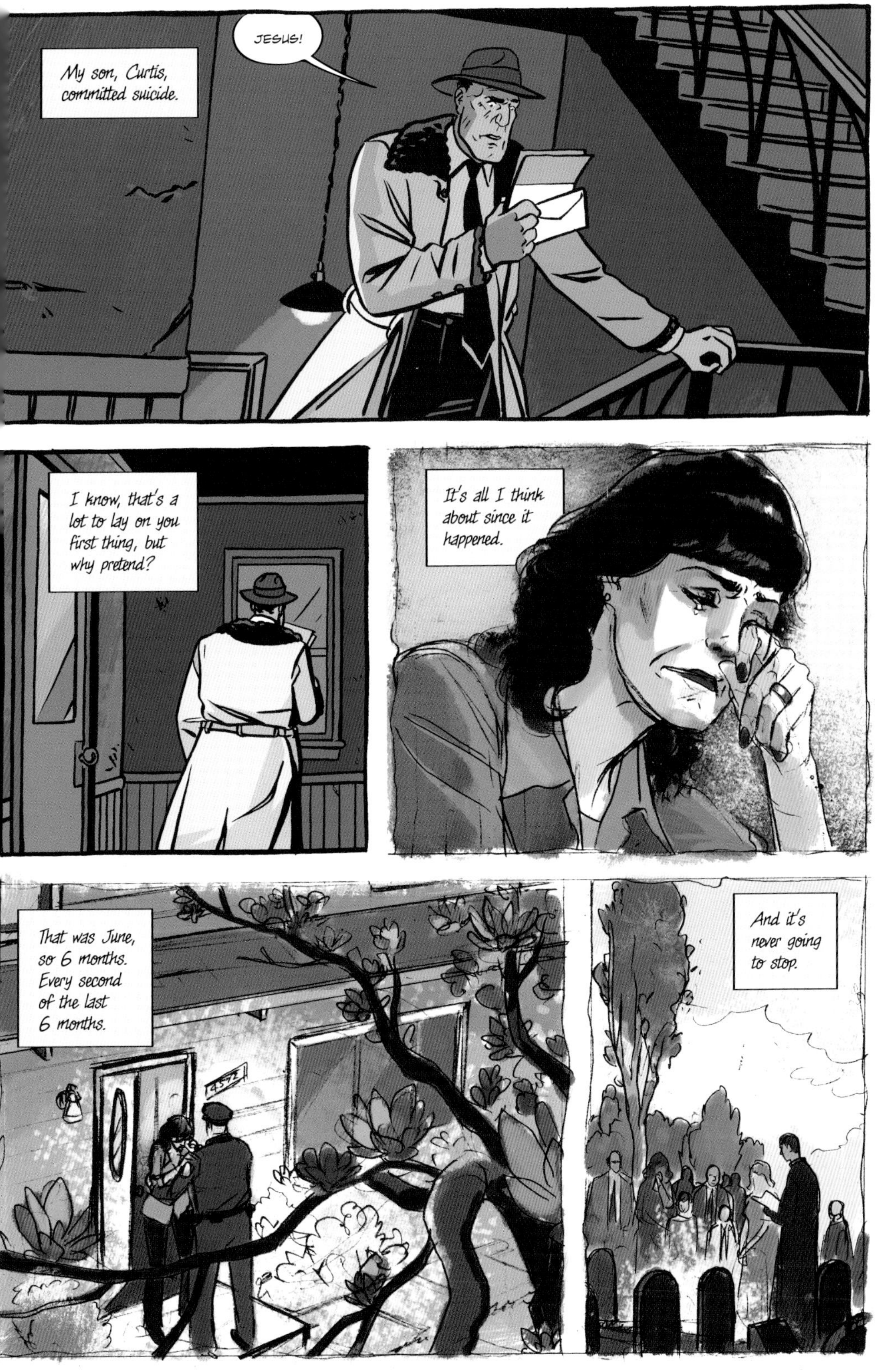
My son, Curtis, committed suicide.
JESUS!
I know, that's a lot to lay on you first thing, but why pretend?
It's all I think about since it happened.
That was June, so 6 months. Every second of the last 6 months.
And it's never going to stop.

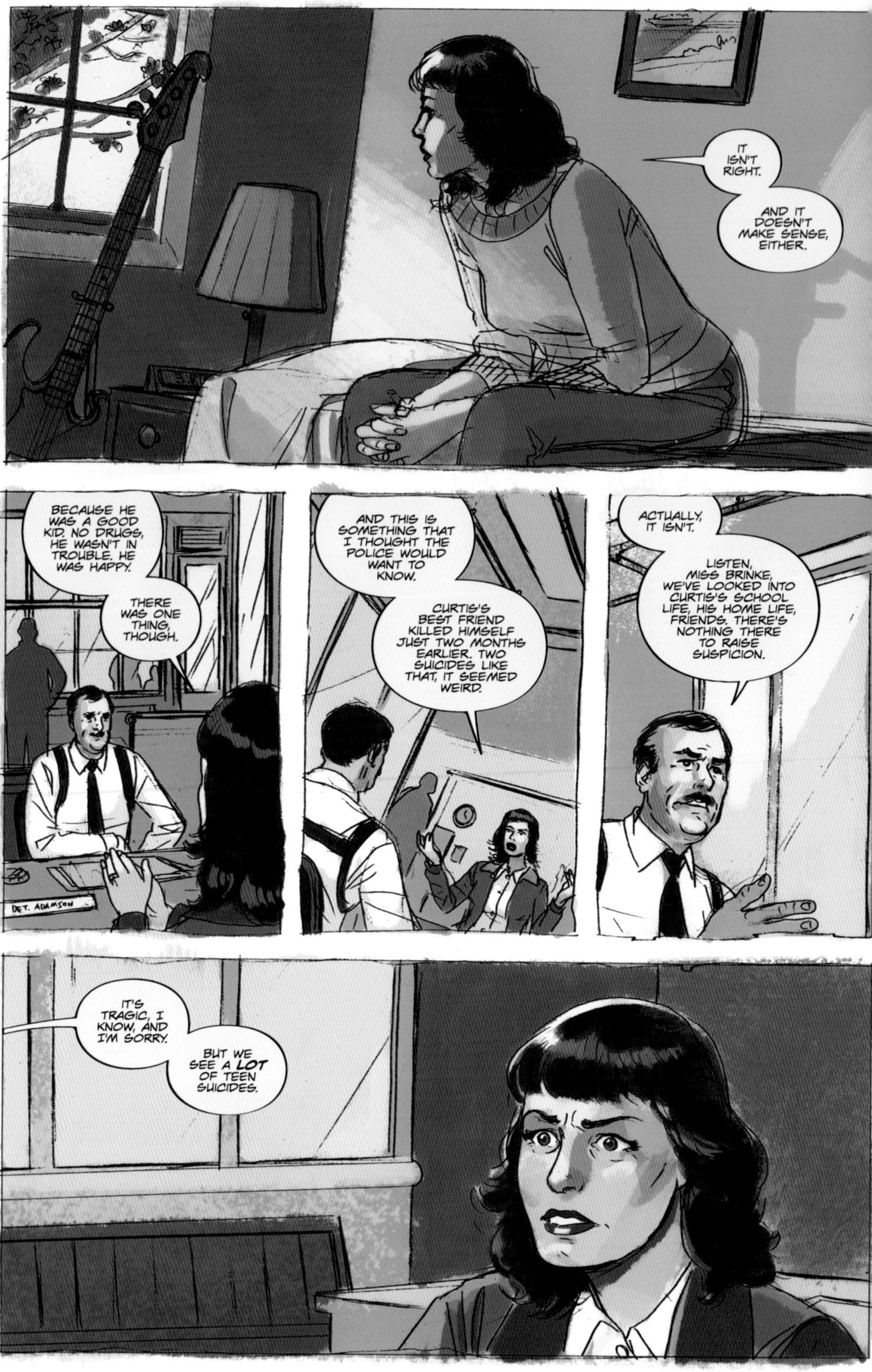
IT ISN'T RIGHT.
AND IT DOESN'T MAKE SENSE, EITHER.
BECAUSE HE WAS A GOOD KID. NO DRUGS, HE WASN'T IN TROUBLE. HE WAS HAPPY.
THERE WAS ONE THING, THOUGH.
DET. ADAMSON
AND THIS IS SOMETHING THAT I THOUGHT THE POLICE WOULD WANT TO KNOW.
CURTIS'S BEST FRIEND KILLED HIMSELF JUST TWO MONTHS EARLIER. TWO SUICIDES LIKE THAT, IT SEEMED WEIRD.
ACTUALLY, IT ISN'T.
LISTEN, MISS BRINKE, WE'VE LOOKED INTO CURTIS'S SCHOOL LIFE, HIS HOME LIFE, FRIENDS. THERE'S NOTHING THERE TO RAISE SUSPICION.
IT'S TRAGIC, I KNOW, AND I'M SORRY.
BUT WE SEE A LOT OF TEEN SUICIDES.

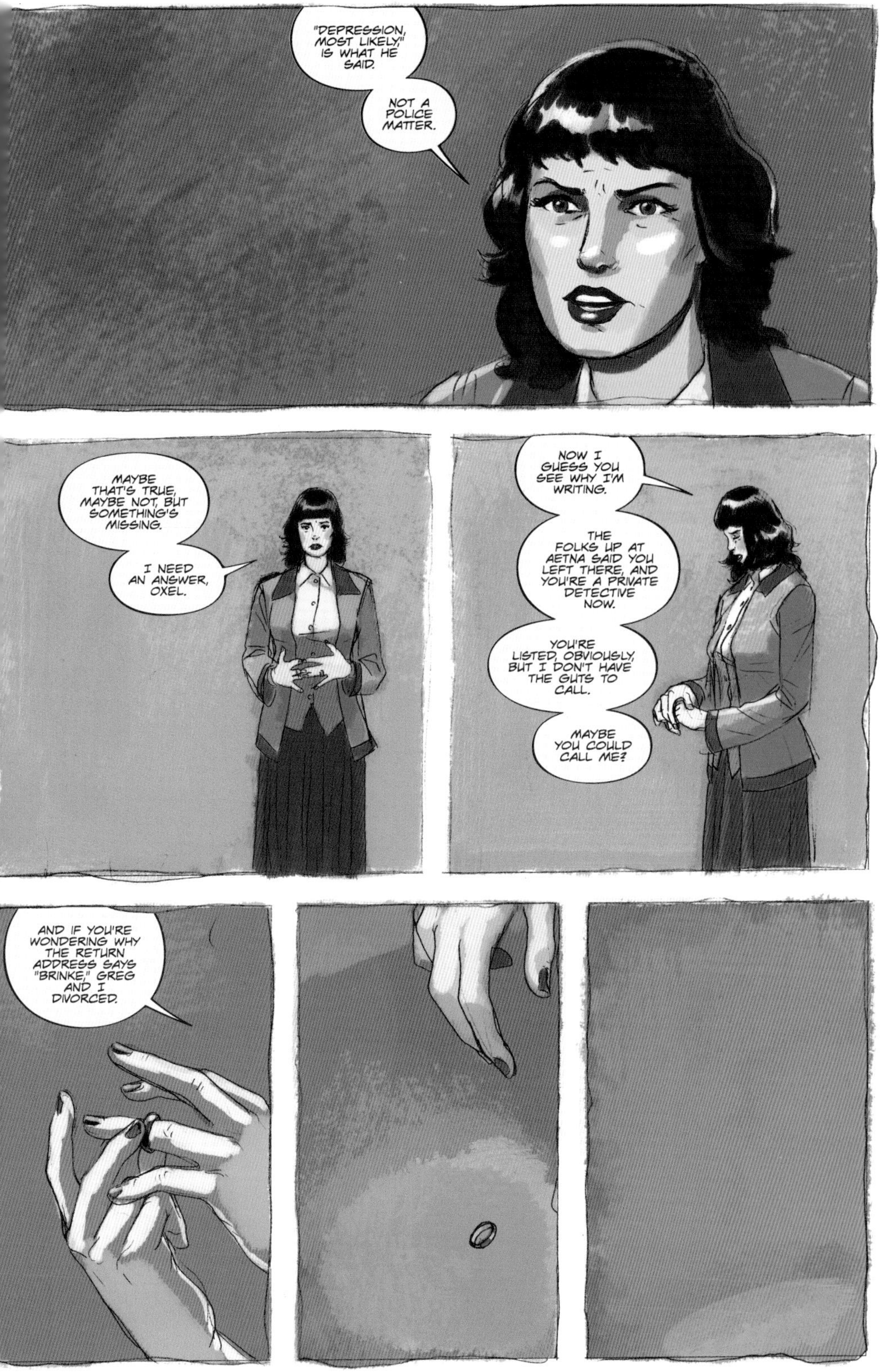
"DEPRESSION, MOST LIKELY," IS WHAT HE SAID.
NOT A POLICE MATTER.
MAYBE THAT'S TRUE, MAYBE NOT, BUT SOMETHING'S MISSING.
I NEED AN ANSWER, OXEL.
NOW I GUESS YOU SEE WHY I'M WRITING.
THE FOLKS UP AT AETNA SAID YOU LEFT THERE, AND YOU'RE A PRIVATE DETECTIVE NOW.
YOU'RE LISTED, OBVIOUSLY, BUT I DON'T HAVE THE GUTS TO CALL.
MAYBE YOU COULD CALL ME?
AND IF YOU'RE WONDERING WHY THE RETURN ADDRESS SAYS "BRINKE," GREG AND I DIVORCED.

I'm sorry, Oxel.

OXEL KARNHUS INVESTIGATIONS

I'm sorry how I treated you, I'm sorry after twenty years I'm finally writing only because I want something.

I'm sorry to disturb your life.

THREE, PAY PHONE BILL.

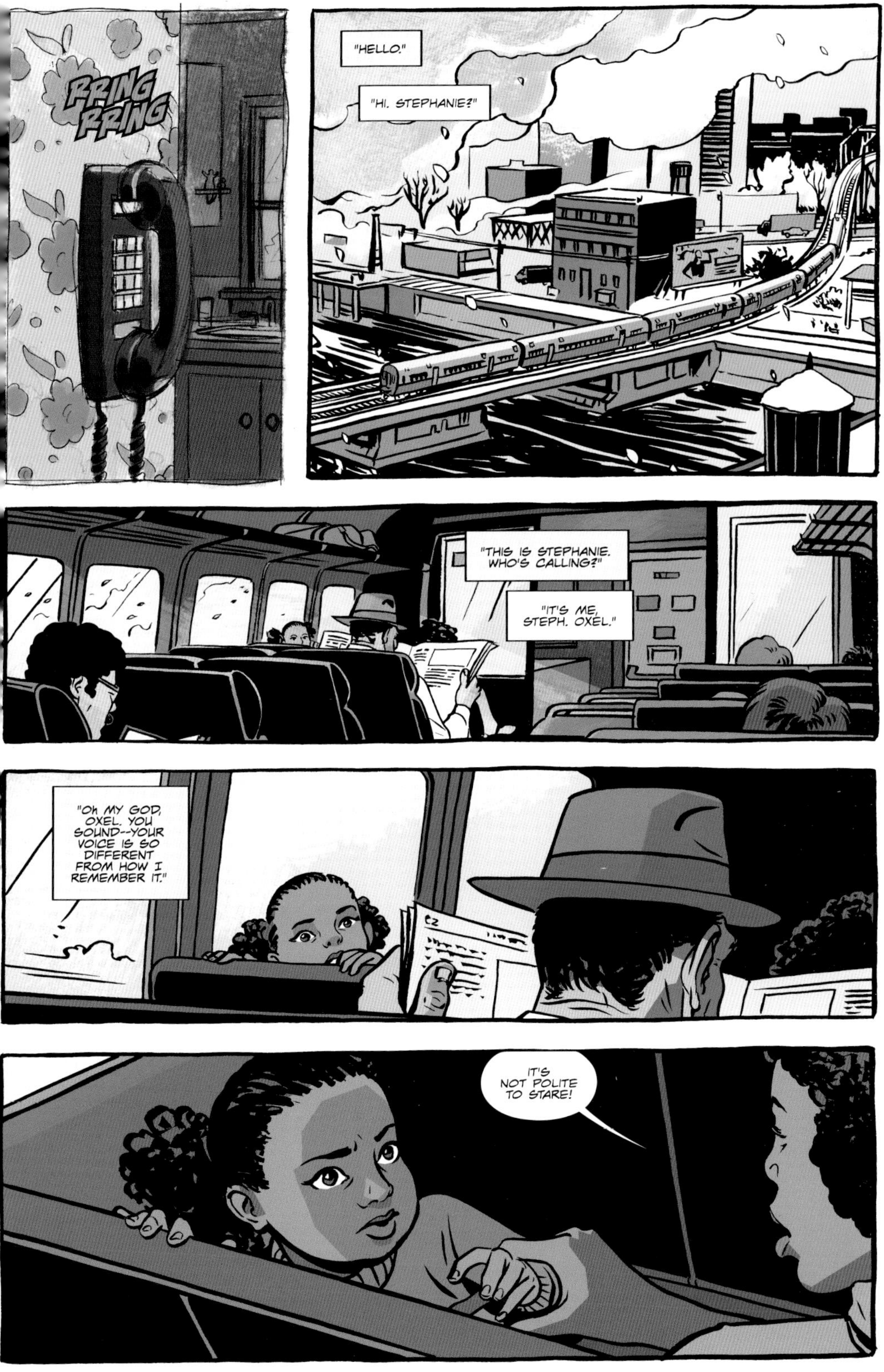
RRING RRING
"HELLO."
"HI. STEPHANIE?"
"THIS IS STEPHANIE. WHO'S CALLING?"
"IT'S ME, STEPH. OXEL."
"Oh MY GOD, OXEL. YOU SOUND--YOUR VOICE IS SO DIFFERENT FROM HOW I REMEMBER IT."
IT'S NOT POLITE TO STARE!

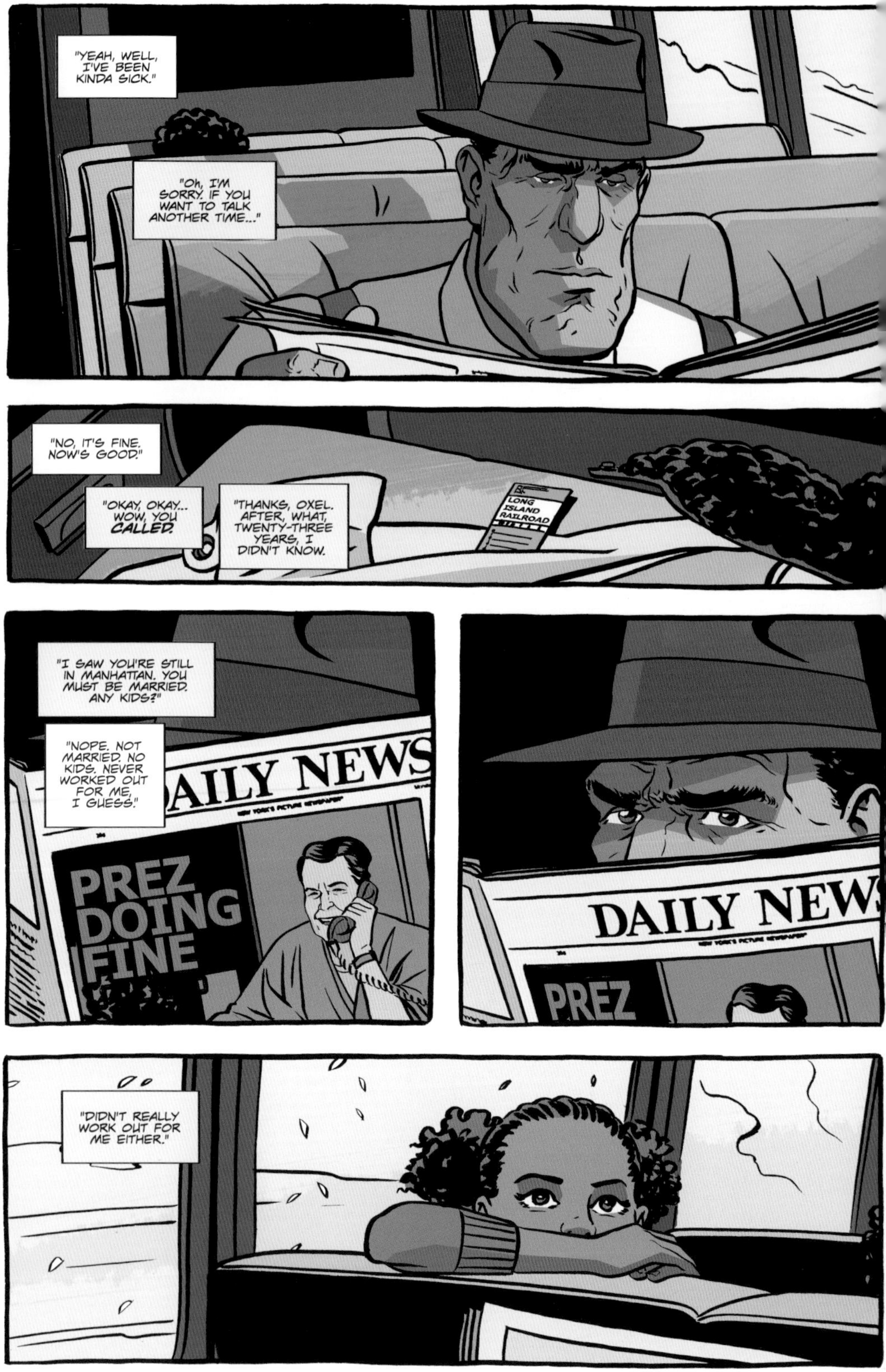
"YEAH, WELL, I'VE BEEN KINDA SICK."
"Oh, I'M SORRY. IF YOU WANT TO TALK ANOTHER TIME..."
"NO, IT'S FINE. NOW'S GOOD."
"OKAY, OKAY... WOW, YOU CALLED."
"THANKS, OXEL. AFTER, WHAT, TWENTY-THREE YEARS, I DIDN'T KNOW.
LONG ISLAND RAILROAD
"I SAW YOU'RE STILL IN MANHATTAN. YOU MUST BE MARRIED. ANY KIDS?"
"NOPE. NOT MARRIED. NO KIDS. NEVER WORKED OUT FOR ME, I GUESS."
DAILY NEWS
NEW YORK'S PICTURE NEWSPAPER
PREZ DOING FINE
DAILY NEWS
NEW YORK'S PICTURE NEWSPAPER
PREZ
"DIDN'T REALLY WORK OUT FOR ME EITHER."

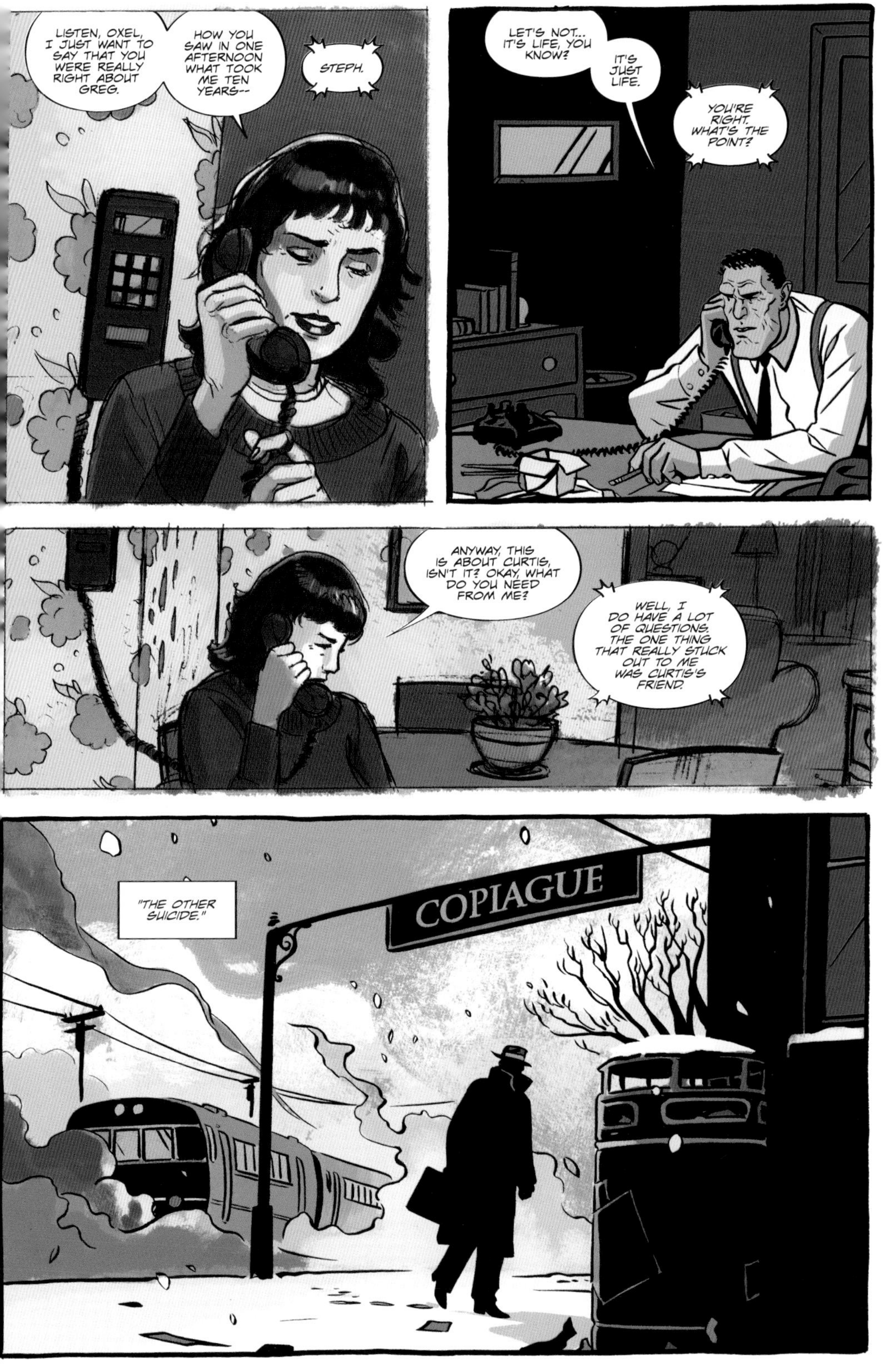
LISTEN, OXEL, I JUST WANT TO SAY THAT YOU WERE REALLY RIGHT ABOUT GREG.
HOW YOU SAW IN ONE AFTERNOON WHAT TOOK ME TEN YEARS--
STEPH.
LET'S NOT... IT'S LIFE, YOU KNOW?
IT'S JUST LIFE.
YOU'RE RIGHT. WHAT'S THE POINT?
ANYWAY, THIS IS ABOUT CURTIS, ISN'T IT? OKAY, WHAT DO YOU NEED FROM ME?
WELL, I DO HAVE A LOT OF QUESTIONS. THE ONE THING THAT REALLY STUCK OUT TO ME WAS CURTIS'S FRIEND.
"THE OTHER SUICIDE."
COPIAGUE

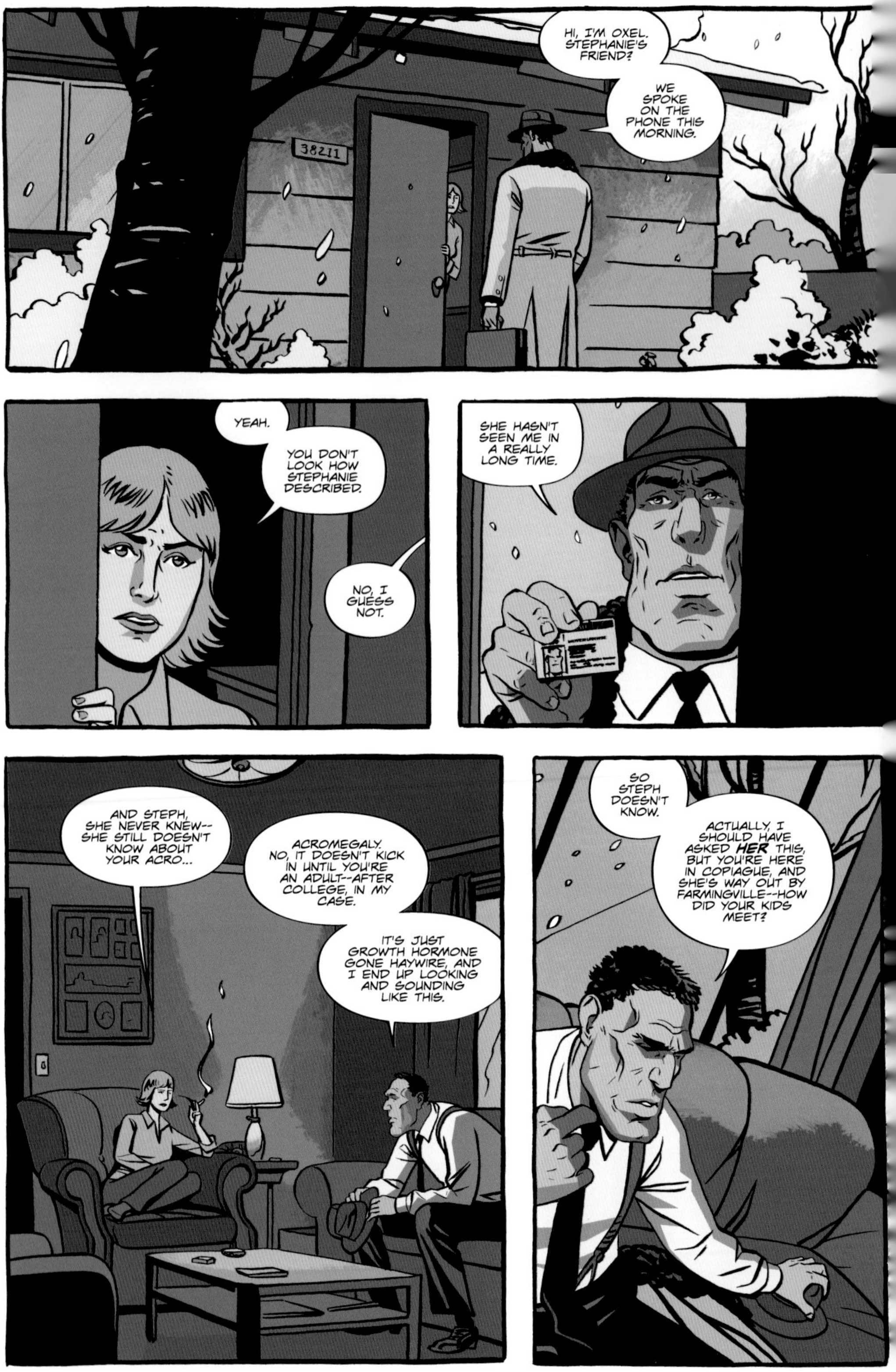
HI, I'M OXEL. STEPHANIE'S FRIEND?
WE SPOKE ON THE PHONE THIS MORNING.
38211
YEAH.
YOU DON'T LOOK HOW STEPHANIE DESCRIBED.
NO, I GUESS NOT.
SHE HASN'T SEEN ME IN A REALLY LONG TIME.
AND STEPH, SHE NEVER KNEW-- SHE STILL DOESN'T KNOW ABOUT YOUR ACRO...
ACROMEGALY. NO, IT DOESN'T KICK IN UNTIL YOU'RE AN ADULT--AFTER COLLEGE, IN MY CASE.
IT'S JUST GROWTH HORMONE GONE HAYWIRE, AND I END UP LOOKING AND SOUNDING LIKE THIS.
SO STEPH DOESN'T KNOW.
ACTUALLY, I SHOULD HAVE ASKED **HER** THIS, BUT YOU'RE HERE IN COPIAGUE, AND SHE'S WAY OUT BY FARMINGVILLE--HOW DID YOUR KIDS MEET?

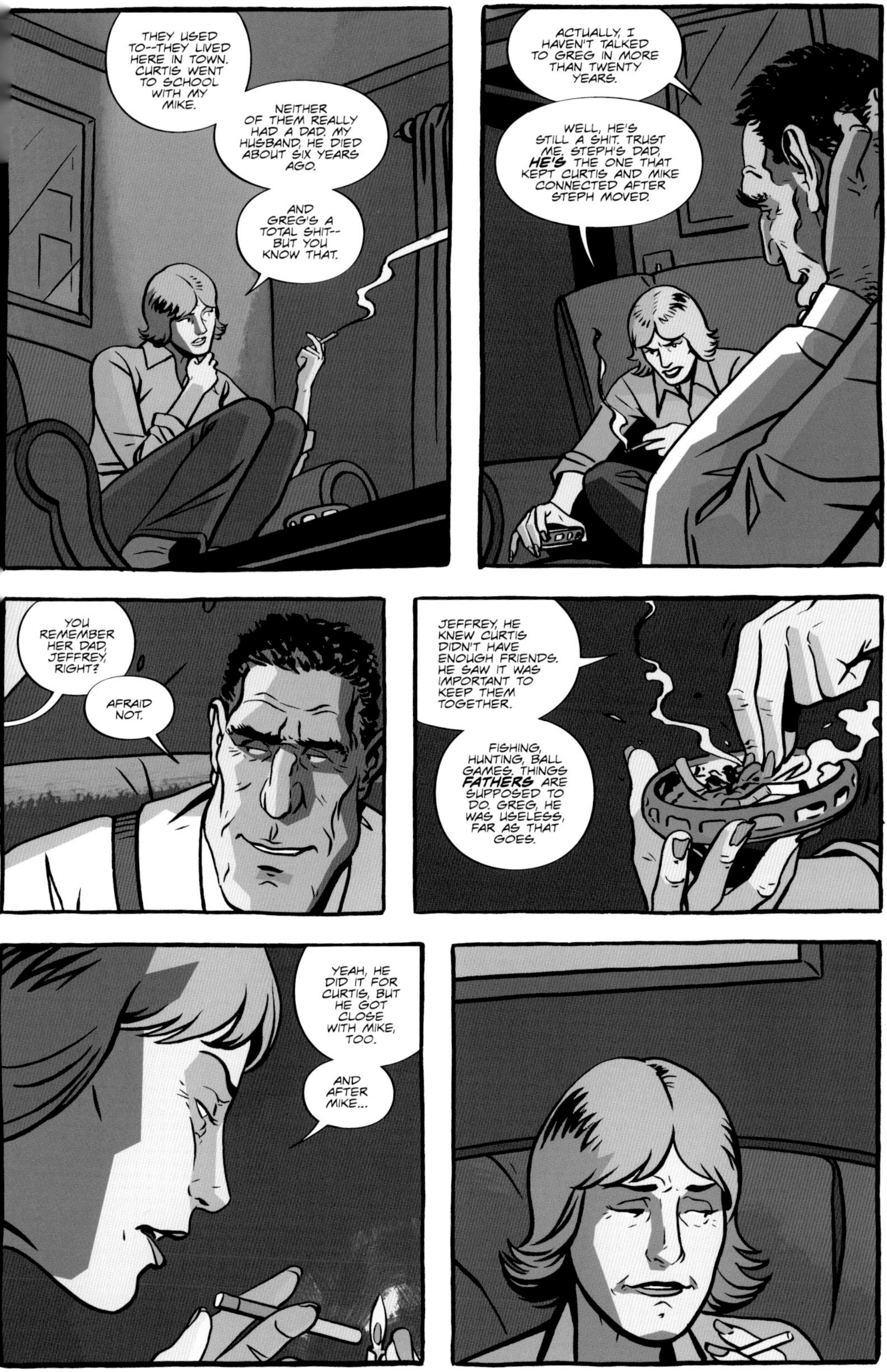
THEY USED TO--THEY LIVED HERE IN TOWN. CURTIS WENT TO SCHOOL WITH MY MIKE.
NEITHER OF THEM REALLY HAD A DAD. MY HUSBAND, HE DIED ABOUT SIX YEARS AGO.
AND GREG'S A TOTAL SHIT-- BUT YOU KNOW THAT.
ACTUALLY, I HAVEN'T TALKED TO GREG IN MORE THAN TWENTY YEARS.
WELL, HE'S STILL A SHIT. TRUST ME. STEPH'S DAD, HE'S THE ONE THAT KEPT CURTIS AND MIKE CONNECTED AFTER STEPH MOVED.
YOU REMEMBER HER DAD, JEFFREY, RIGHT?
AFRAID NOT.
JEFFREY, HE KNEW CURTIS DIDN'T HAVE ENOUGH FRIENDS. HE SAW IT WAS IMPORTANT TO KEEP THEM TOGETHER.
FISHING, HUNTING, BALL GAMES. THINGS FATHERS ARE SUPPOSED TO DO. GREG, HE WAS USELESS, FAR AS THAT GOES.
YEAH, HE DID IT FOR CURTIS, BUT HE GOT CLOSE WITH MIKE, TOO.
AND AFTER MIKE...

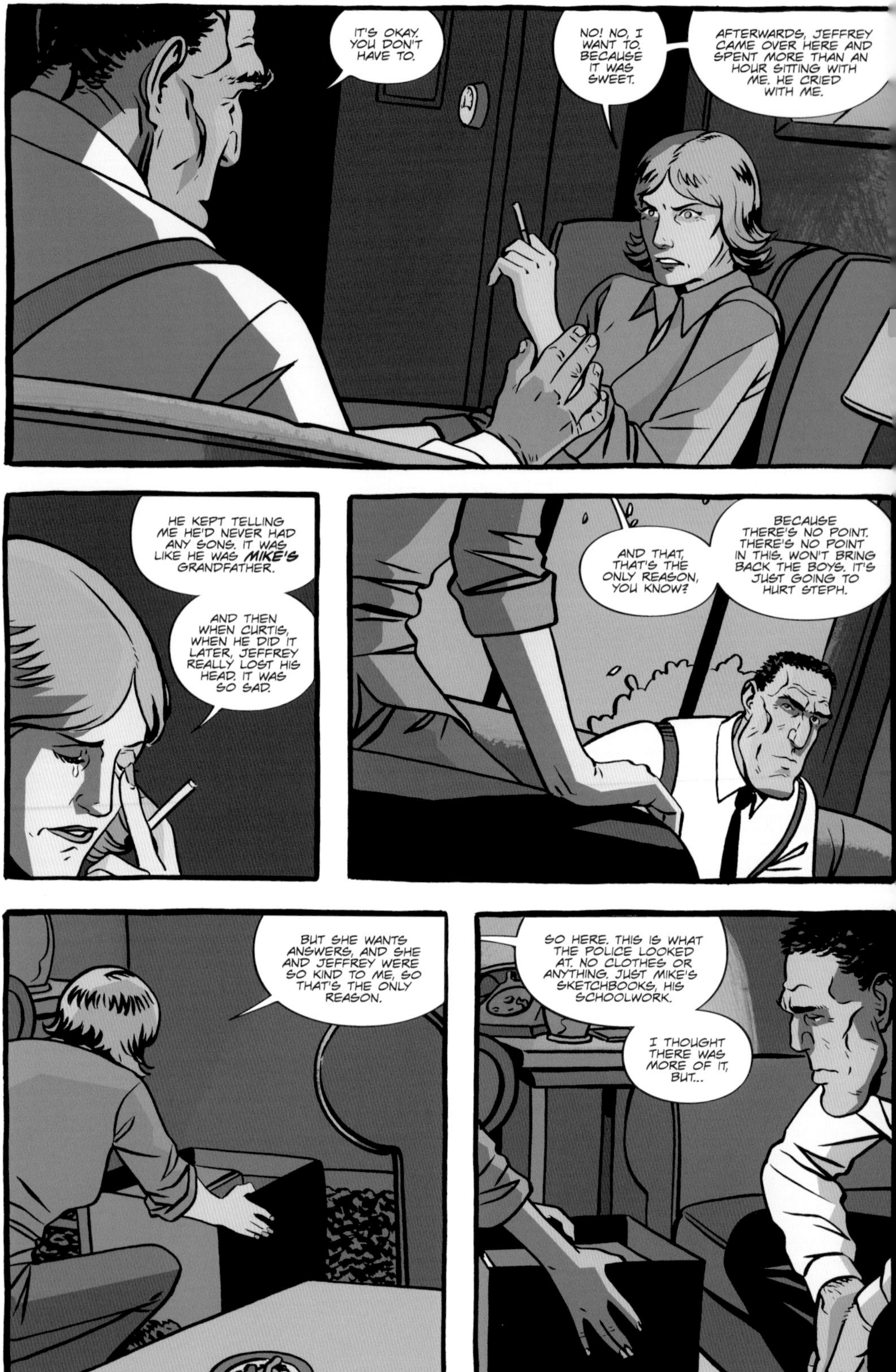
IT'S OKAY. YOU DON'T HAVE TO.
NO! NO, I WANT TO. BECAUSE IT WAS SWEET.
AFTERWARDS, JEFFREY CAME OVER HERE AND SPENT MORE THAN AN HOUR SITTING WITH ME. HE CRIED WITH ME.
HE KEPT TELLING ME HE'D NEVER HAD ANY SONS. IT WAS LIKE HE WAS MIKE'S GRANDFATHER.
AND THEN WHEN CURTIS, WHEN HE DID IT LATER, JEFFREY REALLY LOST HIS HEAD. IT WAS SO SAD.
AND THAT, THAT'S THE ONLY REASON, YOU KNOW?
BECAUSE THERE'S NO POINT. THERE'S NO POINT IN THIS. WON'T BRING BACK THE BOYS. IT'S JUST GOING TO HURT STEPH.
BUT SHE WANTS ANSWERS, AND SHE AND JEFFREY WERE SO KIND TO ME, SO THAT'S THE ONLY REASON.
SO HERE. THIS IS WHAT THE POLICE LOOKED AT. NO CLOTHES OR ANYTHING. JUST MIKE'S SKETCHBOOKS, HIS SCHOOLWORK.
I THOUGHT THERE WAS MORE OF IT, BUT...

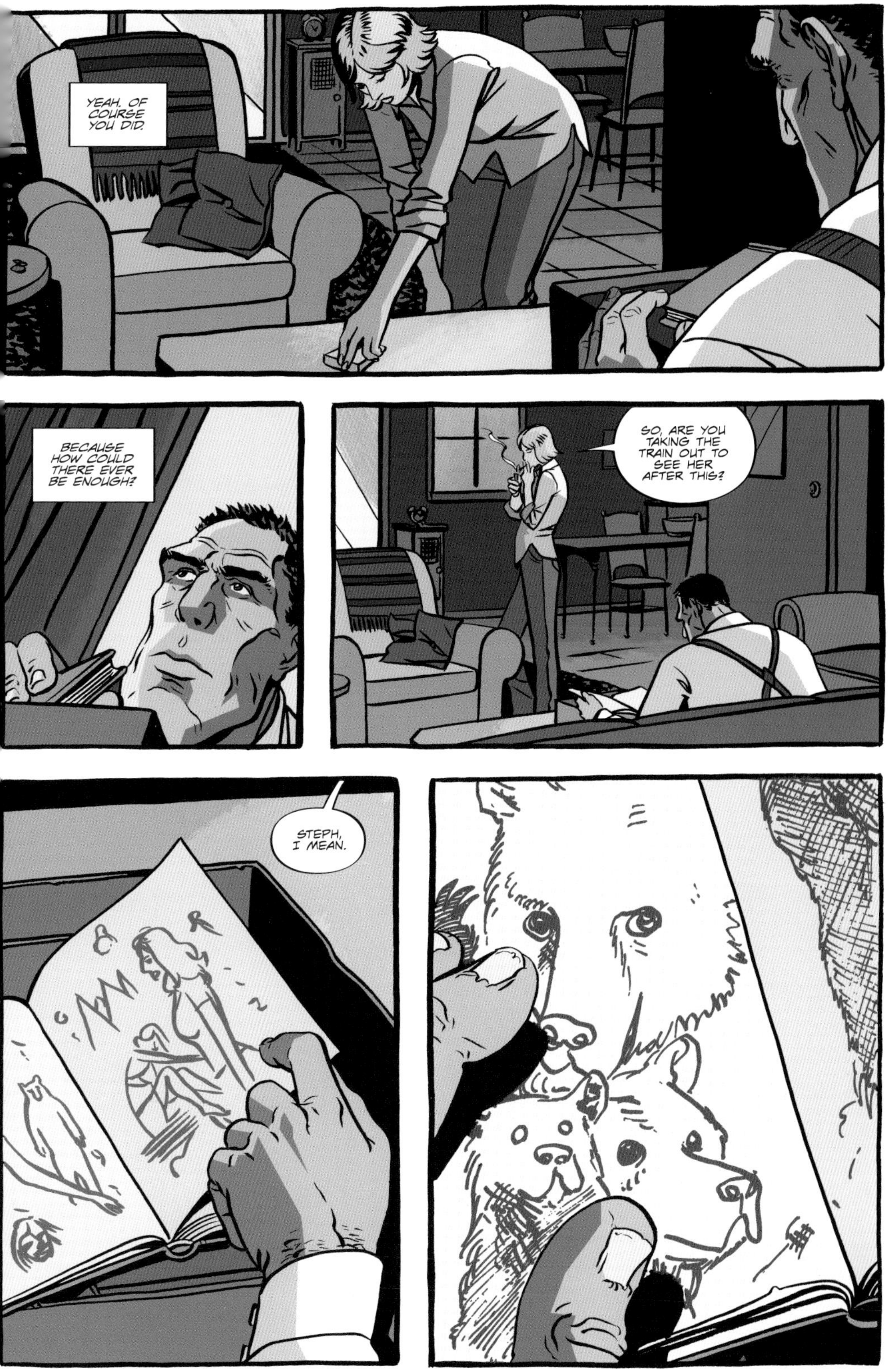
YEAH, OF COURSE YOU DID.
BECAUSE HOW COULD THERE EVER BE ENOUGH?
SO, ARE YOU TAKING THE TRAIN OUT TO SEE HER AFTER THIS?
STEPH, I MEAN.

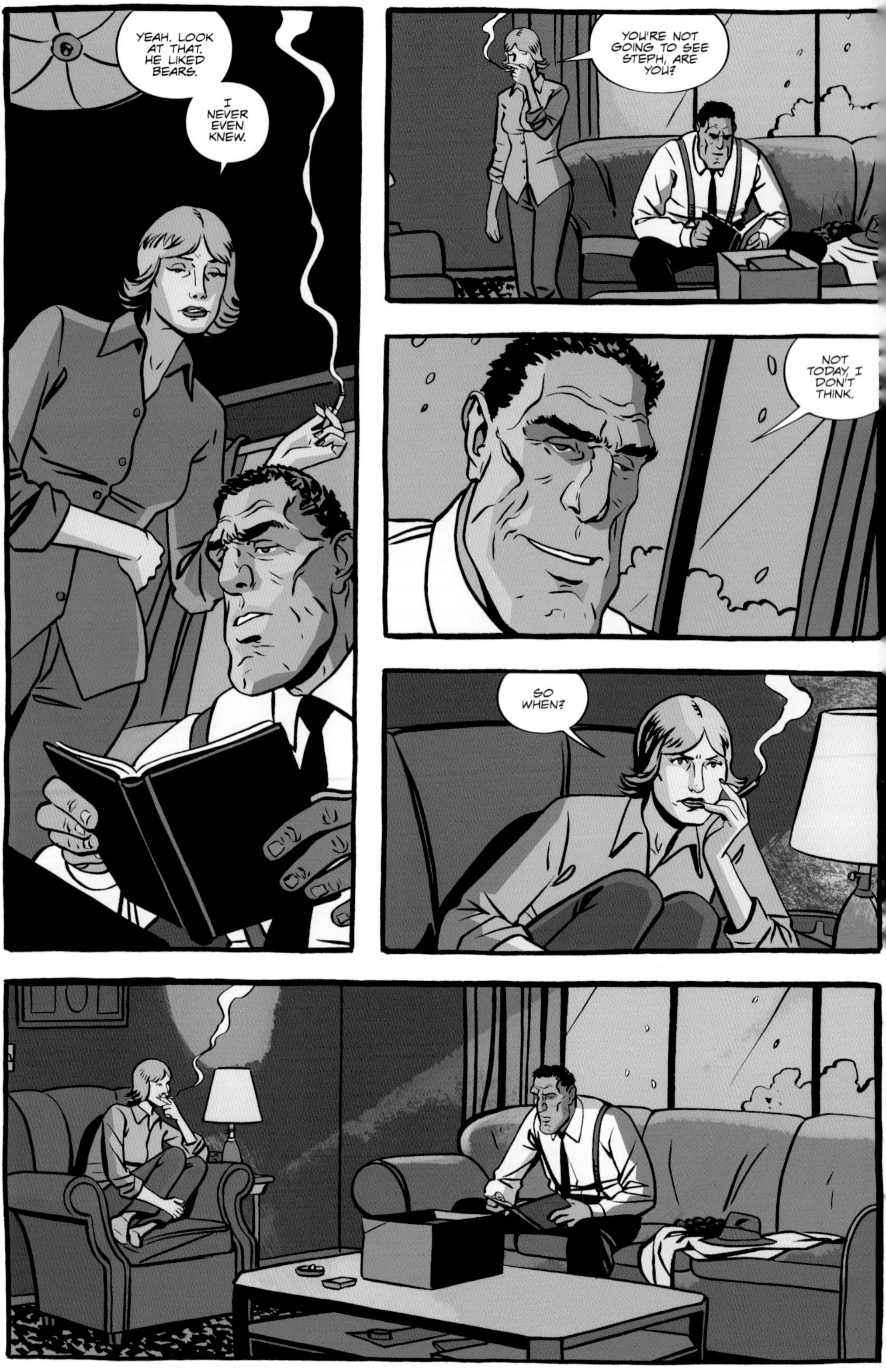
YEAH. LOOK AT THAT. HE LIKED BEARS.
I NEVER EVEN KNEW.
YOU'RE NOT GOING TO SEE STEPH, ARE YOU?
NOT TODAY, I DON'T THINK.
SO WHEN?

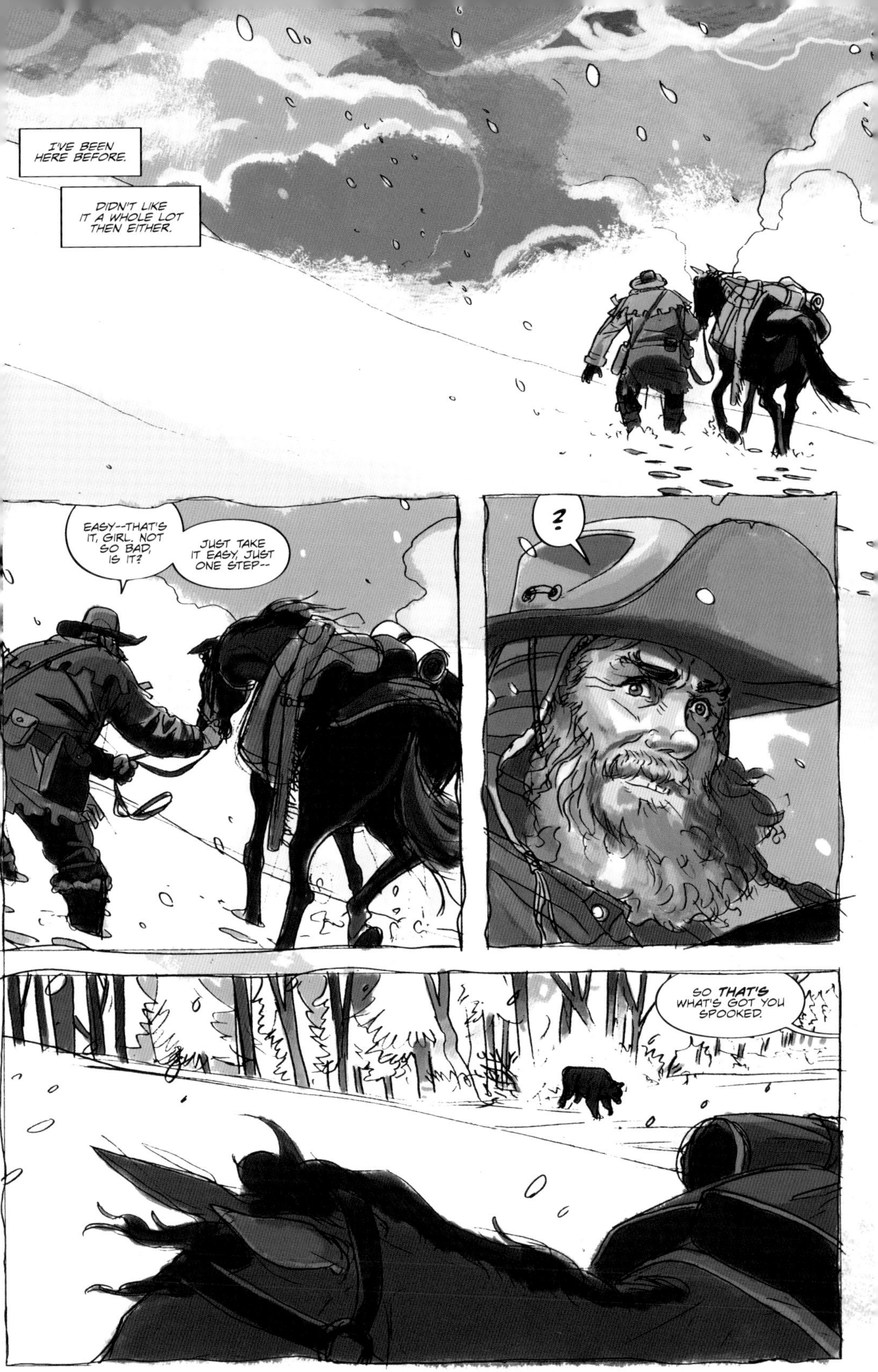
I'VE BEEN HERE BEFORE.
DIDN'T LIKE IT A WHOLE LOT THEN EITHER.
EASY--THAT'S IT, GIRL. NOT SO BAD, IS IT?
JUST TAKE IT EASY, JUST ONE STEP--
?
SO **THAT'S** WHAT'S GOT YOU SPOOKED.

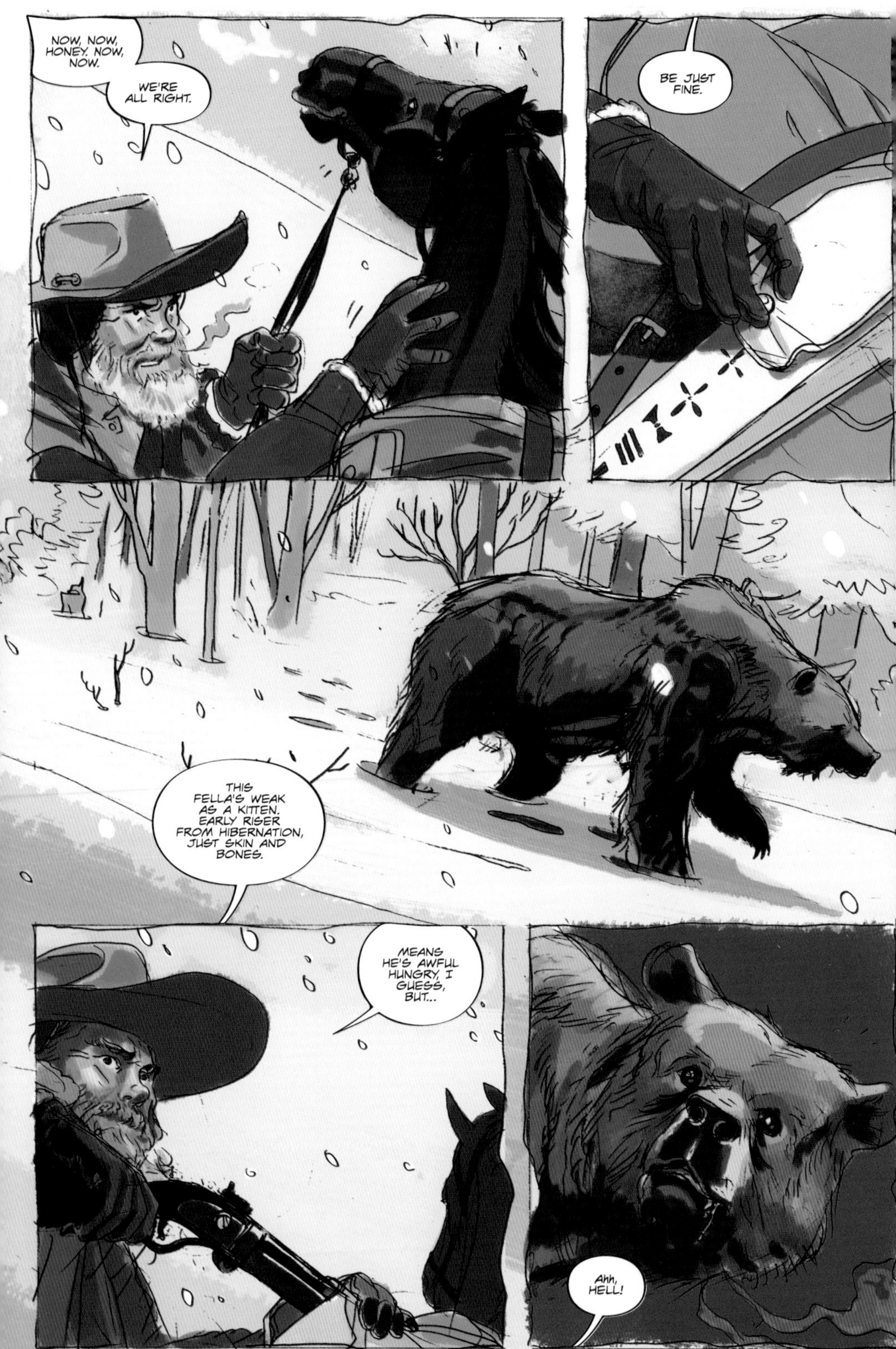
NOW, NOW, HONEY. NOW, NOW.
WE'RE ALL RIGHT.
BE JUST FINE.
THIS FELLA'S WEAK AS A KITTEN. EARLY RISER FROM HIBERNATION, JUST SKIN AND BONES.
MEANS HE'S AWFUL HUNGRY, I GUESS, BUT...
Ahh, HELL!

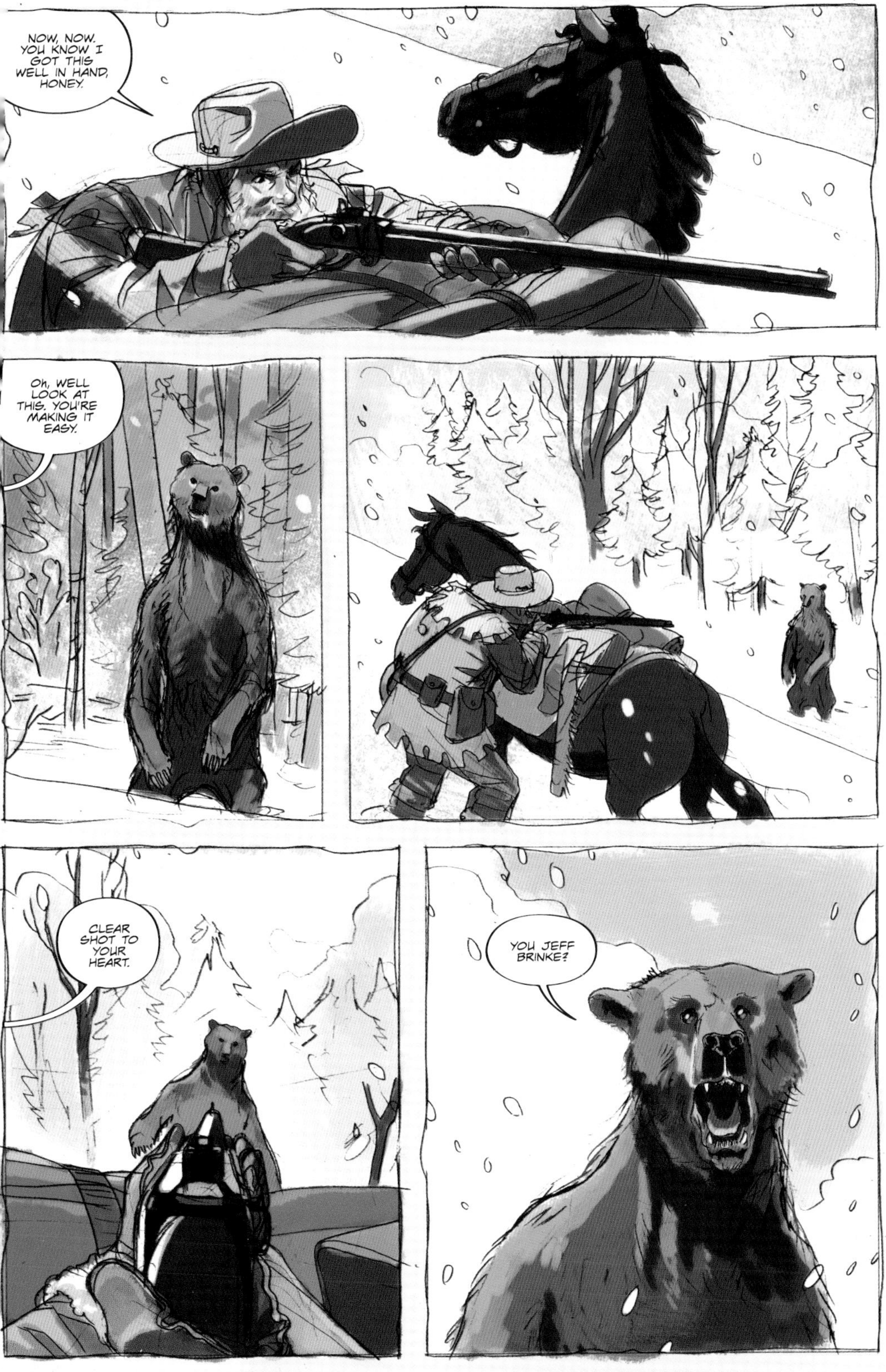
NOW, NOW. YOU KNOW I GOT THIS WELL IN HAND, HONEY.
Oh, WELL LOOK AT THIS. YOU'RE MAKING IT EASY.
CLEAR SHOT TO YOUR HEART.
YOU JEFF BRINKE?

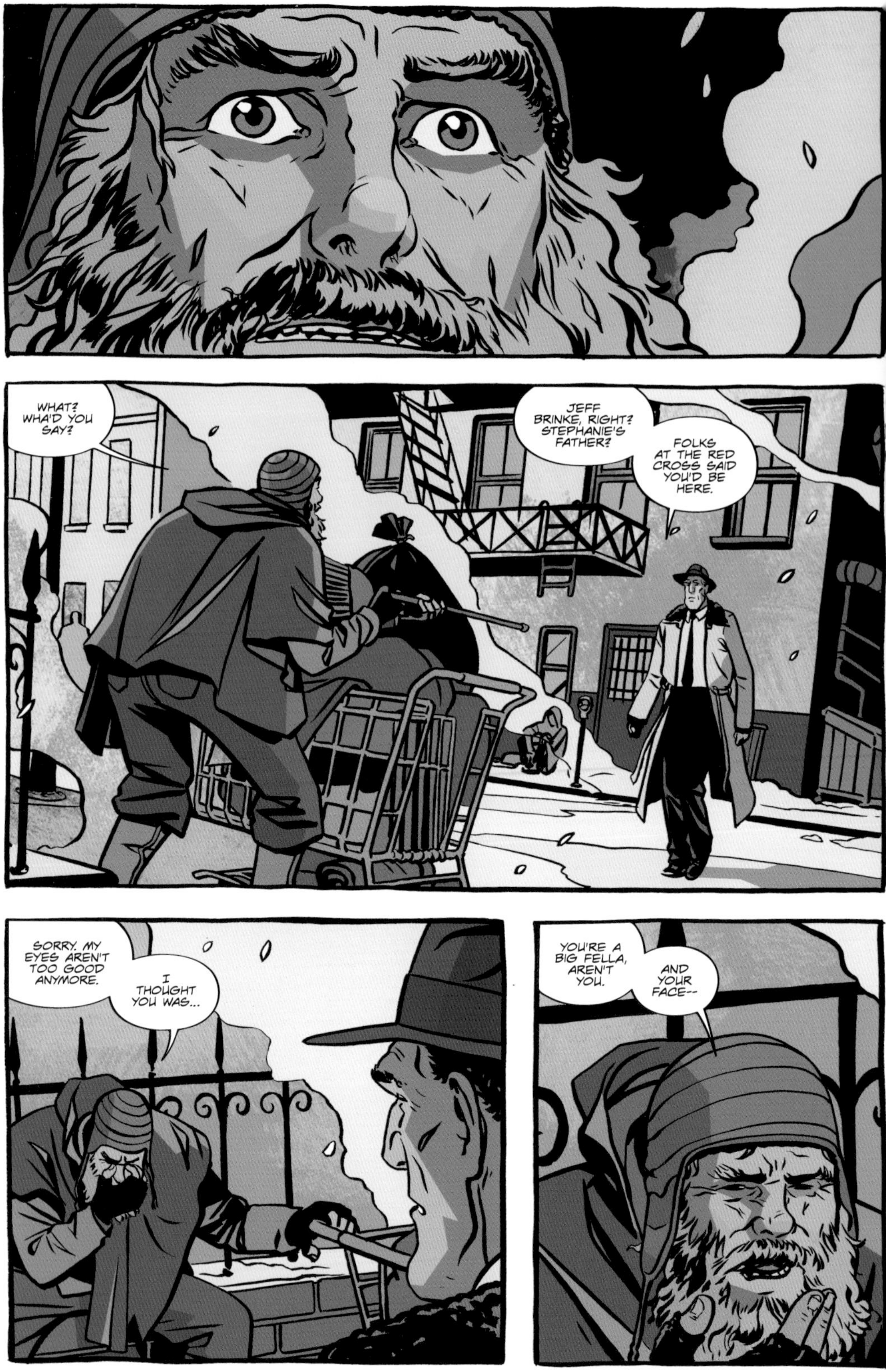

WHAT? WHA'D YOU SAY?
JEFF BRINKE, RIGHT? STEPHANIE'S FATHER?
FOLKS AT THE RED CROSS SAID YOU'D BE HERE.
SORRY. MY EYES AREN'T TOO GOOD ANYMORE.
I THOUGHT YOU WAS...
YOU'RE A BIG FELLA, AREN'T YOU.
AND YOUR FACE--

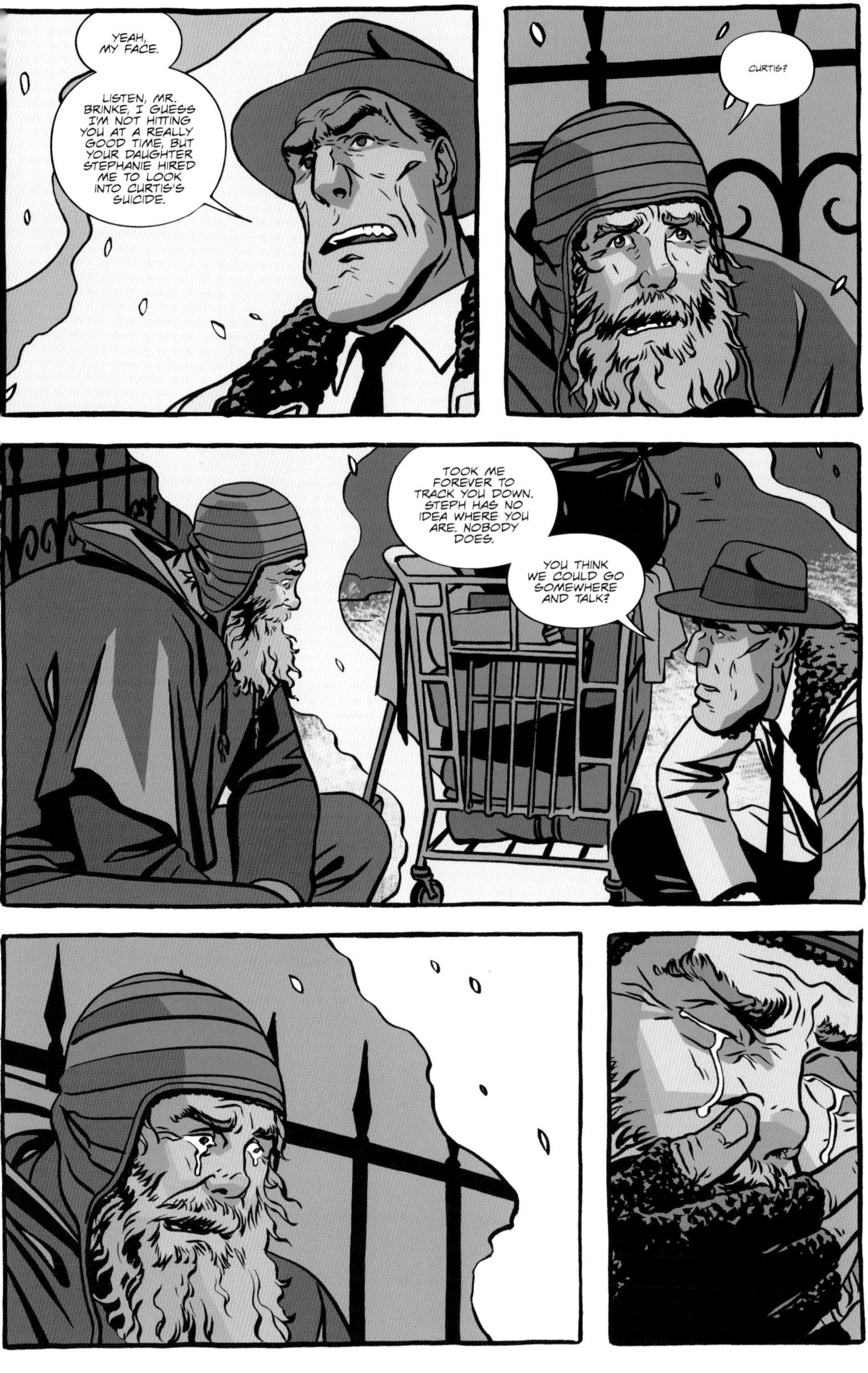
YEAH, MY FACE.
LISTEN, MR. BRINKE, I GUESS I'M NOT HITTING YOU AT A REALLY GOOD TIME, BUT YOUR DAUGHTER STEPHANIE HIRED ME TO LOOK INTO CURTIS'S SUICIDE.
CURTIS?
TOOK ME FOREVER TO TRACK YOU DOWN. STEPH HAS NO IDEA WHERE YOU ARE. NOBODY DOES.
YOU THINK WE COULD GO SOMEWHERE AND TALK?

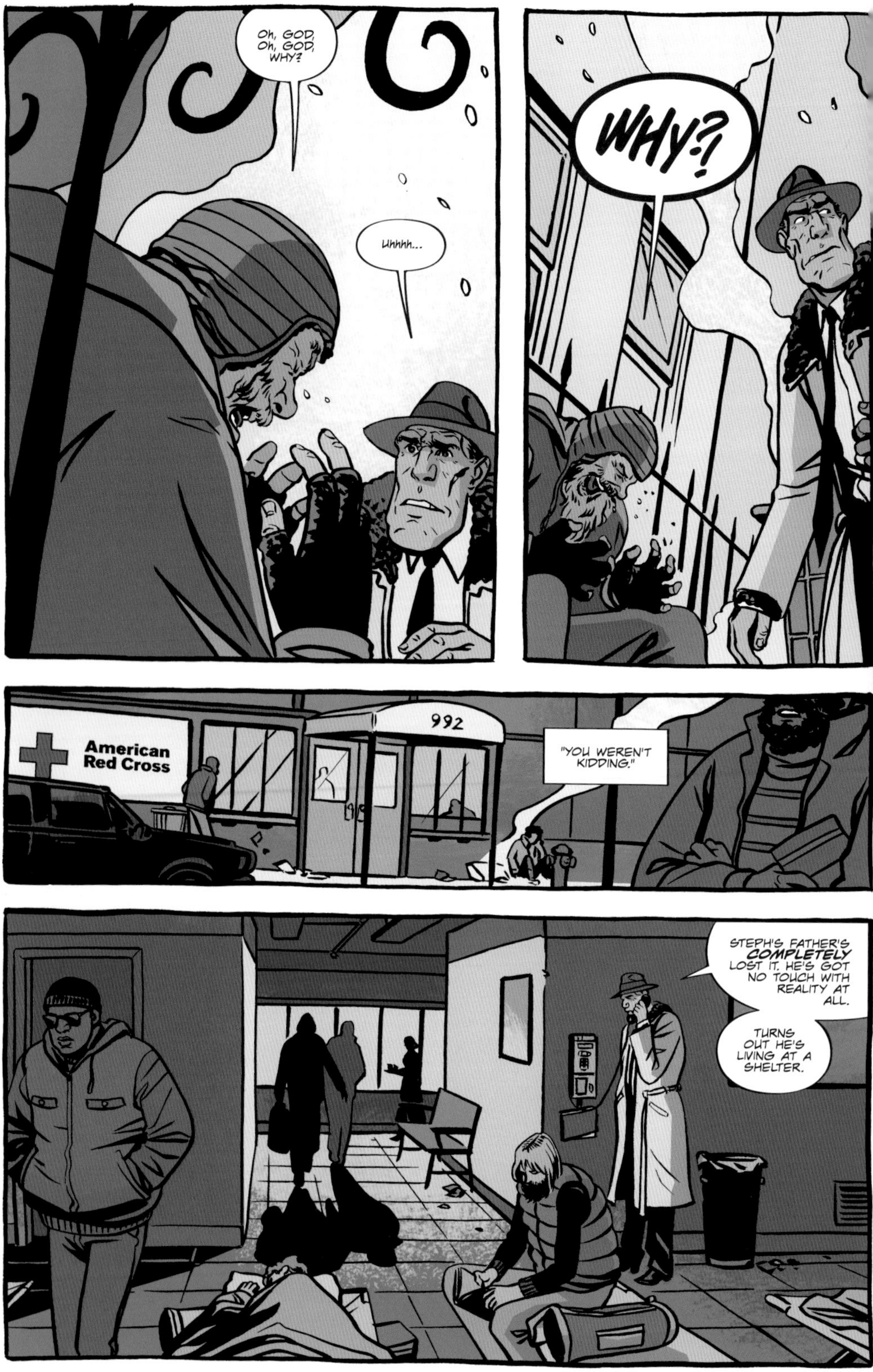
Oh, GOD, Oh, GOD, WHY?
Uhhhh...
WHY?!
American Red Cross
992
"YOU WEREN'T KIDDING."
STEPH'S FATHER'S COMPLETELY LOST IT. HE'S GOT NO TOUCH WITH REALITY AT ALL.
TURNS OUT HE'S LIVING AT A SHELTER.

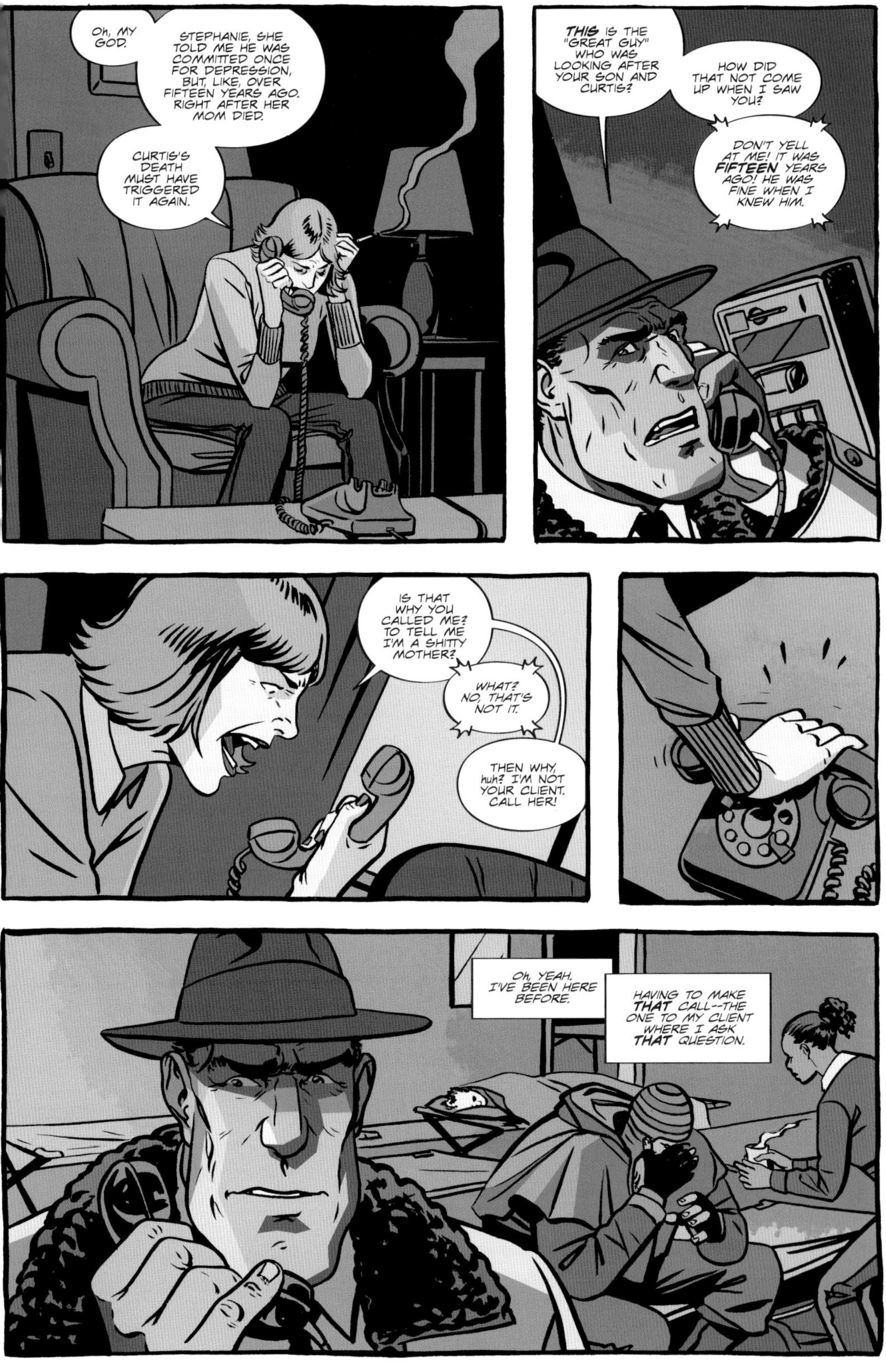
Oh, MY GOD.
STEPHANIE, SHE TOLD ME HE WAS COMMITTED ONCE FOR DEPRESSION, BUT, LIKE, OVER FIFTEEN YEARS AGO. RIGHT AFTER HER MOM DIED.
CURTIS'S DEATH MUST HAVE TRIGGERED IT AGAIN.
THIS IS THE "GREAT GUY" WHO WAS LOOKING AFTER YOUR SON AND CURTIS?
HOW DID THAT NOT COME UP WHEN I SAW YOU?
DON'T YELL AT ME! IT WAS FIFTEEN YEARS AGO! HE WAS FINE WHEN I KNEW HIM.
IS THAT WHY YOU CALLED ME? TO TELL ME I'M A SHITTY MOTHER?
WHAT? NO, THAT'S NOT IT.
THEN WHY, huh? I'M NOT YOUR CLIENT. CALL HER!
Oh, YEAH. I'VE BEEN HERE BEFORE.
HAVING TO MAKE THAT CALL--THE ONE TO MY CLIENT WHERE I ASK THAT QUESTION.

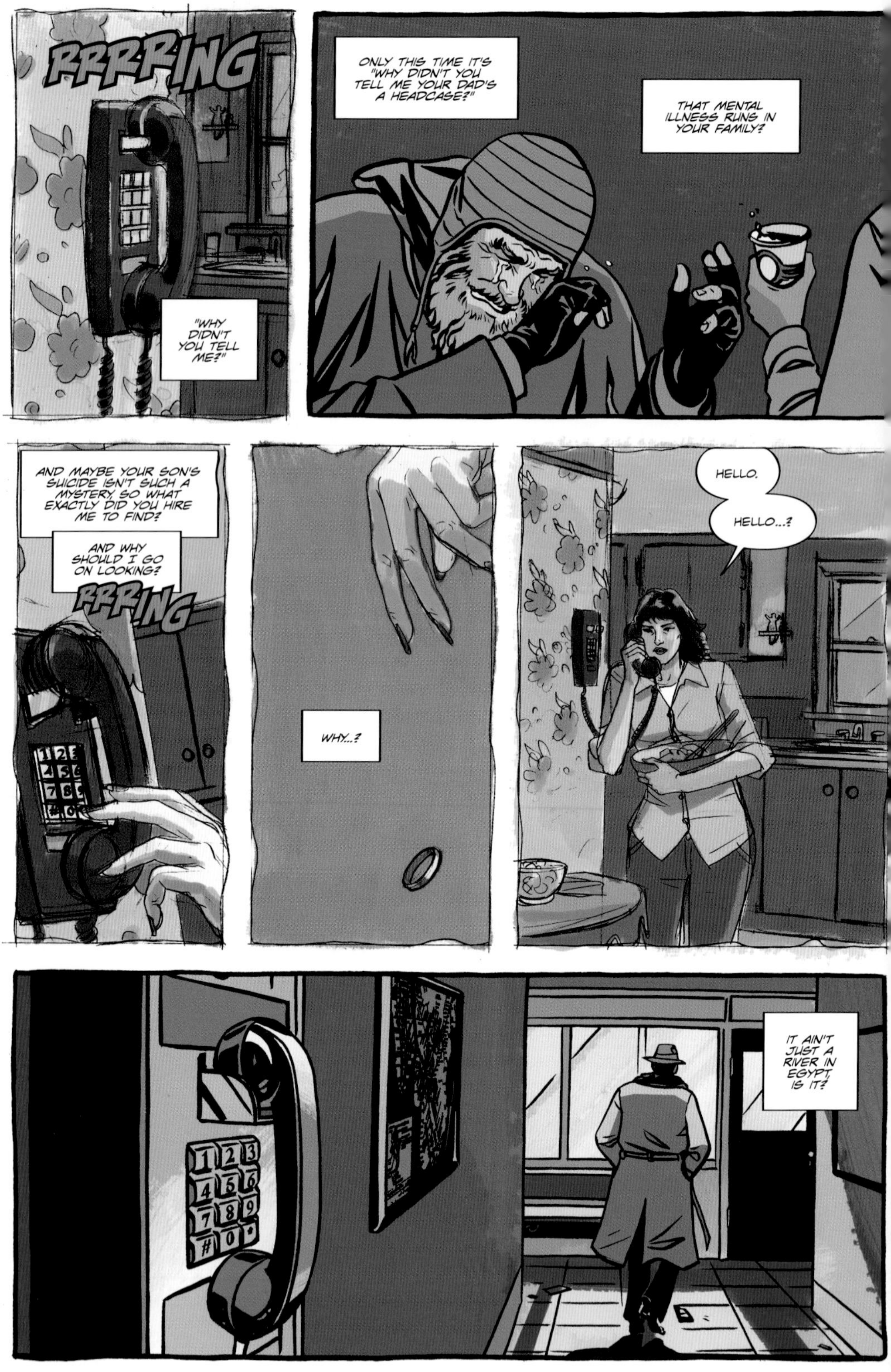
RRRRING
"WHY DIDN'T YOU TELL ME?"
ONLY THIS TIME IT'S "WHY DIDN'T YOU TELL ME YOUR DAD'S A HEADCASE?"
THAT MENTAL ILLNESS RUNS IN YOUR FAMILY?
AND MAYBE YOUR SON'S SUICIDE ISN'T SUCH A MYSTERY, SO WHAT EXACTLY DID YOU HIRE ME TO FIND?
AND WHY SHOULD I GO ON LOOKING?
RRRING
WHY...?
HELLO.
HELLO...?
IT AIN'T JUST A RIVER IN EGYPT, IS IT?

— CHAPTER TWO —

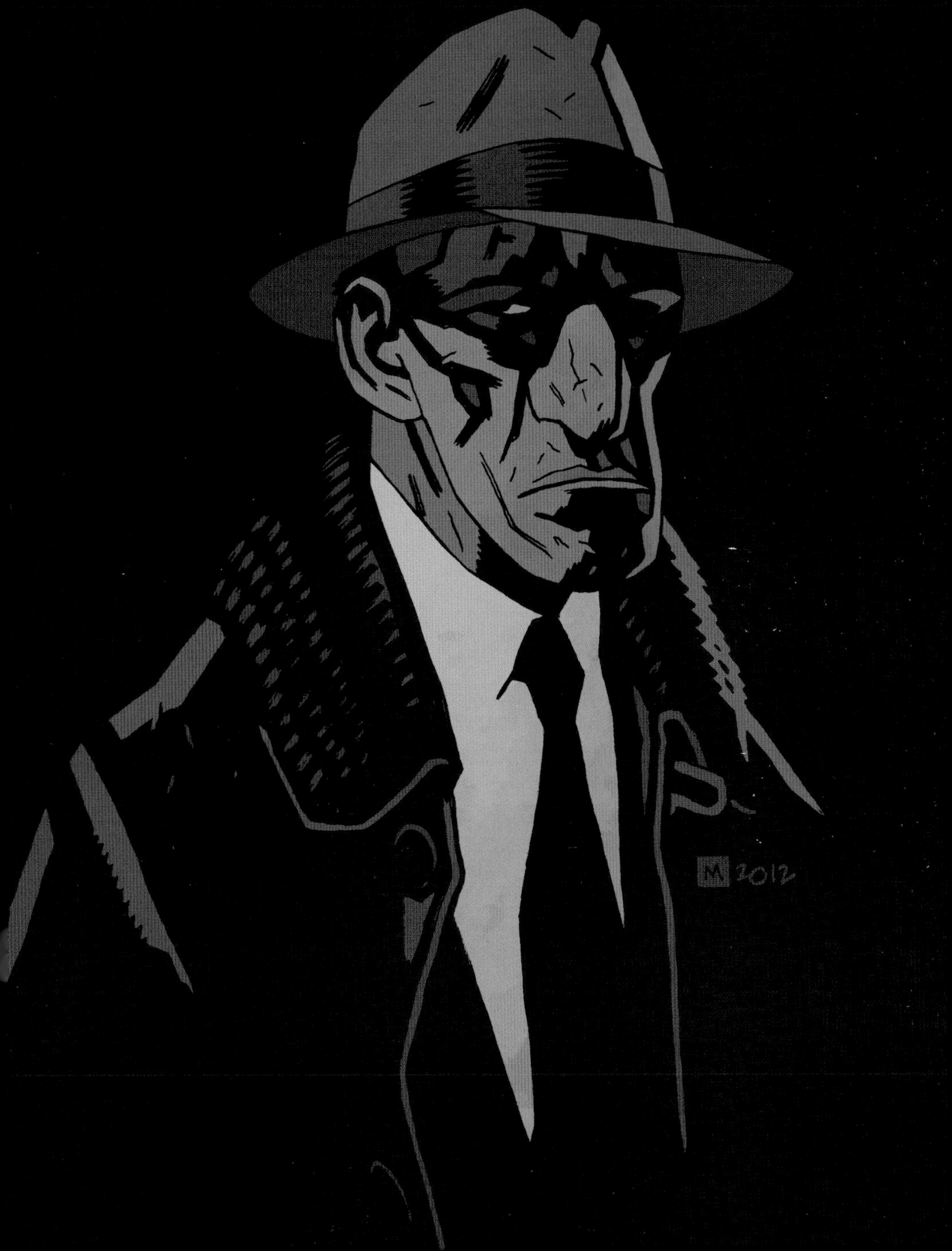
M 2012

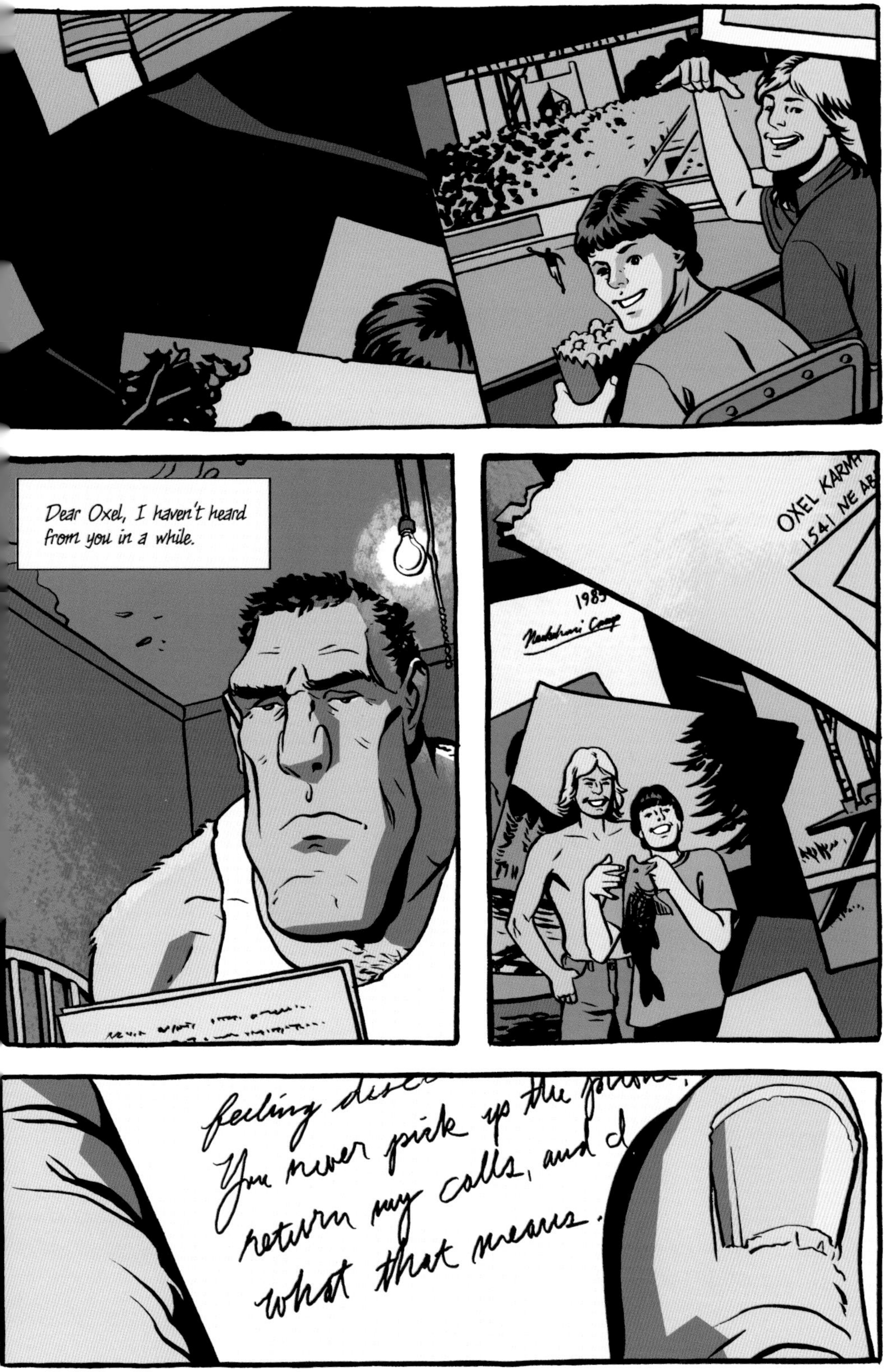
Dear Oxel, I haven't heard from you in a while.
You never pick up the phone,
return my calls, and
what that means.

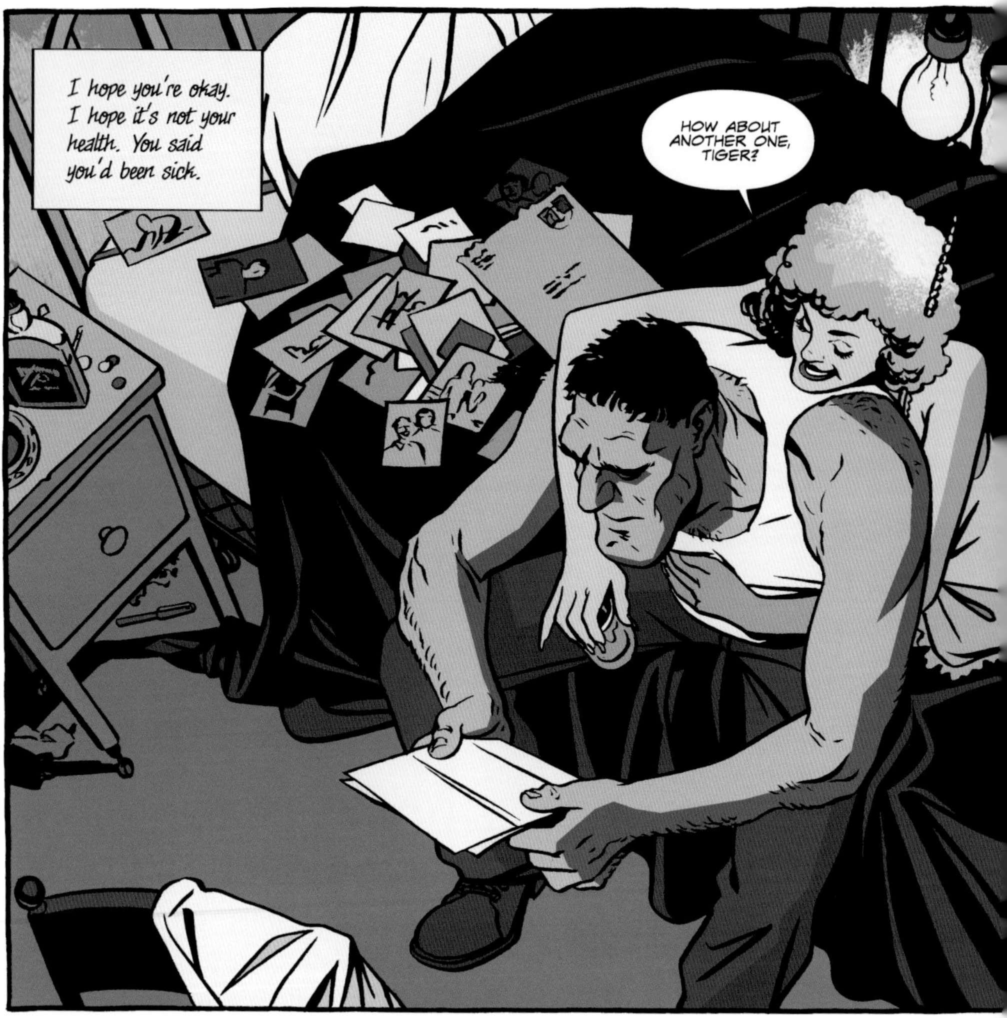
I hope you're okay. I hope it's not your health. You said you'd been sick.
HOW ABOUT ANOTHER ONE, TIGER?

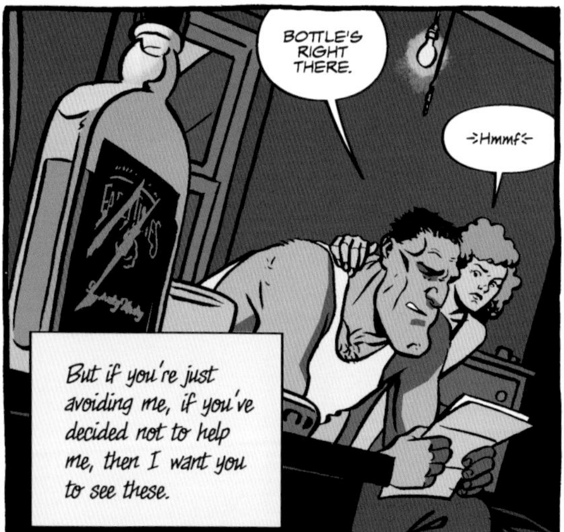
BOTTLE'S RIGHT THERE.
Hmmf
But if you're just avoiding me, if you've decided not to help me, then I want you to see these.

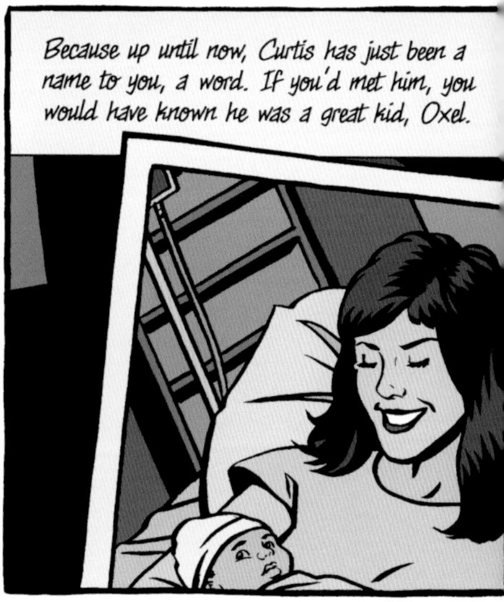
Because up until now, Curtis has just been a name to you, a word. If you'd met him, you would have known he was a great kid, Oxel.

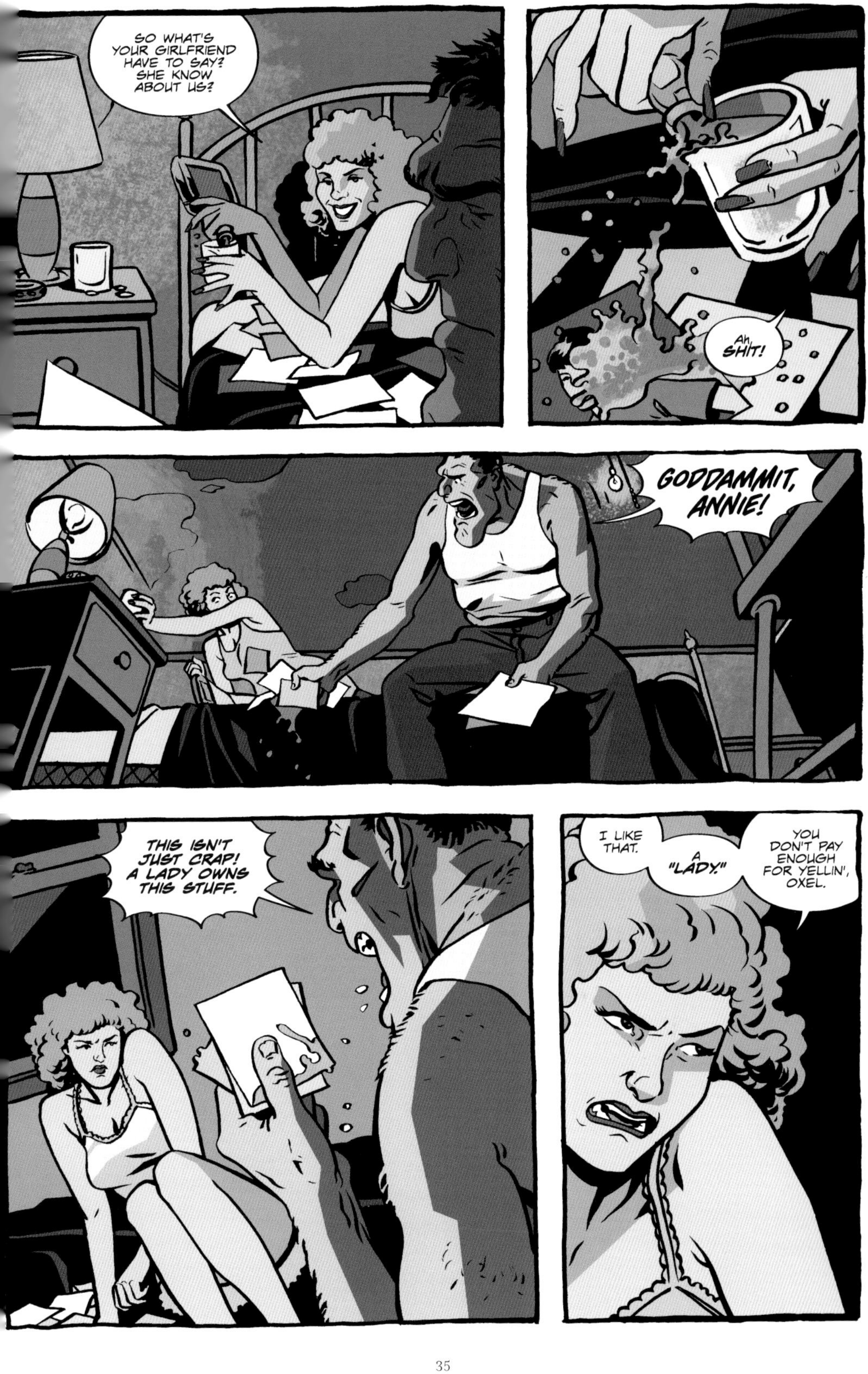
SO WHAT'S YOUR GIRLFRIEND HAVE TO SAY? SHE KNOW ABOUT US?
Ah, SHIT!
GODDAMMIT, ANNIE!
THIS ISN'T JUST CRAP! A LADY OWNS THIS STUFF.
I LIKE THAT.
A "LADY."
YOU DON'T PAY ENOUGH FOR YELLIN', OXEL.

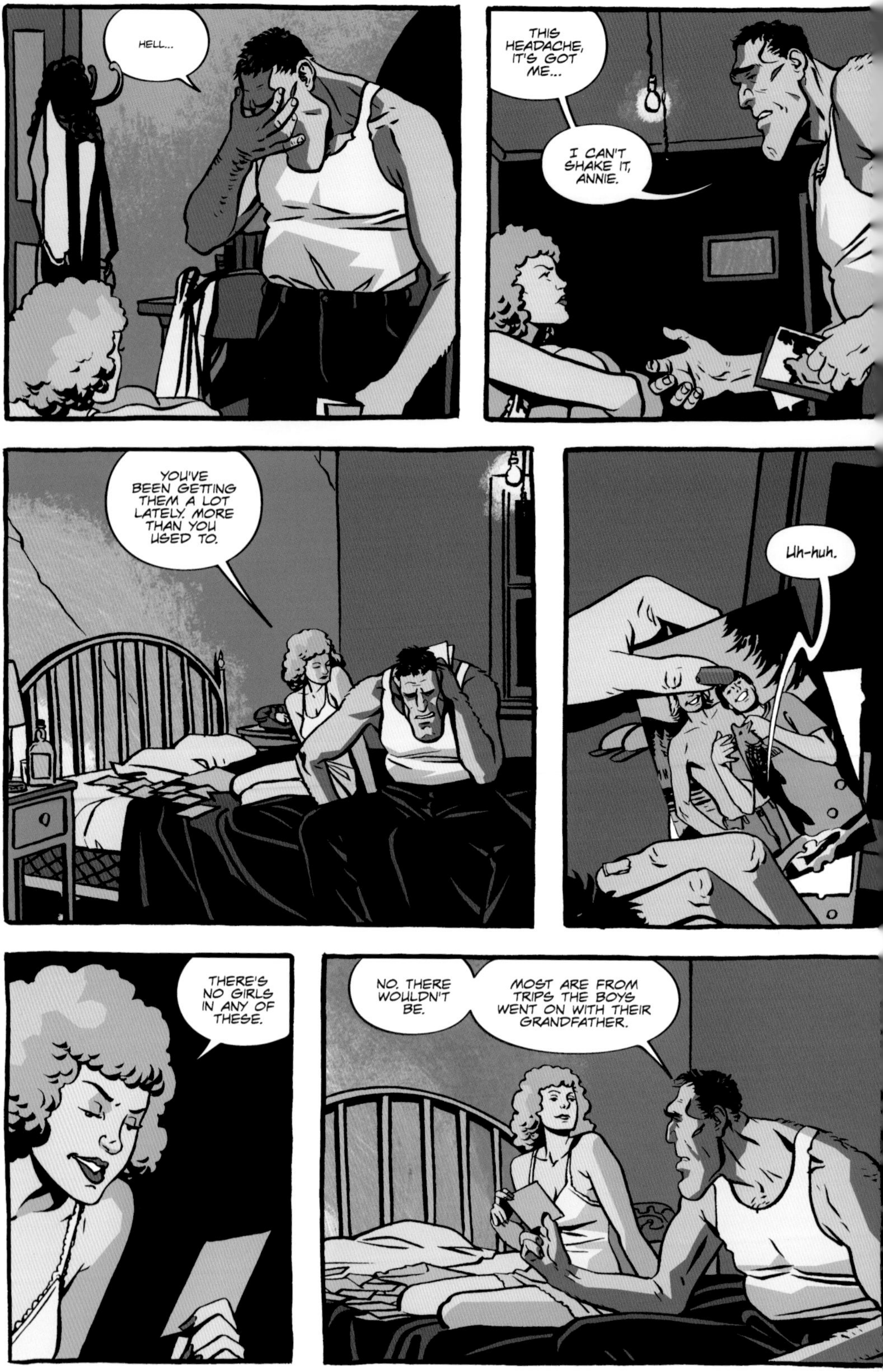
HELL...
THIS HEADACHE, IT'S GOT ME...
I CAN'T SHAKE IT, ANNIE.
YOU'VE BEEN GETTING THEM A LOT LATELY. MORE THAN YOU USED TO.
Uh-huh.
THERE'S NO GIRLS IN ANY OF THESE.
NO. THERE WOULDN'T BE.
MOST ARE FROM TRIPS THE BOYS WENT ON WITH THEIR GRANDFATHER.

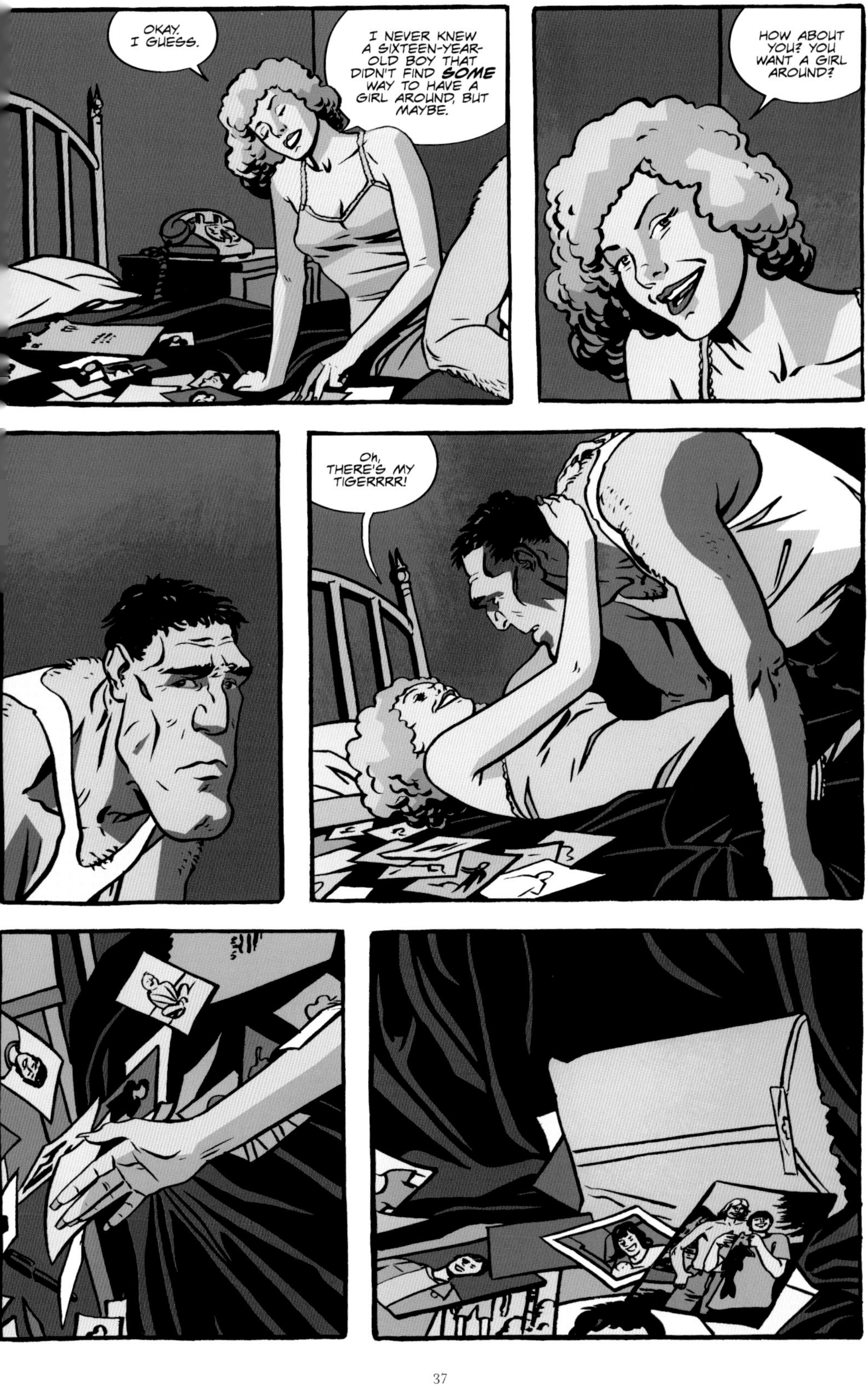
OKAY. I GUESS.
I NEVER KNEW A SIXTEEN-YEAR-OLD BOY THAT DIDN'T FIND SOME WAY TO HAVE A GIRL AROUND, BUT MAYBE.
HOW ABOUT YOU? YOU WANT A GIRL AROUND?
Oh, THERE'S MY TIGERRRR!

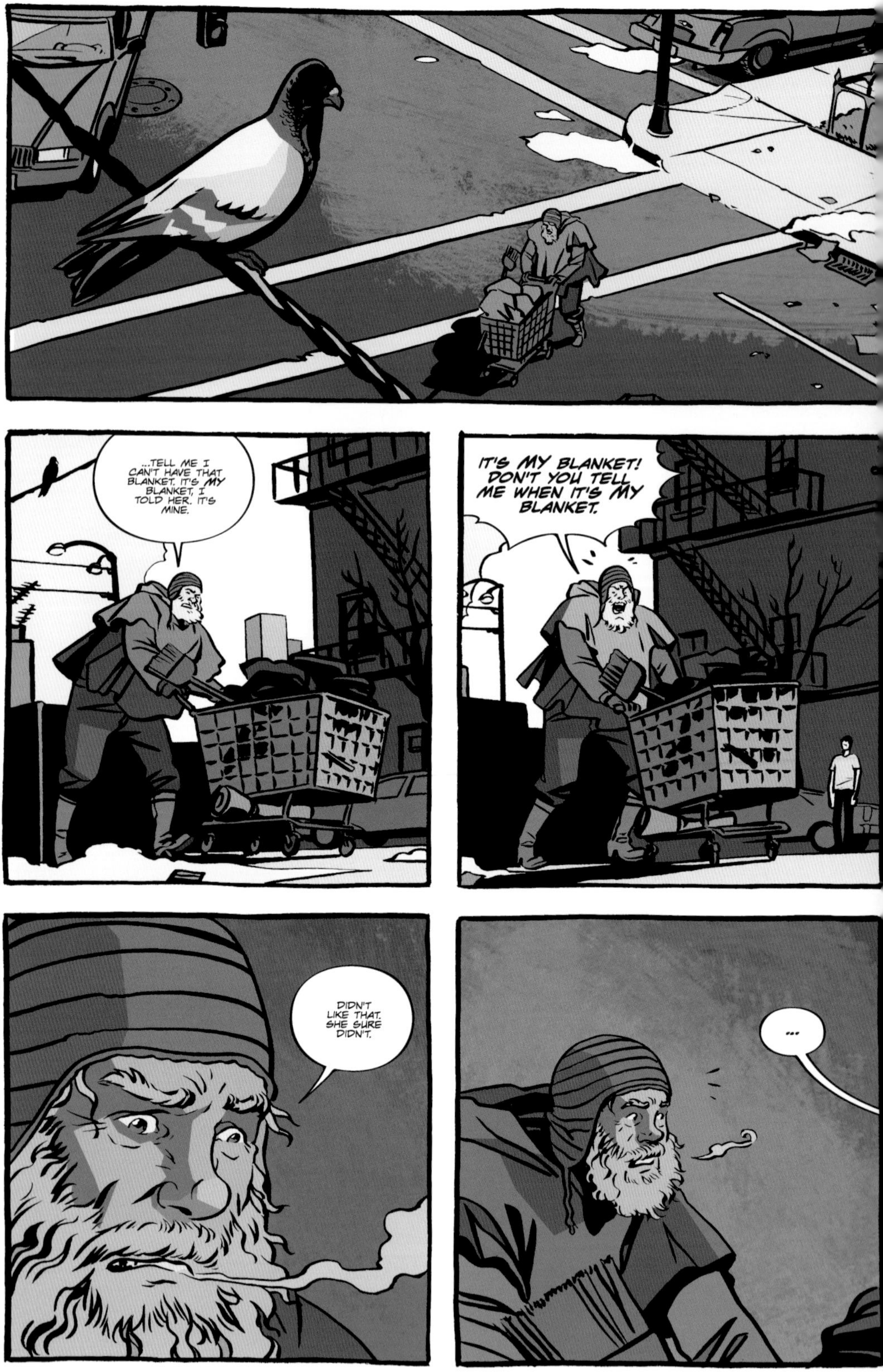
...TELL ME I CAN'T HAVE THAT BLANKET. IT'S MY BLANKET, I TOLD HER. IT'S MINE.
IT'S MY BLANKET! DON'T YOU TELL ME WHEN IT'S MY BLANKET.
DIDN'T LIKE THAT. SHE SURE DIDN'T.
...

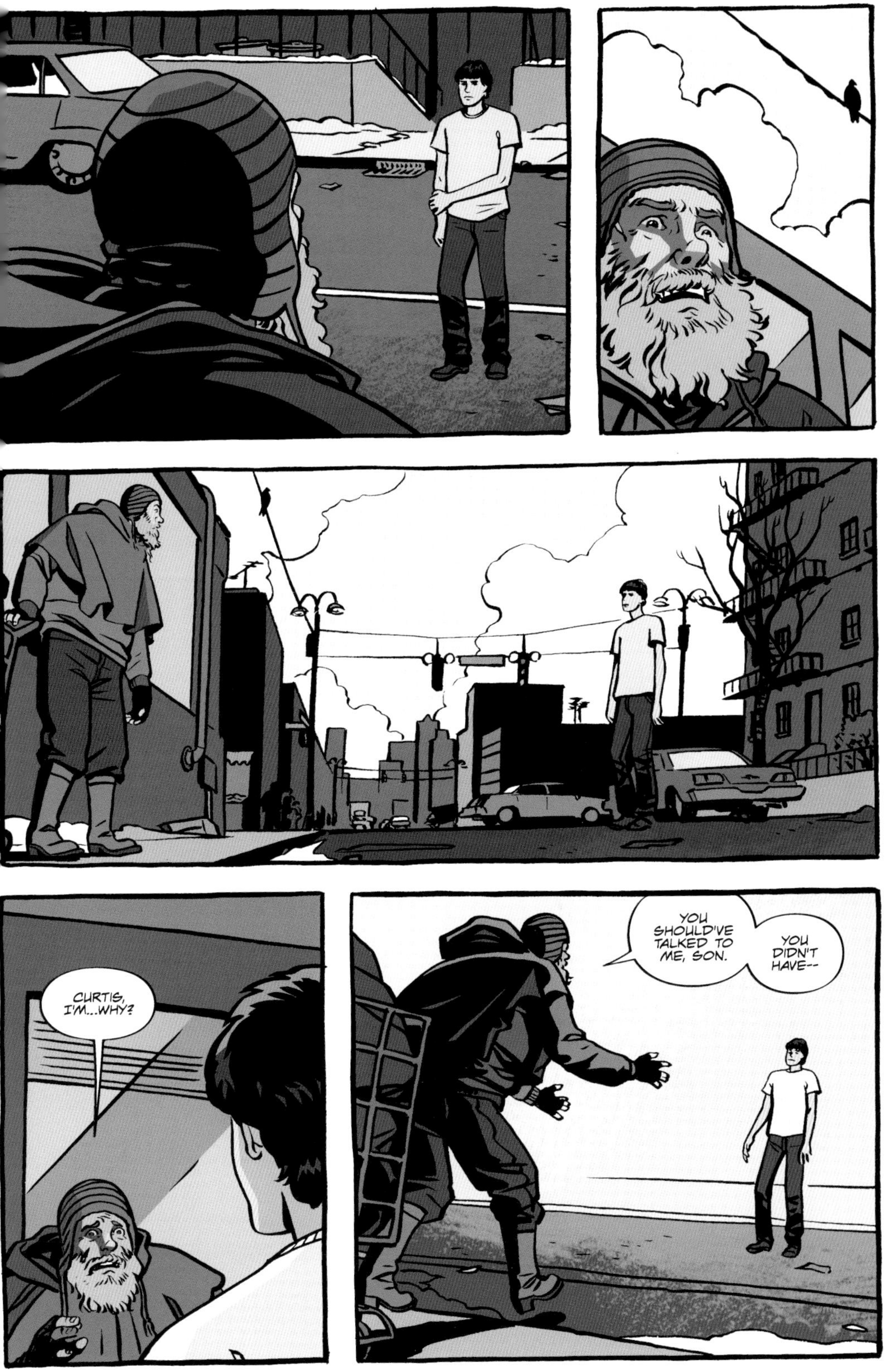
CURTIS, I'M...WHY?
YOU SHOULD'VE TALKED TO ME, SON.
YOU DIDN'T HAVE--

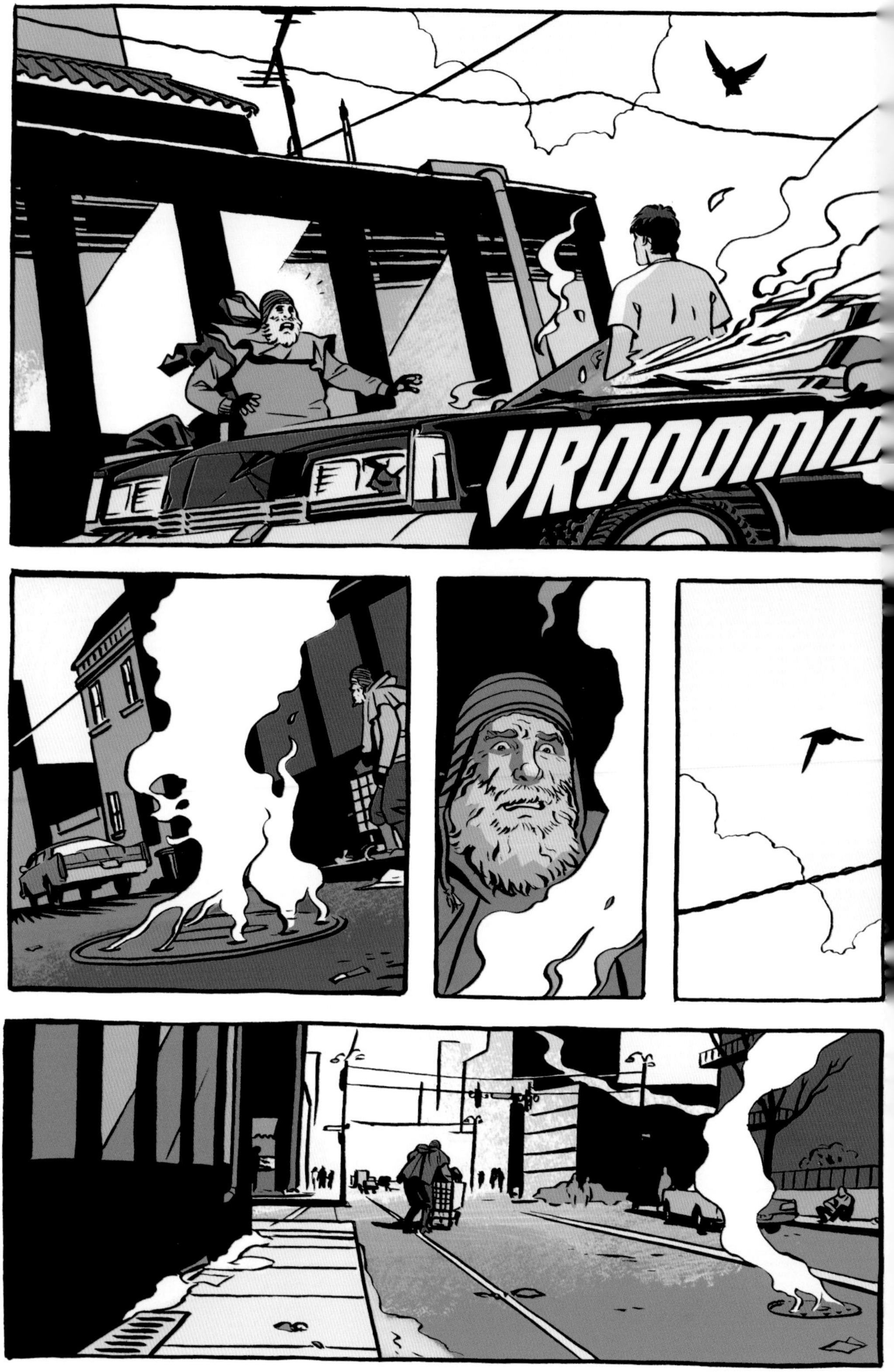
VROOOMM

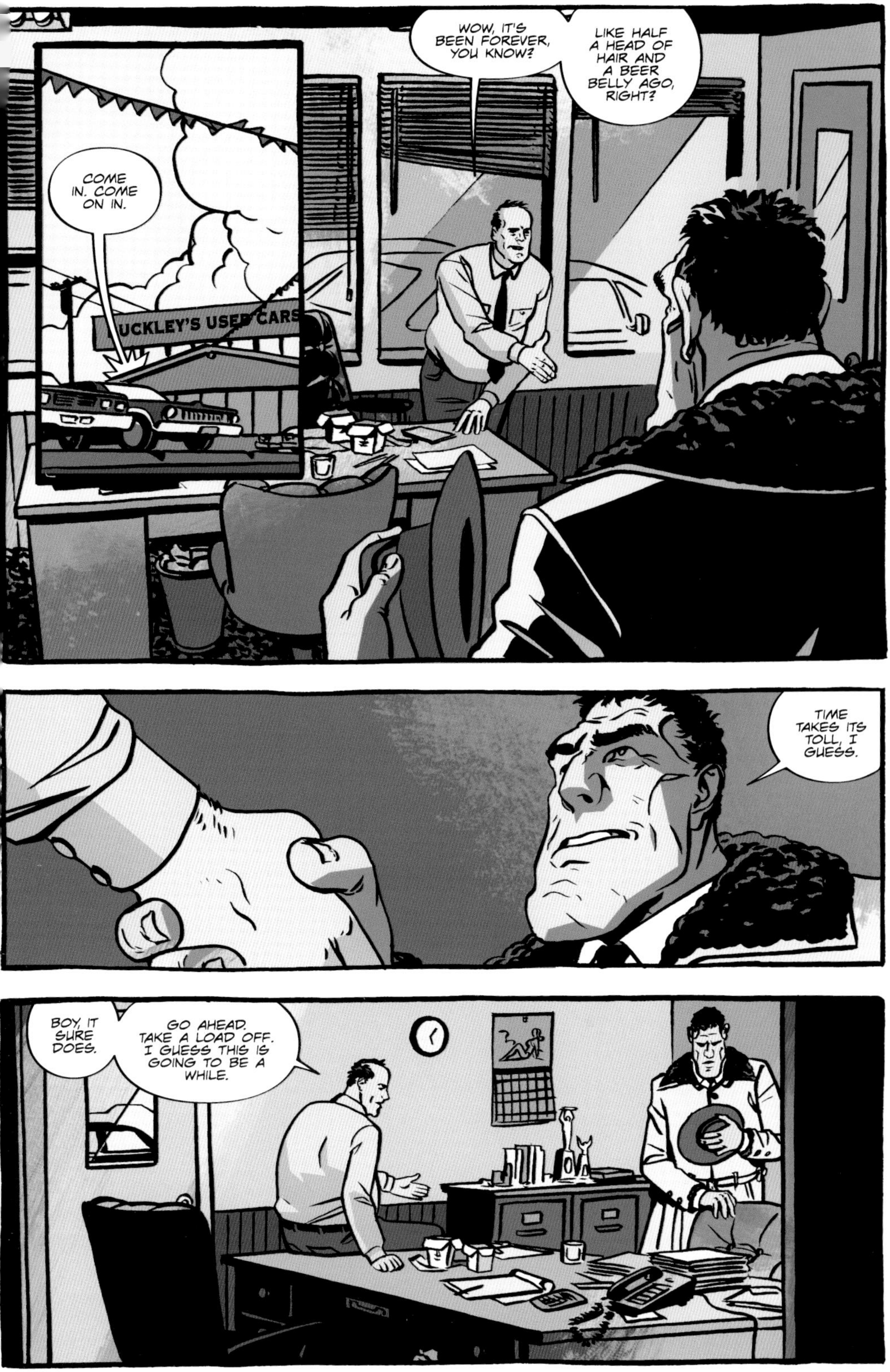
COME IN. COME ON IN.
BUCKLEY'S USED CARS
WOW, IT'S BEEN FOREVER, YOU KNOW?
LIKE HALF A HEAD OF HAIR AND A BEER BELLY AGO, RIGHT?
TIME TAKES ITS TOLL, I GUESS.
BOY, IT SURE DOES.
GO AHEAD. TAKE A LOAD OFF. I GUESS THIS IS GOING TO BE A WHILE.

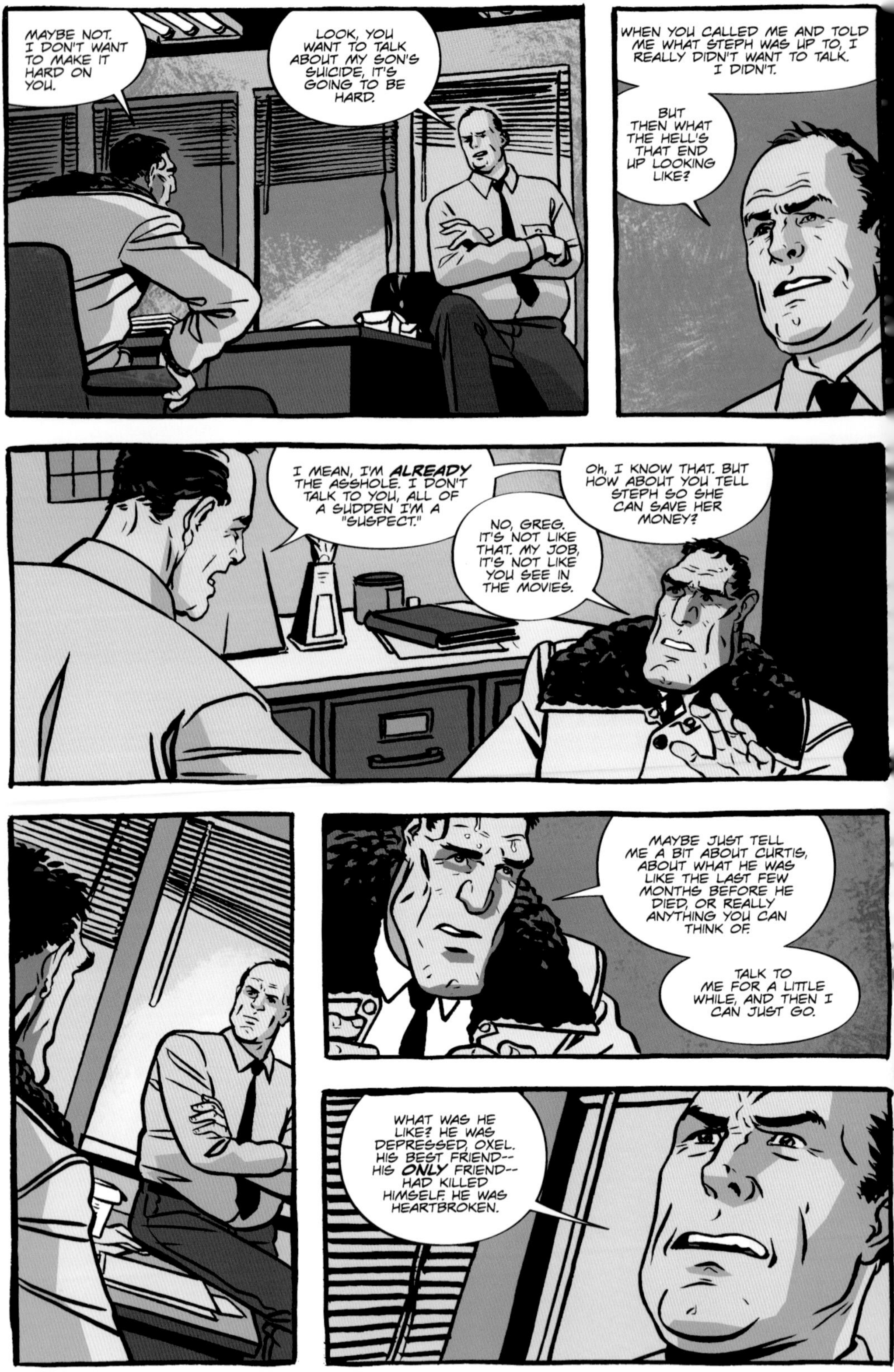
MAYBE NOT. I DON'T WANT TO MAKE IT HARD ON YOU.
LOOK, YOU WANT TO TALK ABOUT MY SON'S SUICIDE, IT'S GOING TO BE HARD.
WHEN YOU CALLED ME AND TOLD ME WHAT STEPH WAS UP TO, I REALLY DIDN'T WANT TO TALK. I DIDN'T.
BUT THEN WHAT THE HELL'S THAT END UP LOOKING LIKE?
I MEAN, I'M ALREADY THE ASSHOLE. I DON'T TALK TO YOU, ALL OF A SUDDEN I'M A "SUSPECT."
NO, GREG. IT'S NOT LIKE THAT. MY JOB, IT'S NOT LIKE YOU SEE IN THE MOVIES.
Oh, I KNOW THAT. BUT HOW ABOUT YOU TELL STEPH SO SHE CAN SAVE HER MONEY?
MAYBE JUST TELL ME A BIT ABOUT CURTIS, ABOUT WHAT HE WAS LIKE THE LAST FEW MONTHS BEFORE HE DIED, OR REALLY ANYTHING YOU CAN THINK OF.
TALK TO ME FOR A LITTLE WHILE, AND THEN I CAN JUST GO.
WHAT WAS HE LIKE? HE WAS DEPRESSED, OXEL. HIS BEST FRIEND-- HIS ONLY FRIEND-- HAD KILLED HIMSELF. HE WAS HEARTBROKEN.

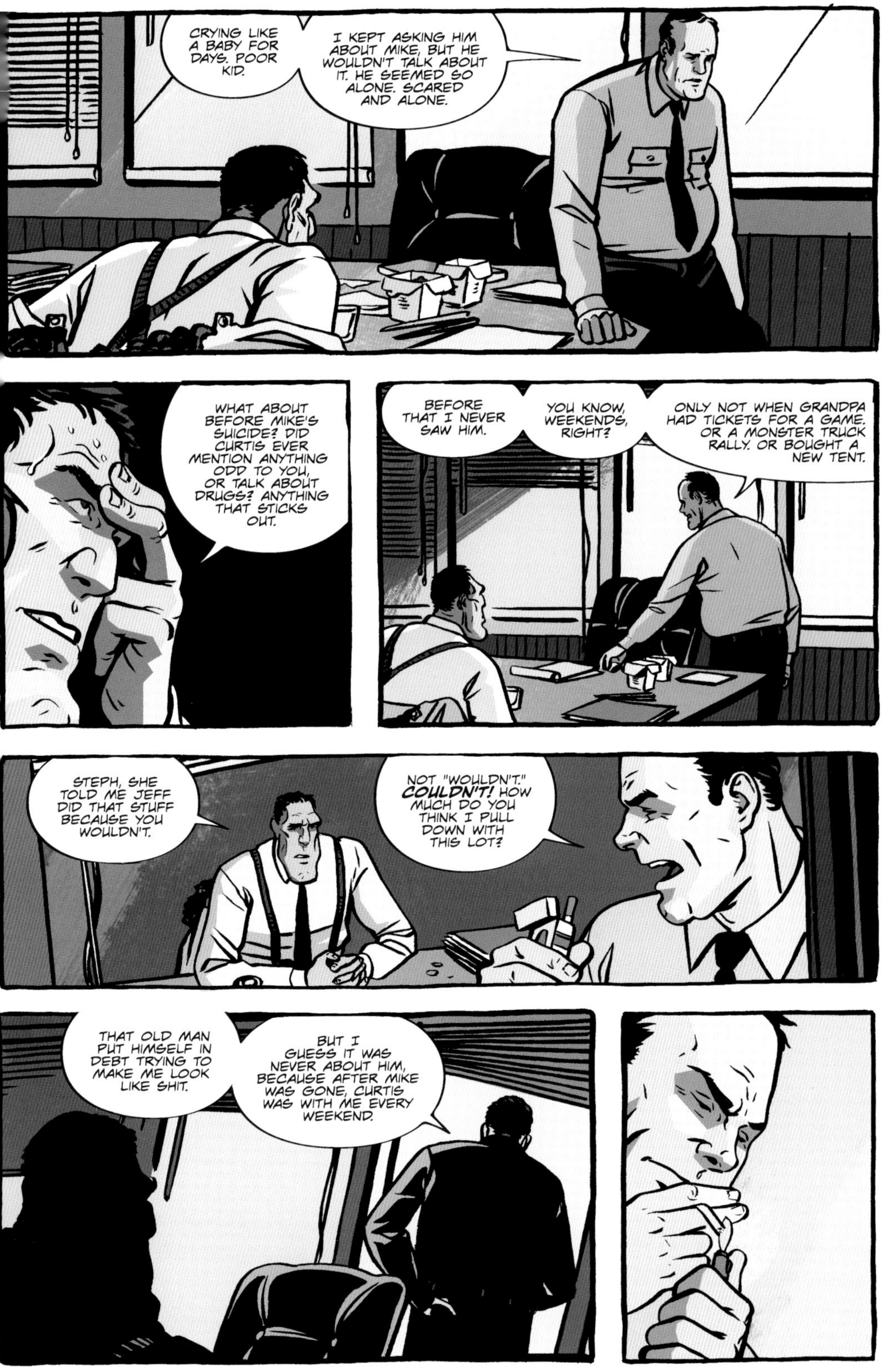
CRYING LIKE A BABY FOR DAYS. POOR KID.
I KEPT ASKING HIM ABOUT MIKE, BUT HE WOULDN'T TALK ABOUT IT. HE SEEMED SO ALONE. SCARED AND ALONE.
WHAT ABOUT BEFORE MIKE'S SUICIDE? DID CURTIS EVER MENTION ANYTHING ODD TO YOU, OR TALK ABOUT DRUGS? ANYTHING THAT STICKS OUT.
BEFORE THAT I NEVER SAW HIM.
YOU KNOW, WEEKENDS, RIGHT?
ONLY NOT WHEN GRANDPA HAD TICKETS FOR A GAME. OR A MONSTER TRUCK RALLY. OR BOUGHT A NEW TENT.
STEPH, SHE TOLD ME JEFF DID THAT STUFF BECAUSE YOU WOULDN'T.
NOT "WOULDN'T." COULDN'T! HOW MUCH DO YOU THINK I PULL DOWN WITH THIS LOT?
THAT OLD MAN PUT HIMSELF IN DEBT TRYING TO MAKE ME LOOK LIKE SHIT.
BUT I GUESS IT WAS NEVER ABOUT HIM, BECAUSE AFTER MIKE WAS GONE, CURTIS WAS WITH ME EVERY WEEKEND.

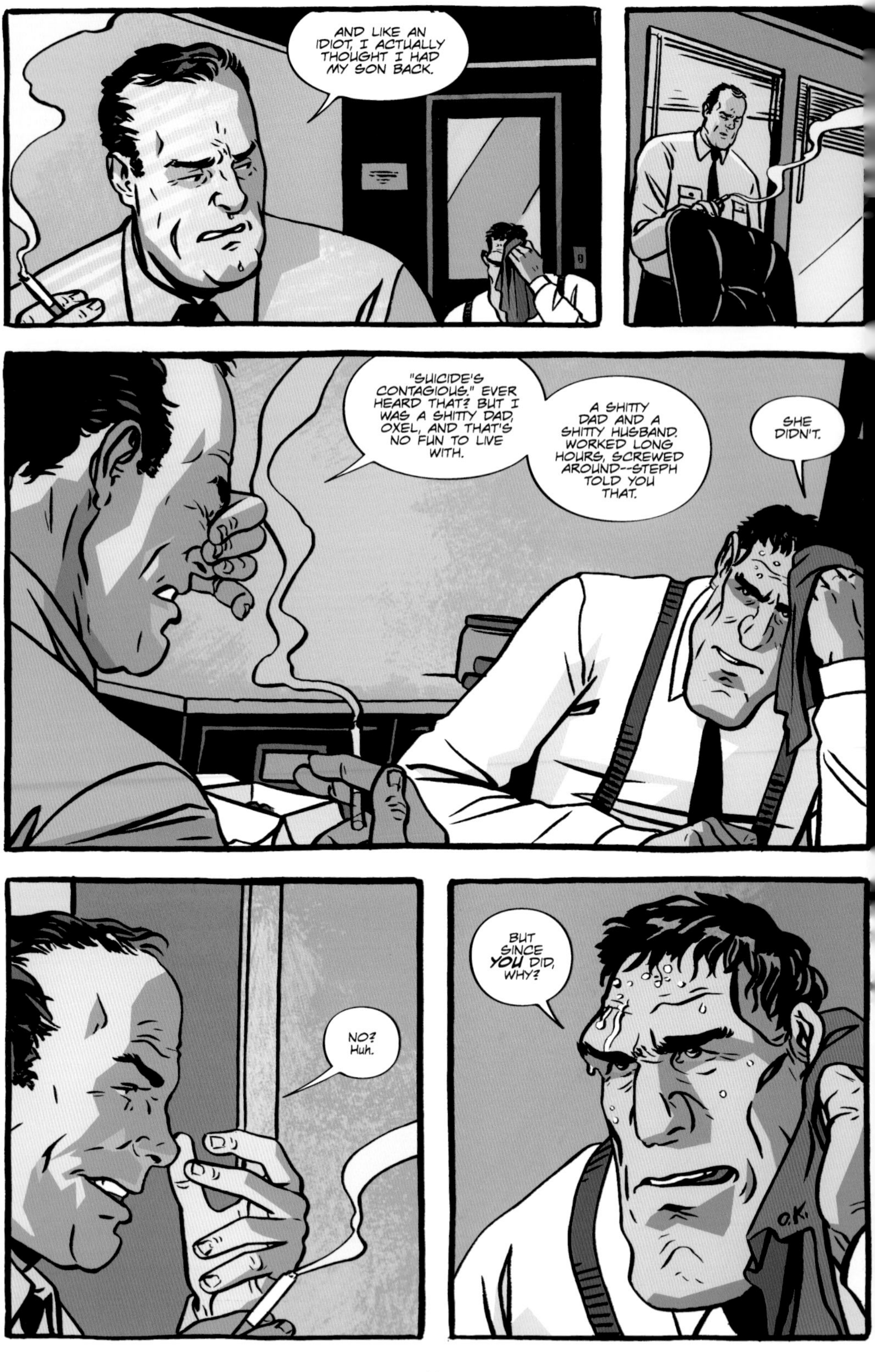
AND LIKE AN IDIOT, I ACTUALLY THOUGHT I HAD MY SON BACK.
"SUICIDE'S CONTAGIOUS." EVER HEARD THAT? BUT I WAS A SHITTY DAD, OXEL, AND THAT'S NO FUN TO LIVE WITH.
A SHITTY DAD AND A SHITTY HUSBAND. WORKED LONG HOURS, SCREWED AROUND--STEPH TOLD YOU THAT.
SHE DIDN'T.
NO? Huh.
BUT SINCE YOU DID, WHY?
O.K.

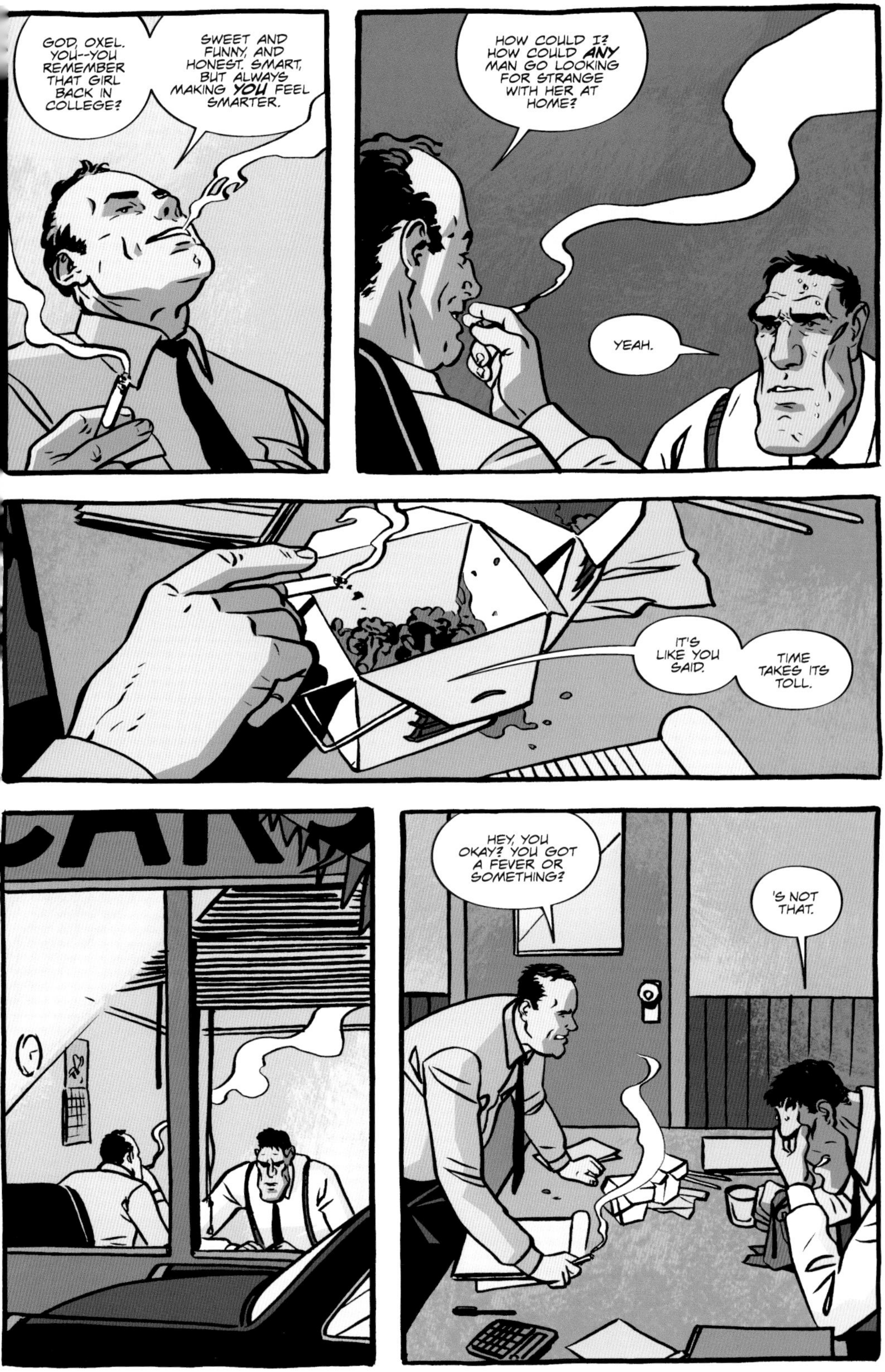
GOD, OXEL. YOU--YOU REMEMBER THAT GIRL BACK IN COLLEGE?
SWEET AND FUNNY, AND HONEST. SMART, BUT ALWAYS MAKING YOU FEEL SMARTER.
HOW COULD I? HOW COULD ANY MAN GO LOOKING FOR STRANGE WITH HER AT HOME?
YEAH.
IT'S LIKE YOU SAID.
TIME TAKES ITS TOLL.
HEY, YOU OKAY? YOU GOT A FEVER OR SOMETHING?
'S NOT THAT.

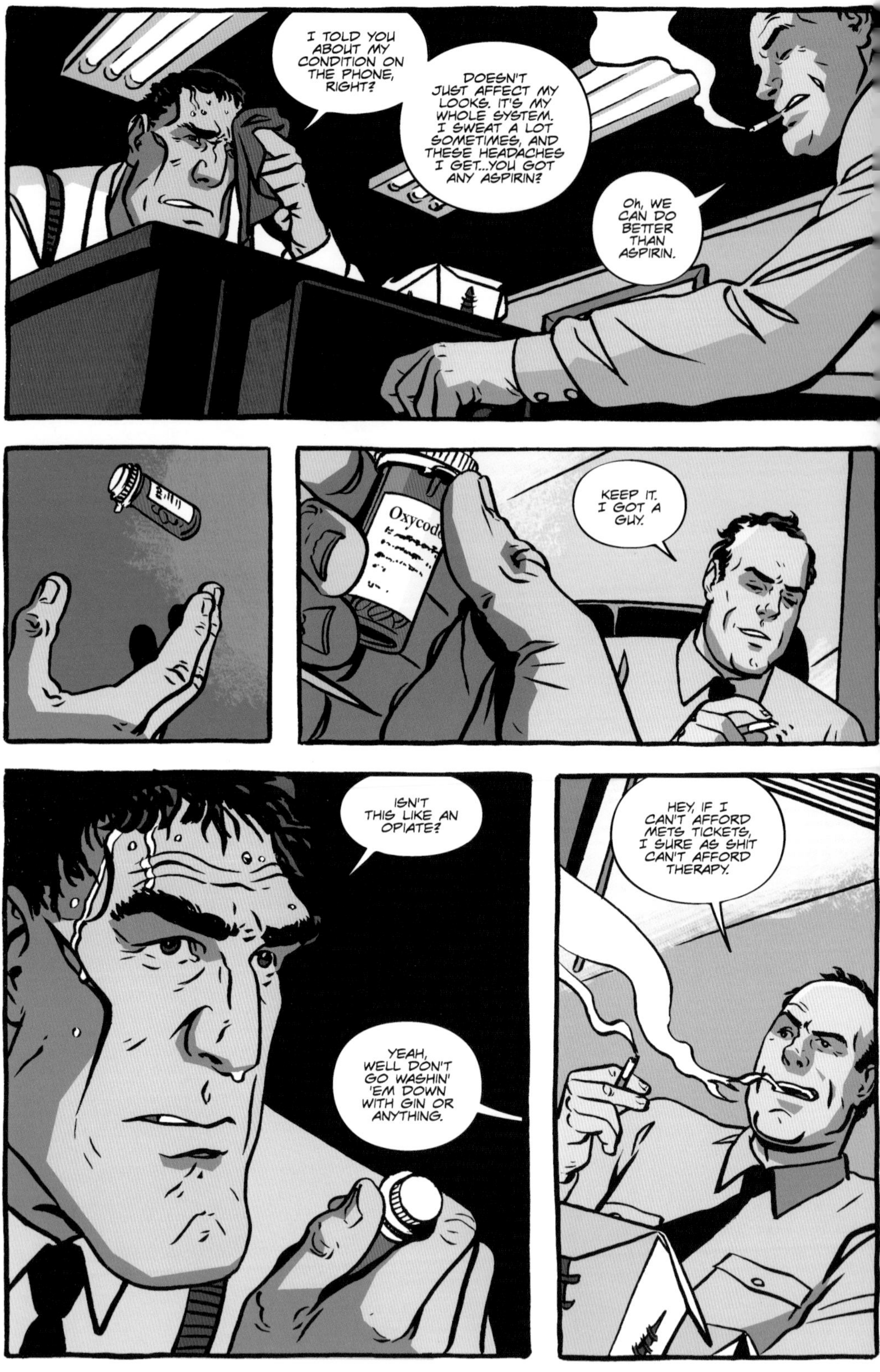
I TOLD YOU ABOUT MY CONDITION ON THE PHONE, RIGHT?
DOESN'T JUST AFFECT MY LOOKS. IT'S MY WHOLE SYSTEM. I SWEAT A LOT SOMETIMES, AND THESE HEADACHES I GET...YOU GOT ANY ASPIRIN?
Oh, WE CAN DO BETTER THAN ASPIRIN.
Oxycode
KEEP IT. I GOT A GUY.
ISN'T THIS LIKE AN OPIATE?
YEAH, WELL DON'T GO WASHIN' 'EM DOWN WITH GIN OR ANYTHING.
HEY, IF I CAN'T AFFORD METS TICKETS, I SURE AS SHIT CAN'T AFFORD THERAPY.

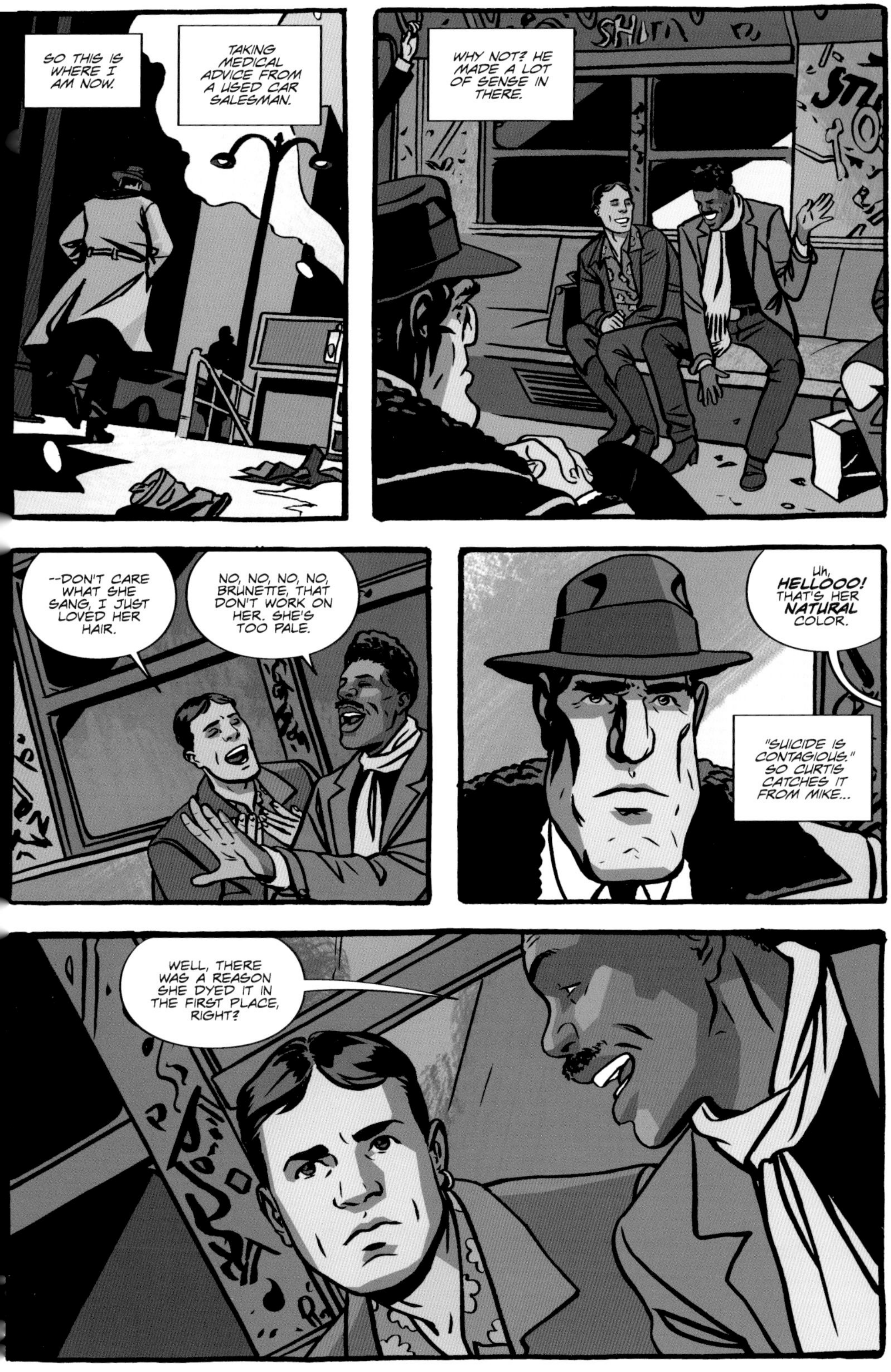

SO THIS IS WHERE I AM NOW.
TAKING MEDICAL ADVICE FROM A USED CAR SALESMAN.
WHY NOT? HE MADE A LOT OF SENSE IN THERE.
--DON'T CARE WHAT SHE SANG, I JUST LOVED HER HAIR.
NO, NO, NO, NO, BRUNETTE, THAT DON'T WORK ON HER. SHE'S TOO PALE.
Uh, HELLOOO! THAT'S HER NATURAL COLOR.
"SUICIDE IS CONTAGIOUS." SO CURTIS CATCHES IT FROM MIKE...
WELL, THERE WAS A REASON SHE DYED IT IN THE FIRST PLACE, RIGHT?

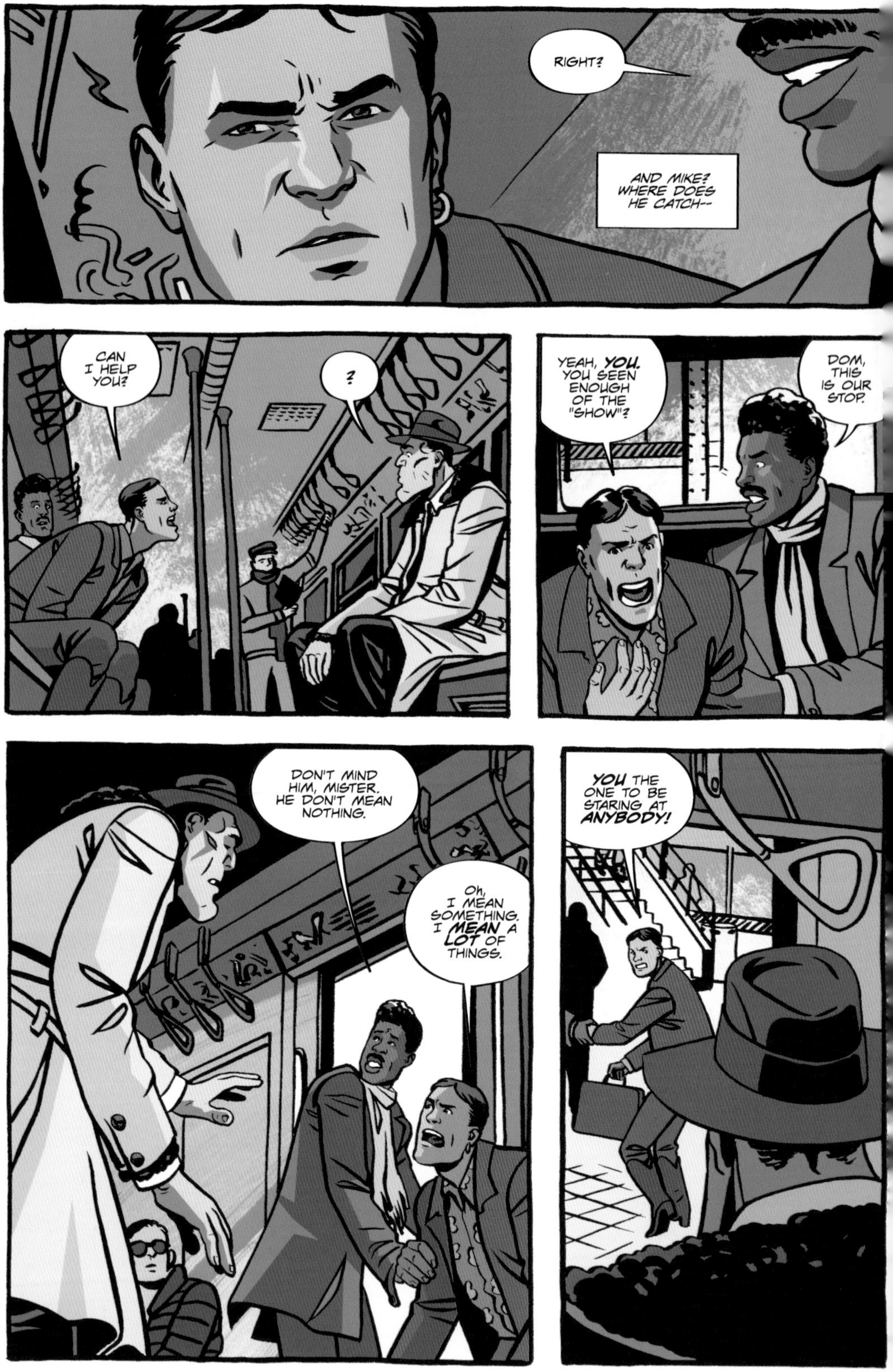
RIGHT?
AND MIKE? WHERE DOES HE CATCH--
CAN I HELP YOU?
?
YEAH, YOU. YOU SEEN ENOUGH OF THE "SHOW"?
DOM, THIS IS OUR STOP.
DON'T MIND HIM, MISTER. HE DON'T MEAN NOTHING.
Oh, I MEAN SOMETHING. I MEAN A LOT OF THINGS.
YOU THE ONE TO BE STARING AT ANYBODY!

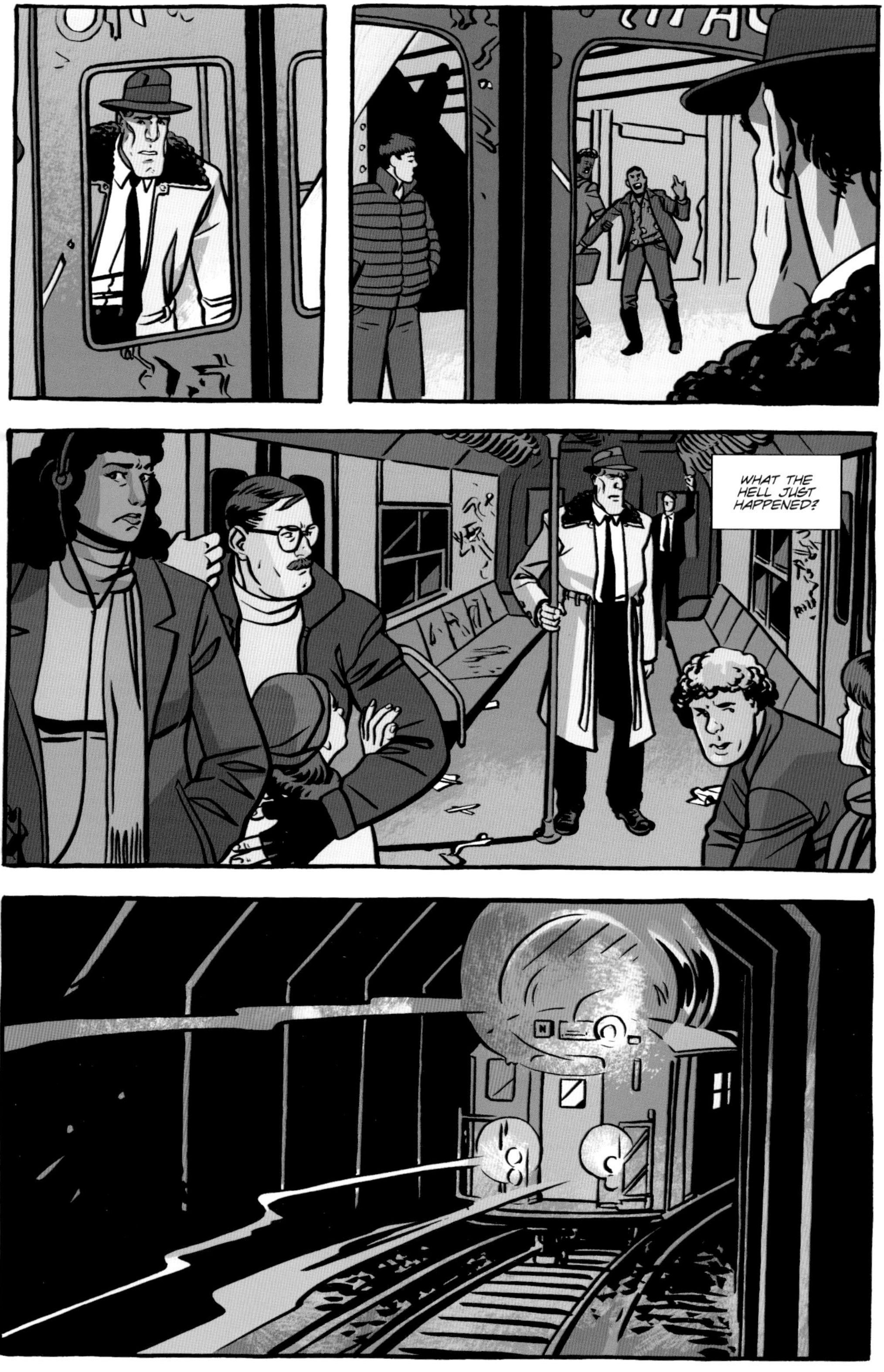
WHAT THE HELL JUST HAPPENED?

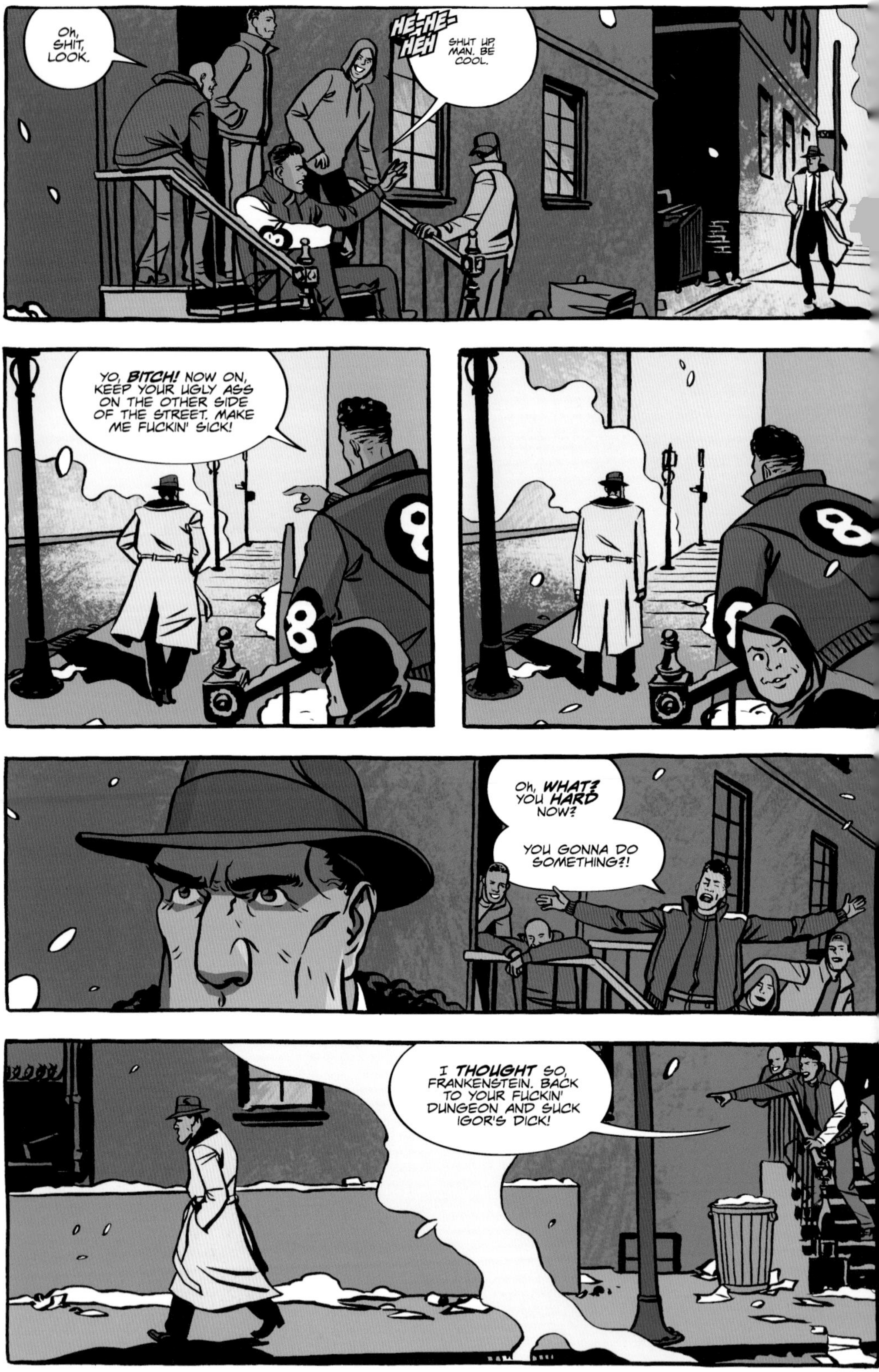
Oh, SHIT, LOOK.
HE-HE-HEH
SHUT UP, MAN. BE COOL.
YO, BITCH! NOW ON, KEEP YOUR UGLY ASS ON THE OTHER SIDE OF THE STREET. MAKE ME FUCKIN' SICK!
Oh, WHAT? YOU HARD NOW?
YOU GONNA DO SOMETHING?!
I THOUGHT SO, FRANKENSTEIN. BACK TO YOUR FUCKIN' DUNGEON AND SUCK IGOR'S DICK!

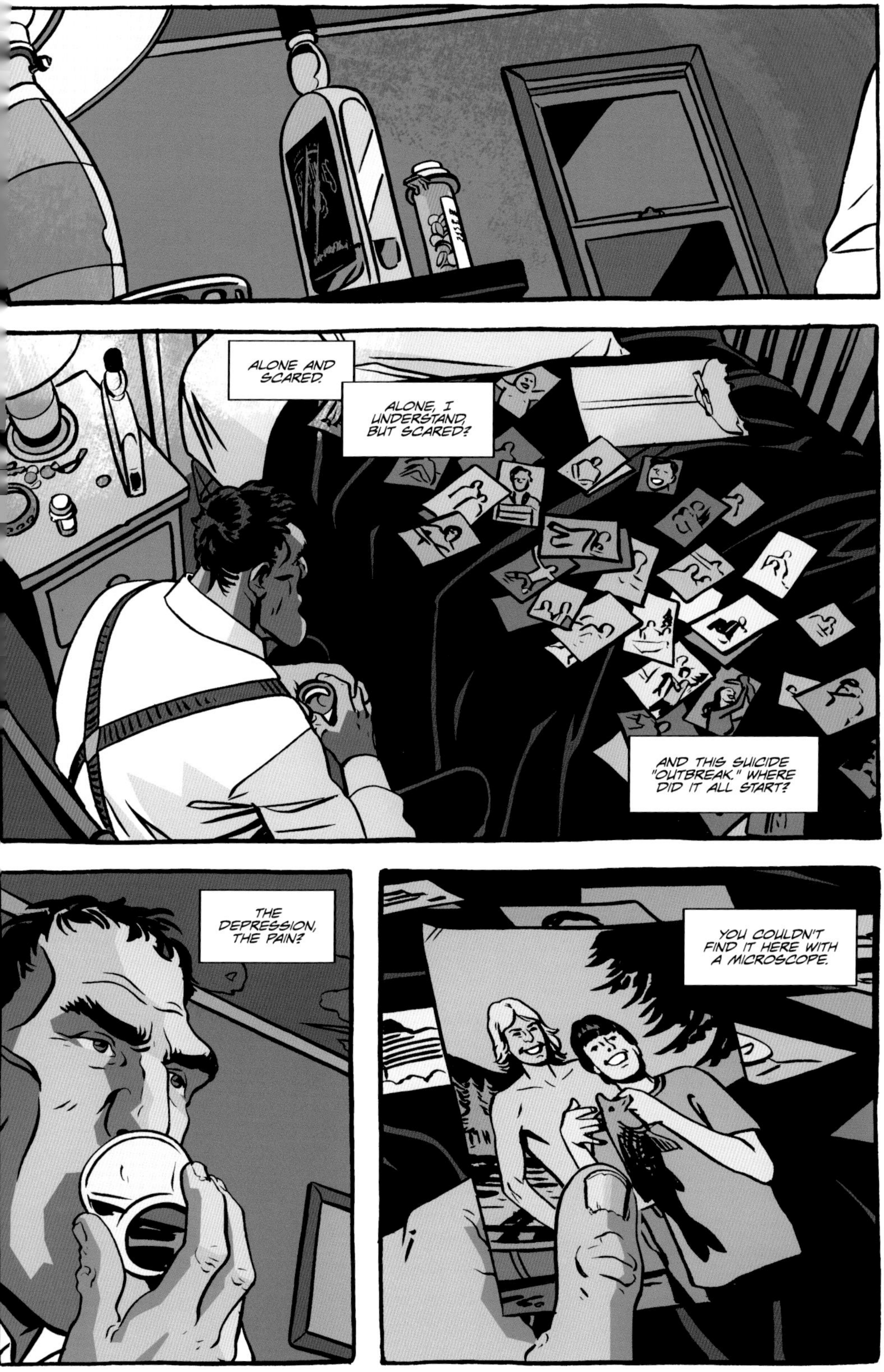
ALONE AND SCARED.
ALONE, I UNDERSTAND, BUT SCARED?
AND THIS SUICIDE "OUTBREAK." WHERE DID IT ALL START?
THE DEPRESSION, THE PAIN?
YOU COULDN'T FIND IT HERE WITH A MICROSCOPE.

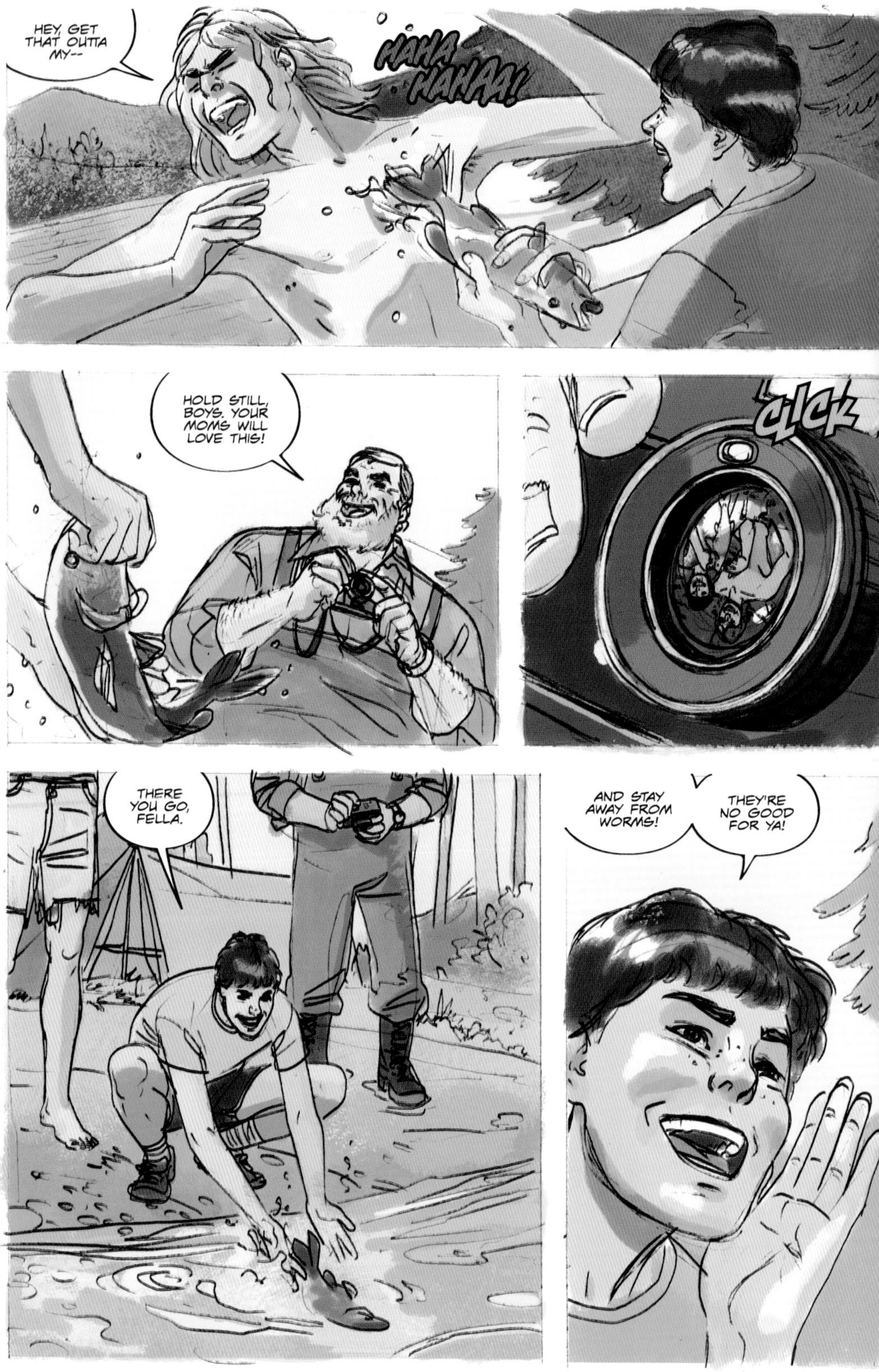
HEY, GET THAT OUTTA MY--
HAHA HAHAA!
HOLD STILL, BOYS. YOUR MOMS WILL LOVE THIS!
CLICK
THERE YOU GO, FELLA.
AND STAY AWAY FROM WORMS!
THEY'RE NO GOOD FOR YA!

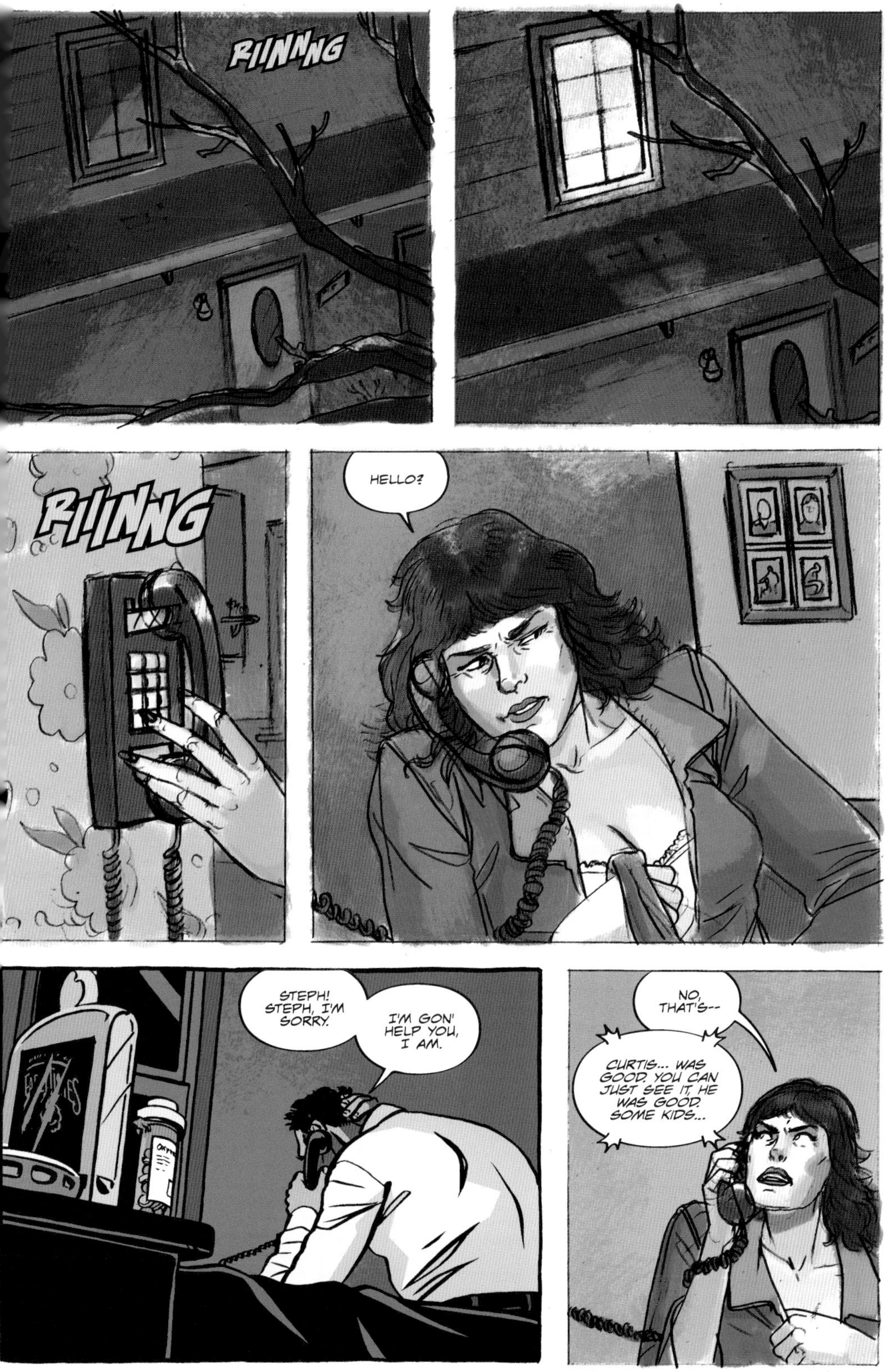
RIINNNG
RIINNG
HELLO?
STEPH! STEPH, I'M SORRY.
I'M GON' HELP YOU, I AM.
NO, THAT'S--
CURTIS... WAS GOOD. YOU CAN JUST SEE IT, HE WAS GOOD. SOME KIDS...

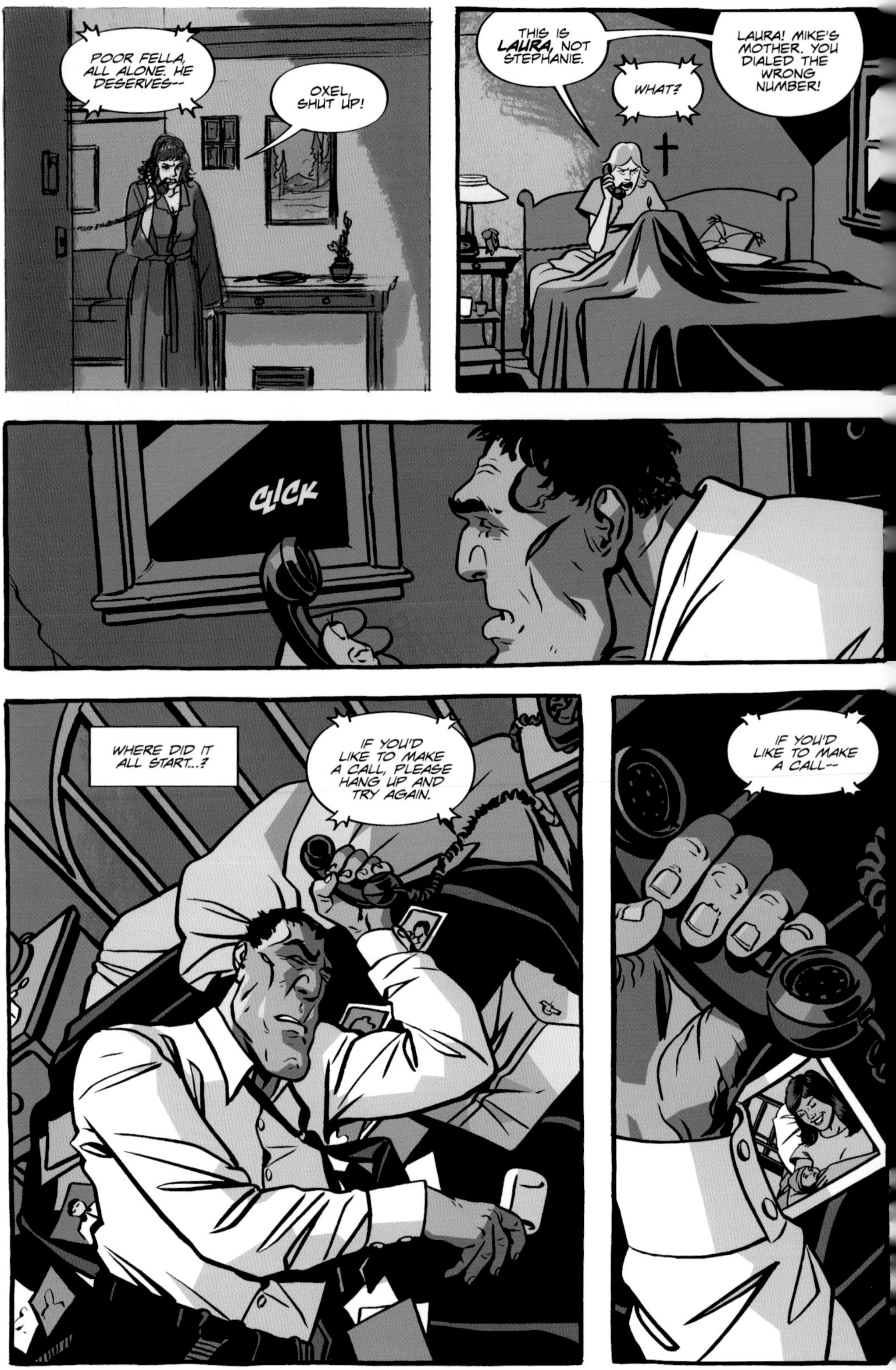
POOR FELLA, ALL ALONE. HE DESERVES--
OXEL, SHUT UP!
THIS IS LAURA, NOT STEPHANIE.
WHAT?
LAURA! MIKE'S MOTHER. YOU DIALED THE WRONG NUMBER!
CLICK
WHERE DID IT ALL START...?
IF YOU'D LIKE TO MAKE A CALL, PLEASE HANG UP AND TRY AGAIN.
IF YOU'D LIKE TO MAKE A CALL--

— CHAPTER THREE —

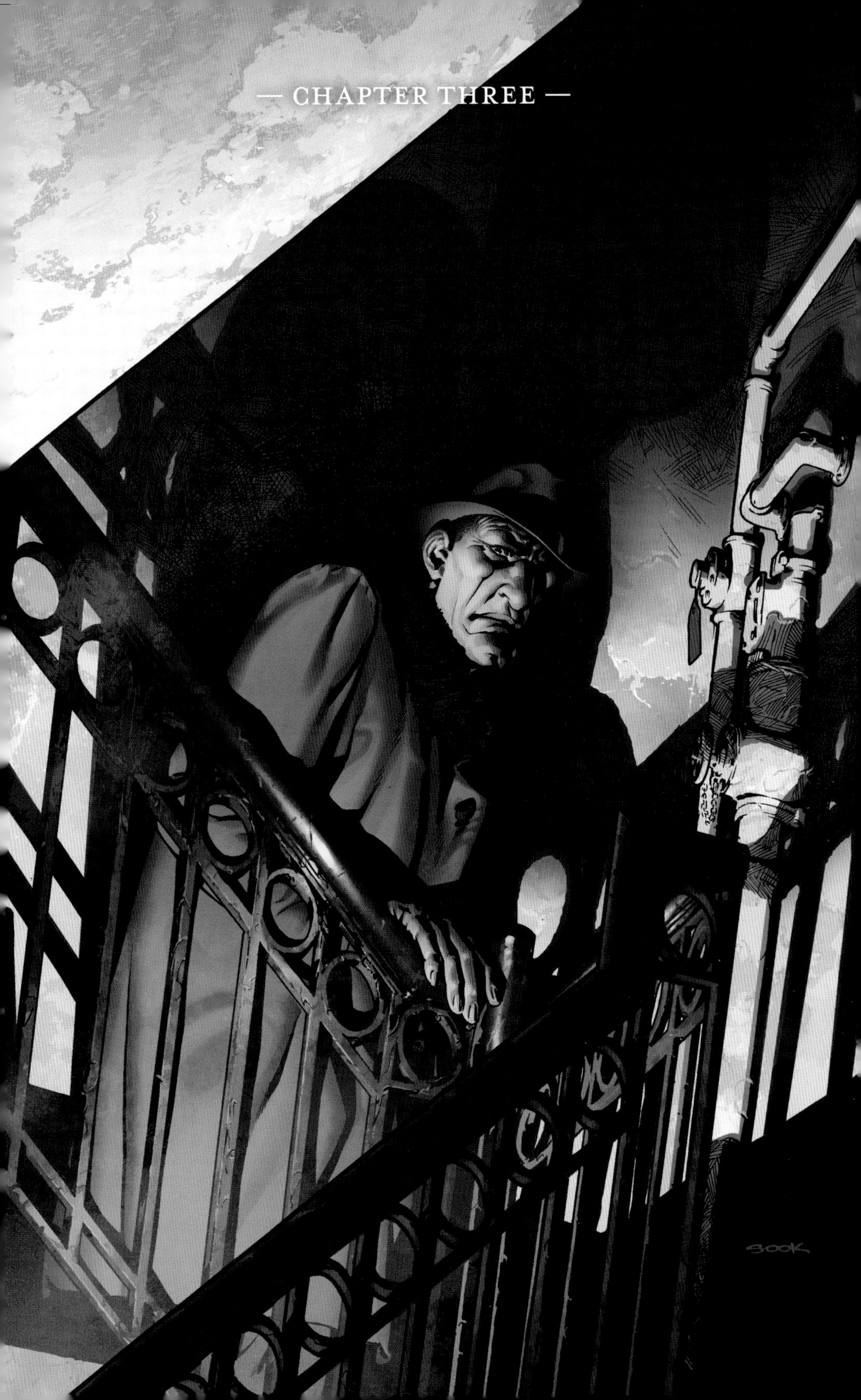
SOOK

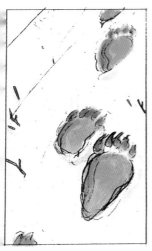

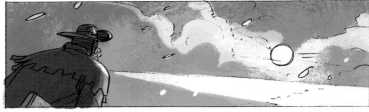

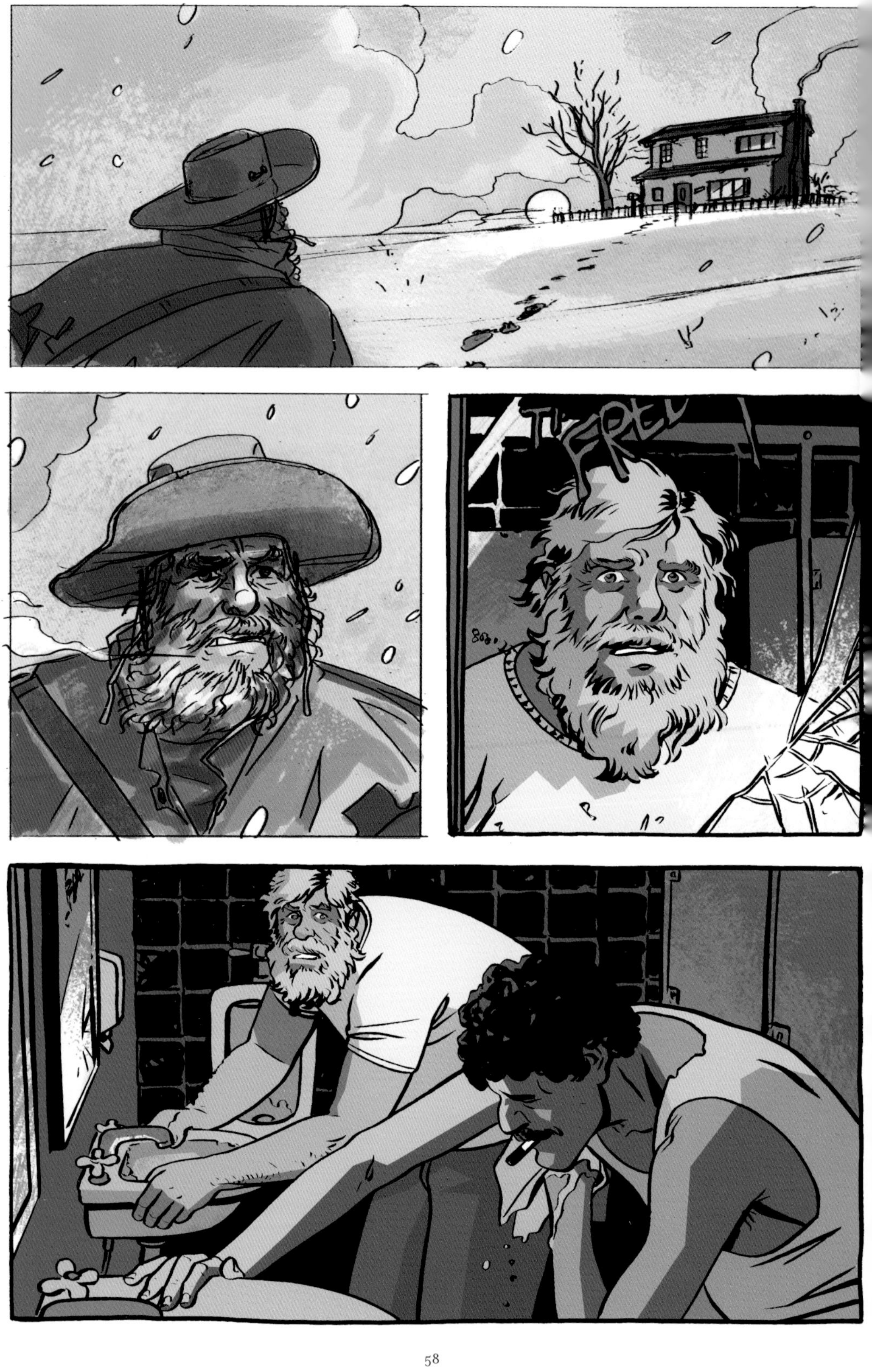

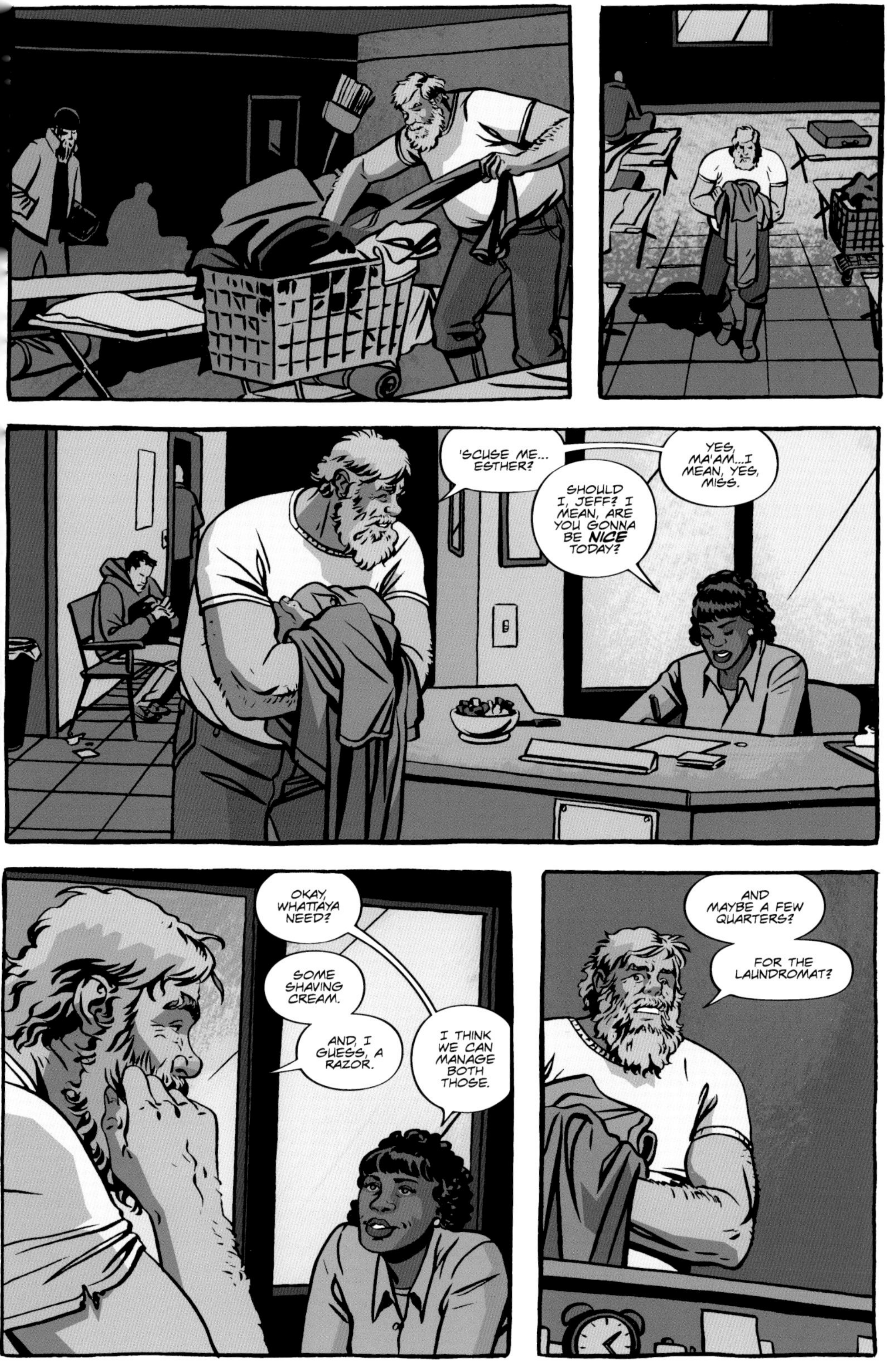
'SCUSE ME... ESTHER?
SHOULD I, JEFF? I MEAN, ARE YOU GONNA BE NICE TODAY?
YES, MA'AM...I MEAN, YES, MISS.
OKAY, WHATTAYA NEED?
SOME SHAVING CREAM.
AND, I GUESS, A RAZOR.
I THINK WE CAN MANAGE BOTH THOSE.
AND MAYBE A FEW QUARTERS?
FOR THE LAUNDROMAT?

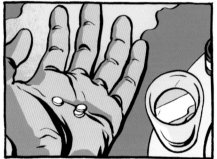

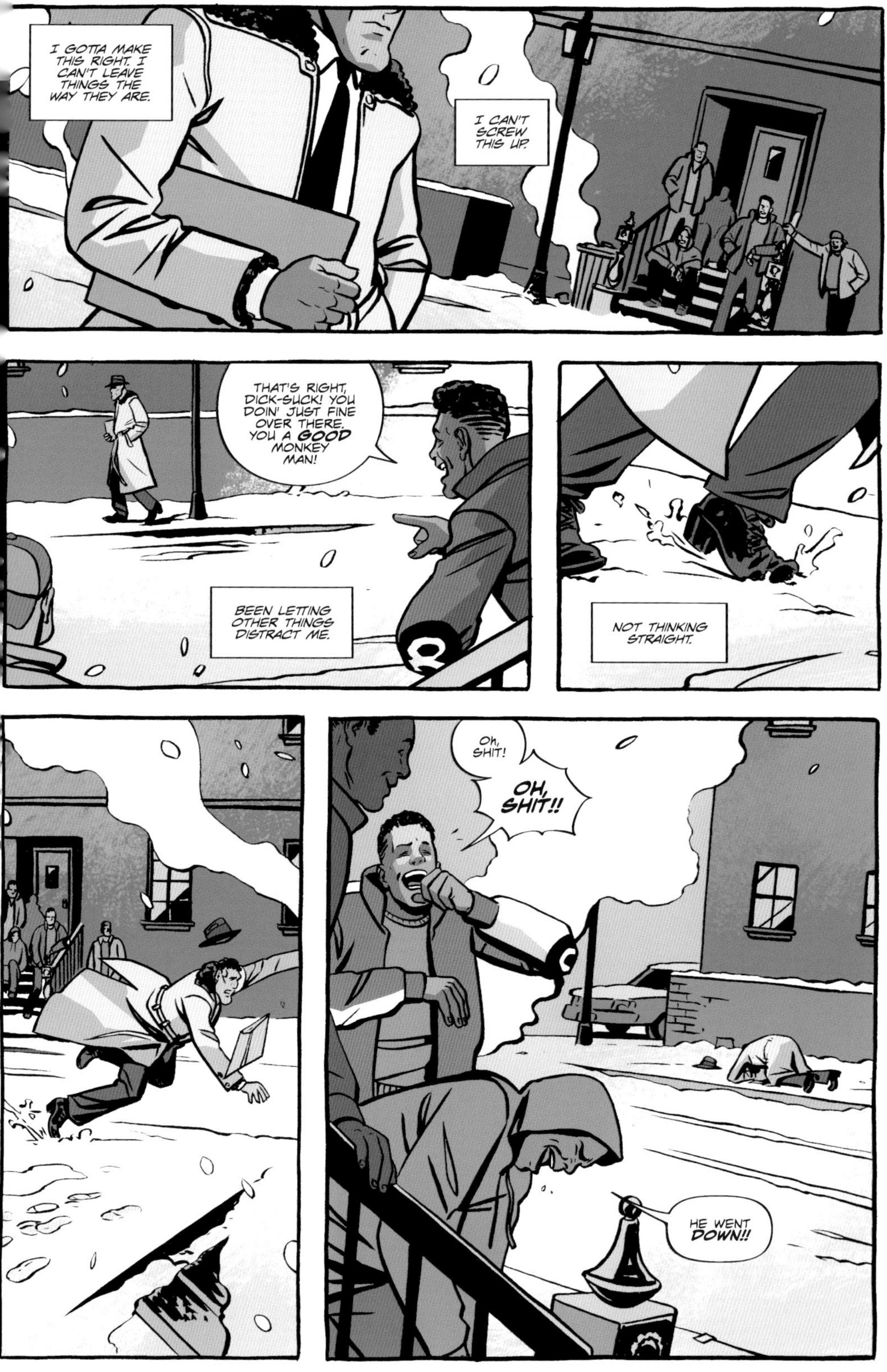
I GOTTA MAKE THIS RIGHT. I CAN'T LEAVE THINGS THE WAY THEY ARE.
I CAN'T SCREW THIS UP.
THAT'S RIGHT, DICK-SUCK! YOU DOIN' JUST FINE OVER THERE. YOU A GOOD MONKEY MAN!
BEEN LETTING OTHER THINGS DISTRACT ME.
NOT THINKING STRAIGHT.
Oh, SHIT!
OH, SHIT!!
HE WENT DOWN!!

DOWN LIKE
A *MOTHER-
FUCKER!!*

IT'S ALL
RIGHT. IT'S
OKAY.

PILLS
KICK IN
SOON.

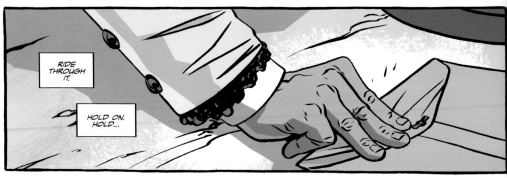

RIDE
THROUGH
IT.

HOLD ON.
HOLD...

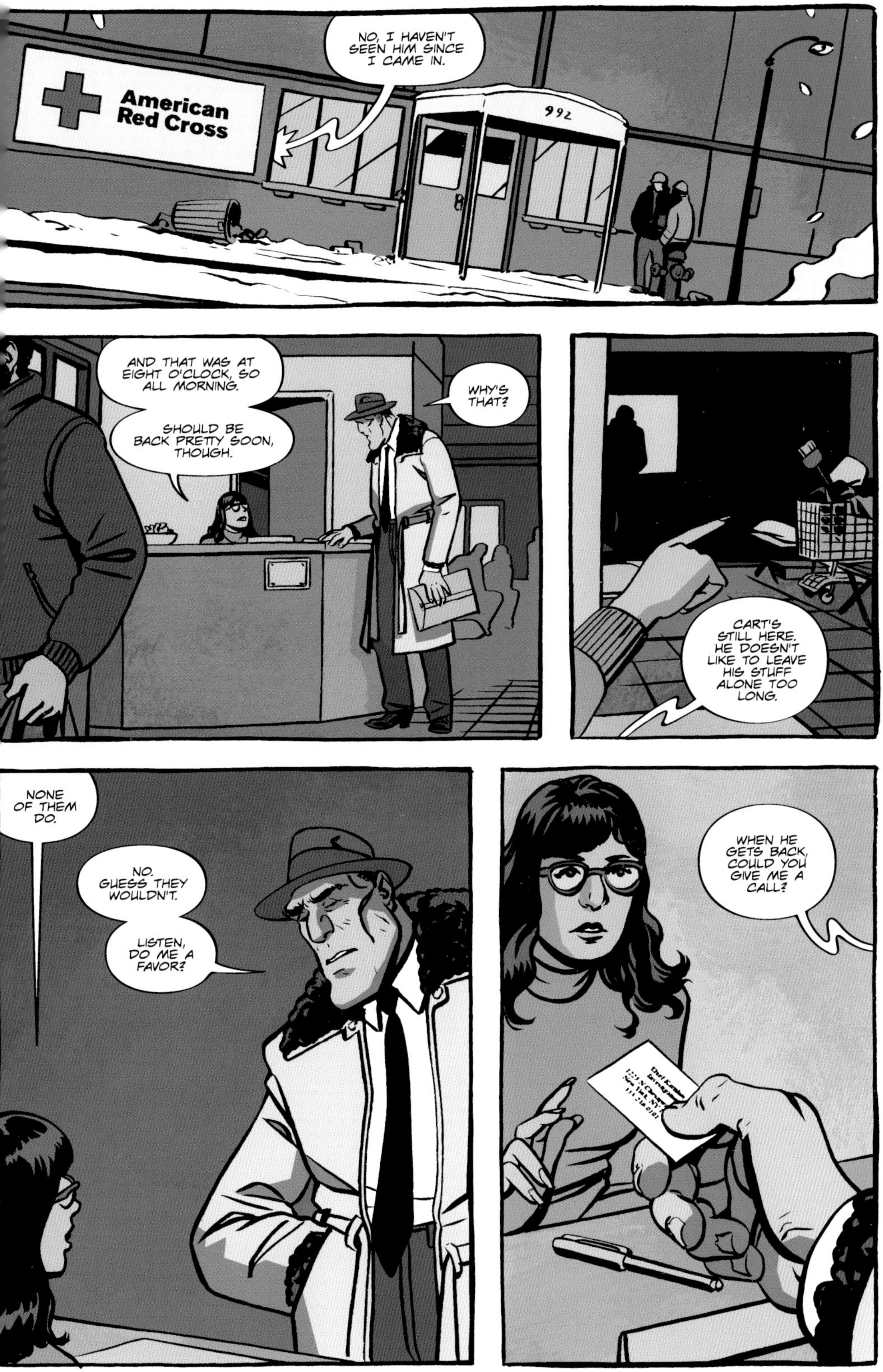
American Red Cross
992
NO, I HAVEN'T SEEN HIM SINCE I CAME IN.
AND THAT WAS AT EIGHT O'CLOCK, SO ALL MORNING.
SHOULD BE BACK PRETTY SOON, THOUGH.
WHY'S THAT?
CART'S STILL HERE. HE DOESN'T LIKE TO LEAVE HIS STUFF ALONE TOO LONG.
NONE OF THEM DO.
NO. GUESS THEY WOULDN'T.
LISTEN, DO ME A FAVOR?
WHEN HE GETS BACK, COULD YOU GIVE ME A CALL?

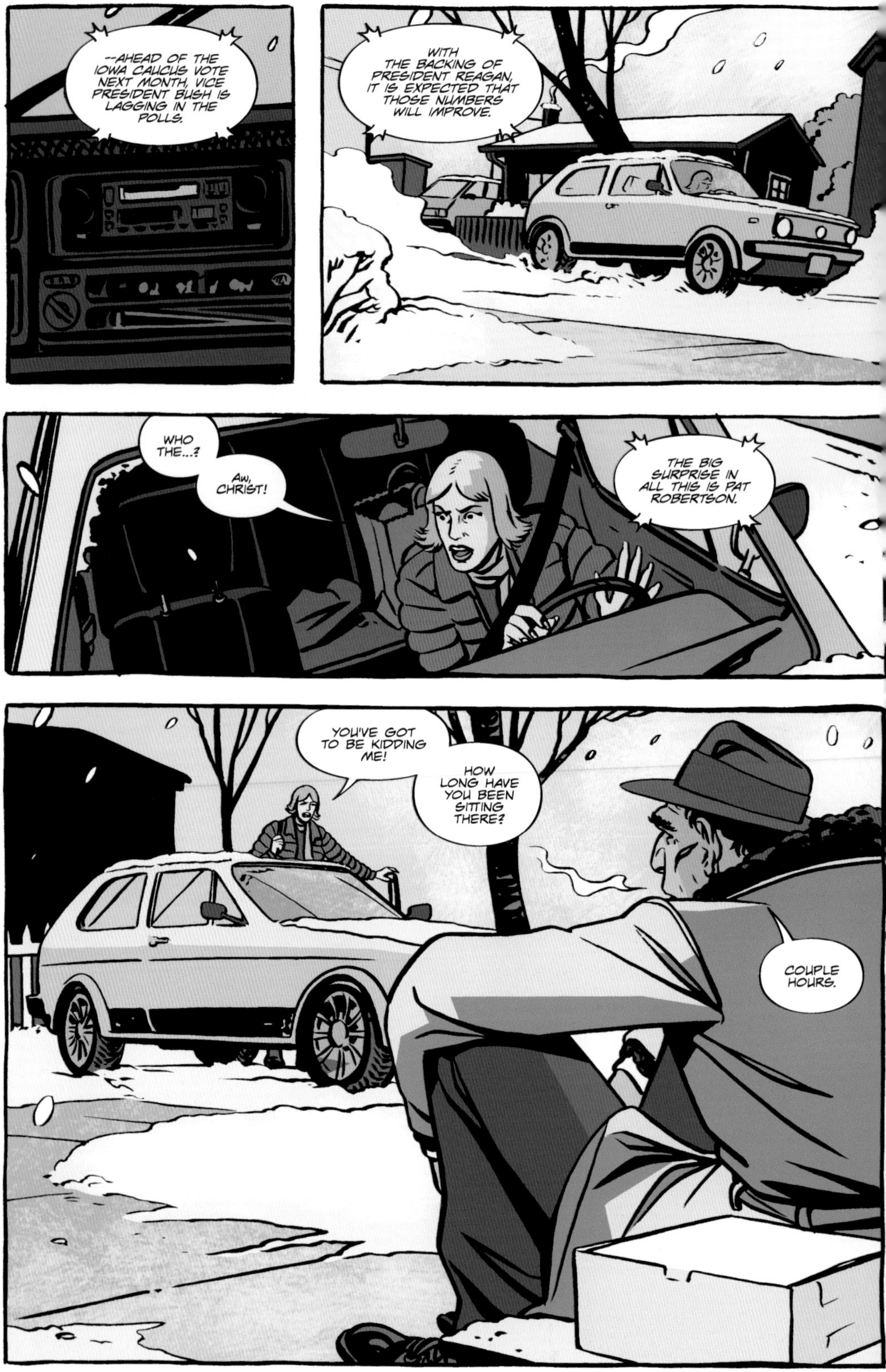
--AHEAD OF THE IOWA CAUCUS VOTE NEXT MONTH, VICE PRESIDENT BUSH IS LAGGING IN THE POLLS.
WITH THE BACKING OF PRESIDENT REAGAN, IT IS EXPECTED THAT THOSE NUMBERS WILL IMPROVE.
WHO THE...?
AW, CHRIST!
THE BIG SURPRISE IN ALL THIS IS PAT ROBERTSON.
YOU'VE GOT TO BE KIDDING ME!
HOW LONG HAVE YOU BEEN SITTING THERE?
COUPLE HOURS.

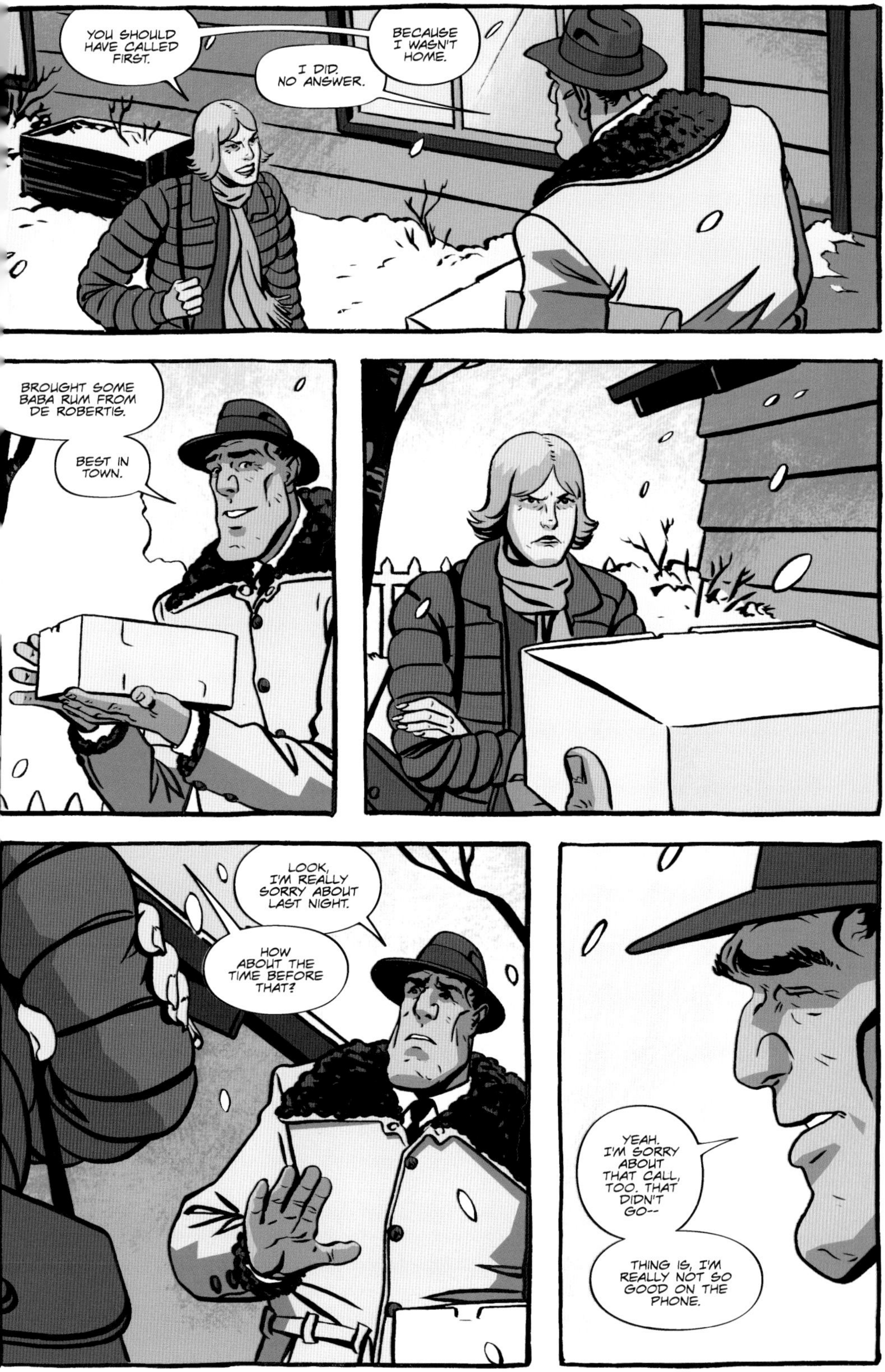
YOU SHOULD HAVE CALLED FIRST.
I DID. NO ANSWER.
BECAUSE I WASN'T HOME.
BROUGHT SOME BABA RUM FROM DE ROBERTIS.
BEST IN TOWN.
LOOK, I'M REALLY SORRY ABOUT LAST NIGHT.
HOW ABOUT THE TIME BEFORE THAT?
YEAH. I'M SORRY ABOUT THAT CALL, TOO. THAT DIDN'T GO--
THING IS, I'M REALLY NOT SO GOOD ON THE PHONE.

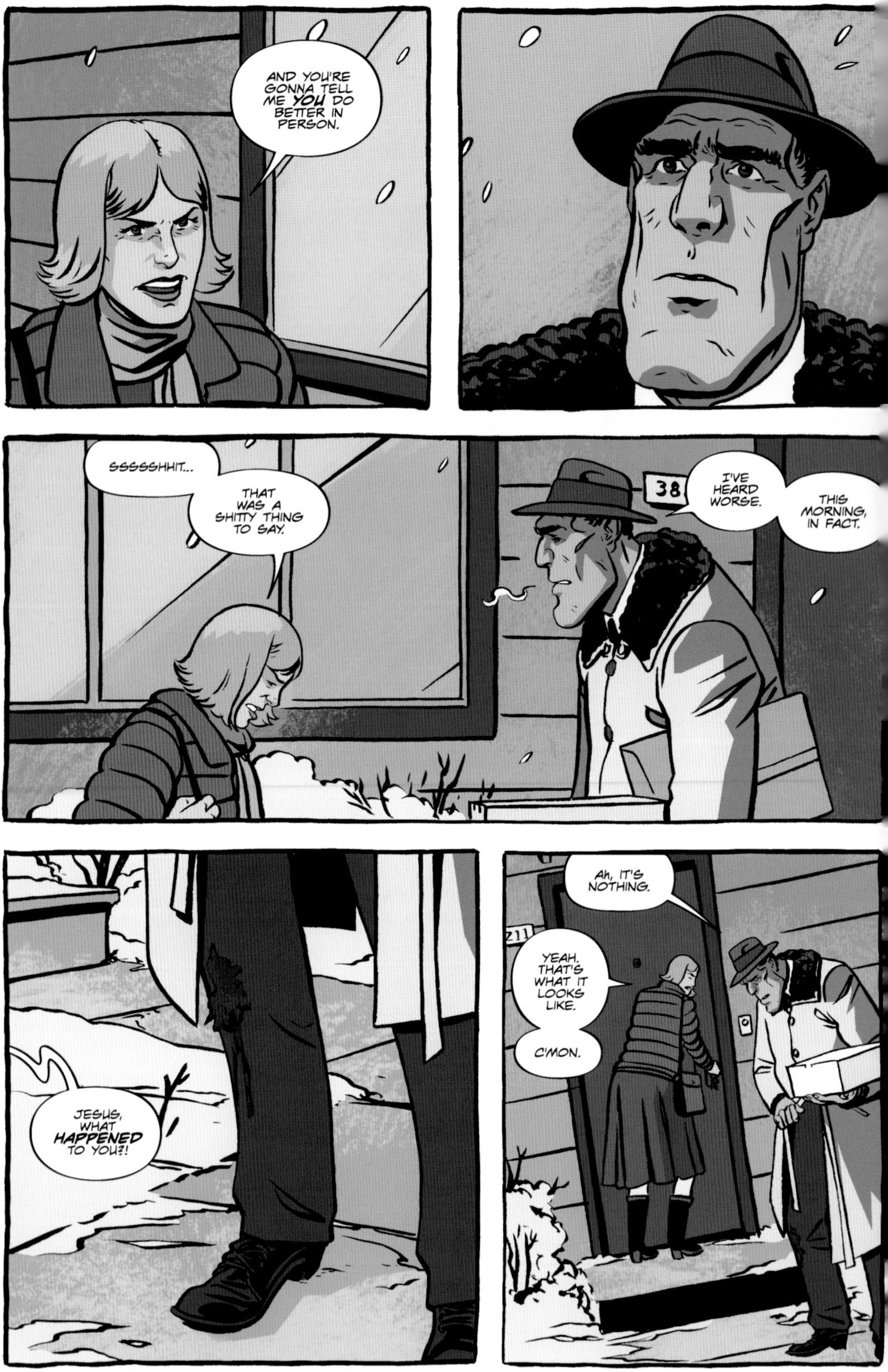
AND YOU'RE GONNA TELL ME YOU DO BETTER IN PERSON.
SSSSSHHIT...
THAT WAS A SHITTY THING TO SAY.
I'VE HEARD WORSE.
THIS MORNING, IN FACT.
JESUS, WHAT HAPPENED TO YOU?!
Ah, IT'S NOTHING.
YEAH. THAT'S WHAT IT LOOKS LIKE.
C'MON.

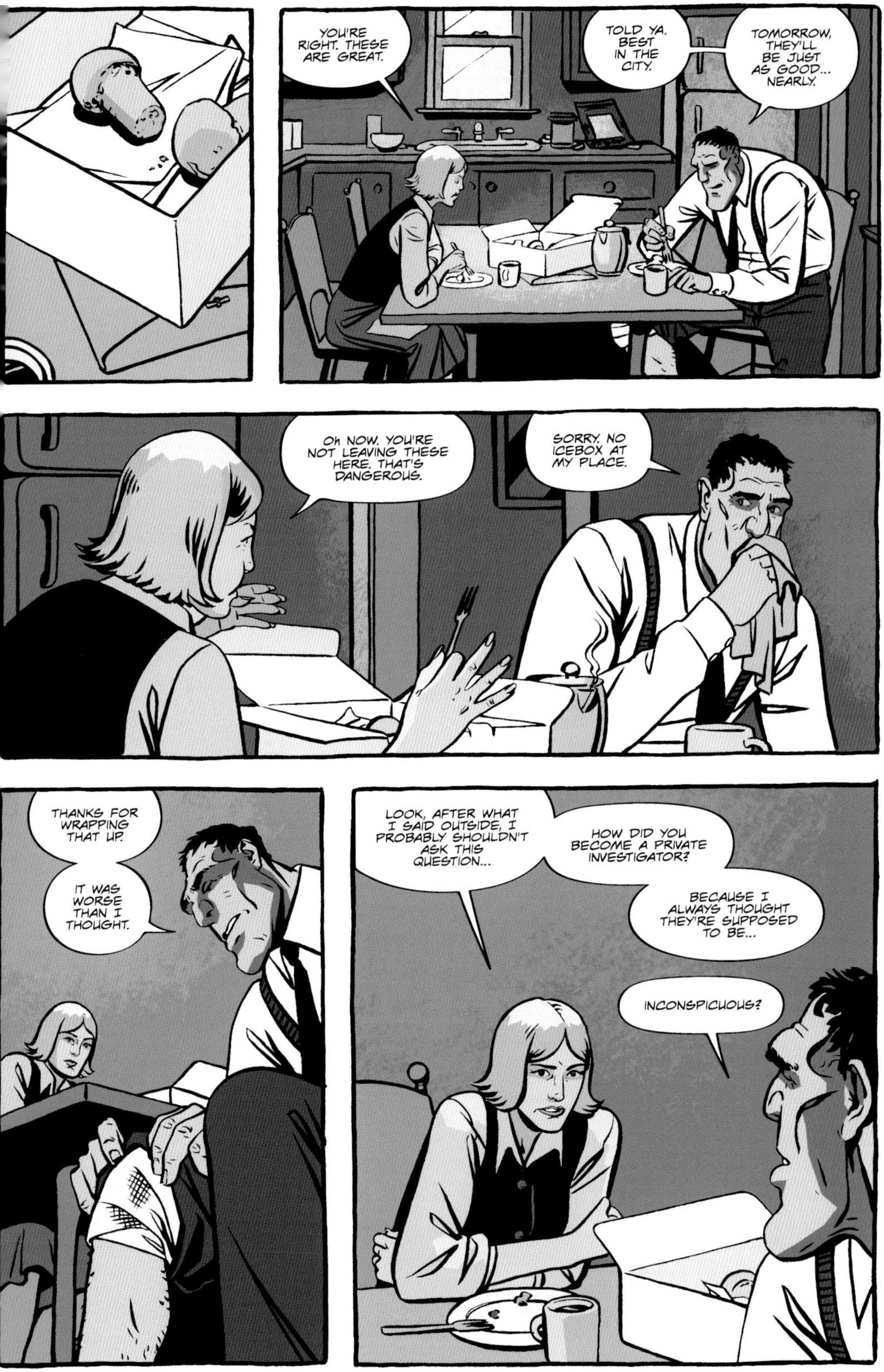
YOU'RE RIGHT. THESE ARE GREAT.
TOLD YA. BEST IN THE CITY.
TOMORROW, THEY'LL BE JUST AS GOOD... NEARLY.
Oh NOW. YOU'RE NOT LEAVING THESE HERE. THAT'S DANGEROUS.
SORRY. NO ICEBOX AT MY PLACE.
THANKS FOR WRAPPING THAT UP.
IT WAS WORSE THAN I THOUGHT.
LOOK, AFTER WHAT I SAID OUTSIDE, I PROBABLY SHOULDN'T ASK THIS QUESTION...
HOW DID YOU BECOME A PRIVATE INVESTIGATOR?
BECAUSE I ALWAYS THOUGHT THEY'RE SUPPOSED TO BE...
INCONSPICUOUS?

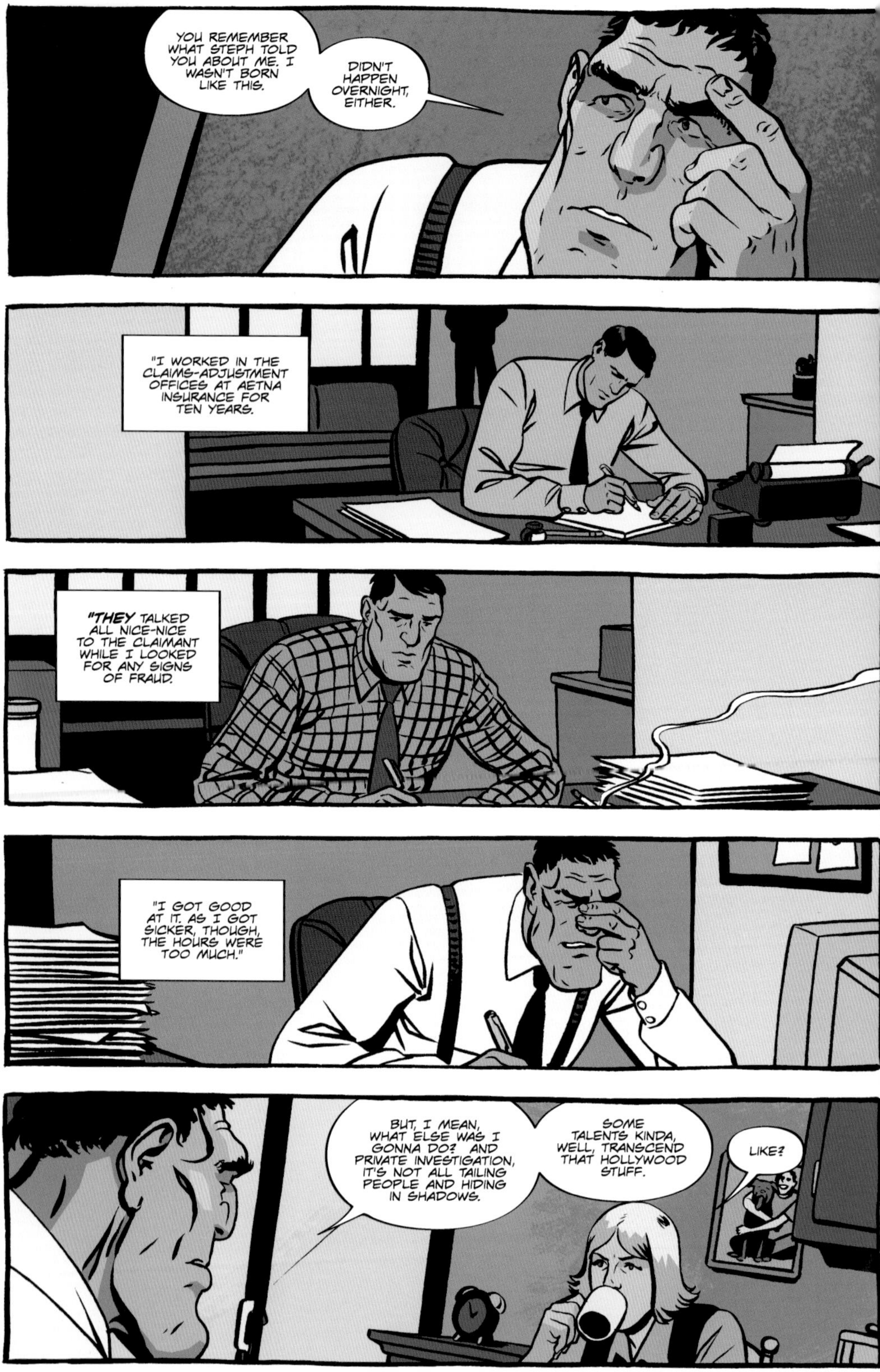
YOU REMEMBER WHAT STEPH TOLD YOU ABOUT ME. I WASN'T BORN LIKE THIS.
DIDN'T HAPPEN OVERNIGHT, EITHER.
"I WORKED IN THE CLAIMS-ADJUSTMENT OFFICES AT AETNA INSURANCE FOR TEN YEARS.
"THEY TALKED ALL NICE-NICE TO THE CLAIMANT WHILE I LOOKED FOR ANY SIGNS OF FRAUD.
"I GOT GOOD AT IT. AS I GOT SICKER, THOUGH, THE HOURS WERE TOO MUCH."
BUT, I MEAN, WHAT ELSE WAS I GONNA DO? AND PRIVATE INVESTIGATION, IT'S NOT ALL TAILING PEOPLE AND HIDING IN SHADOWS.
SOME TALENTS KINDA, WELL, TRANSCEND THAT HOLLYWOOD STUFF.
LIKE?

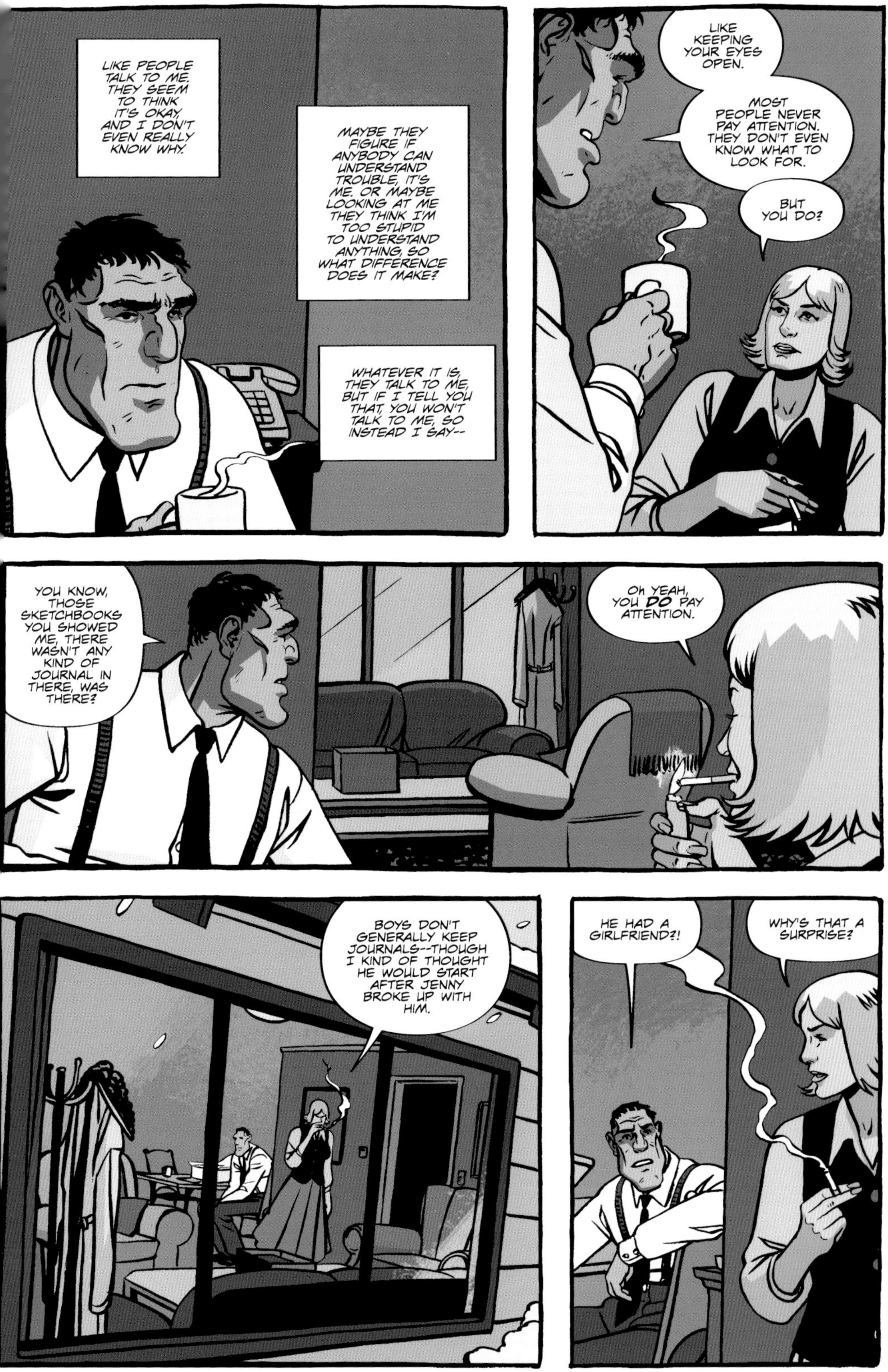
LIKE PEOPLE TALK TO ME. THEY SEEM TO THINK IT'S OKAY, AND I DON'T EVEN REALLY KNOW WHY.
MAYBE THEY FIGURE IF ANYBODY CAN UNDERSTAND TROUBLE, IT'S ME. OR MAYBE LOOKING AT ME THEY THINK I'M TOO STUPID TO UNDERSTAND ANYTHING, SO WHAT DIFFERENCE DOES IT MAKE?
WHATEVER IT IS, THEY TALK TO ME, BUT IF I TELL YOU THAT, YOU WON'T TALK TO ME, SO INSTEAD I SAY--
LIKE KEEPING YOUR EYES OPEN.
MOST PEOPLE NEVER PAY ATTENTION. THEY DON'T EVEN KNOW WHAT TO LOOK FOR.
BUT YOU DO?
YOU KNOW, THOSE SKETCHBOOKS YOU SHOWED ME, THERE WASN'T ANY KIND OF JOURNAL IN THERE, WAS THERE?
Oh YEAH, YOU DO PAY ATTENTION.
BOYS DON'T GENERALLY KEEP JOURNALS--THOUGH I KIND OF THOUGHT HE WOULD START AFTER JENNY BROKE UP WITH HIM.
HE HAD A GIRLFRIEND?!
WHY'S THAT A SURPRISE?

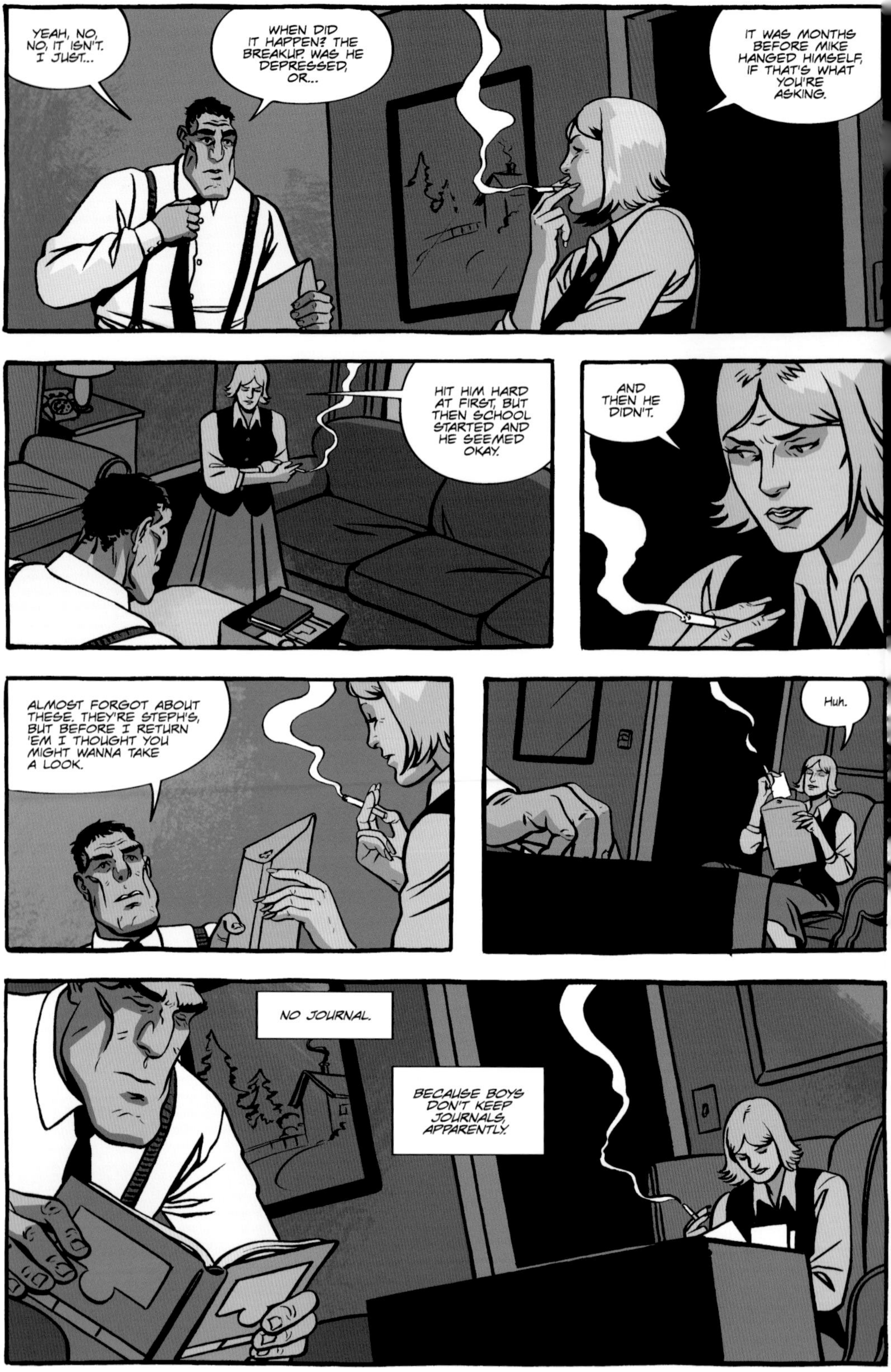
YEAH, NO, NO, IT ISN'T. I JUST...
WHEN DID IT HAPPEN? THE BREAKUP. WAS HE DEPRESSED, OR...
IT WAS MONTHS BEFORE MIKE HANGED HIMSELF, IF THAT'S WHAT YOU'RE ASKING.
HIT HIM HARD AT FIRST, BUT THEN SCHOOL STARTED AND HE SEEMED OKAY.
AND THEN HE DIDN'T.
ALMOST FORGOT ABOUT THESE. THEY'RE STEPH'S, BUT BEFORE I RETURN 'EM I THOUGHT YOU MIGHT WANNA TAKE A LOOK.
Huh.
NO JOURNAL.
BECAUSE BOYS DON'T KEEP JOURNALS, APPARENTLY.

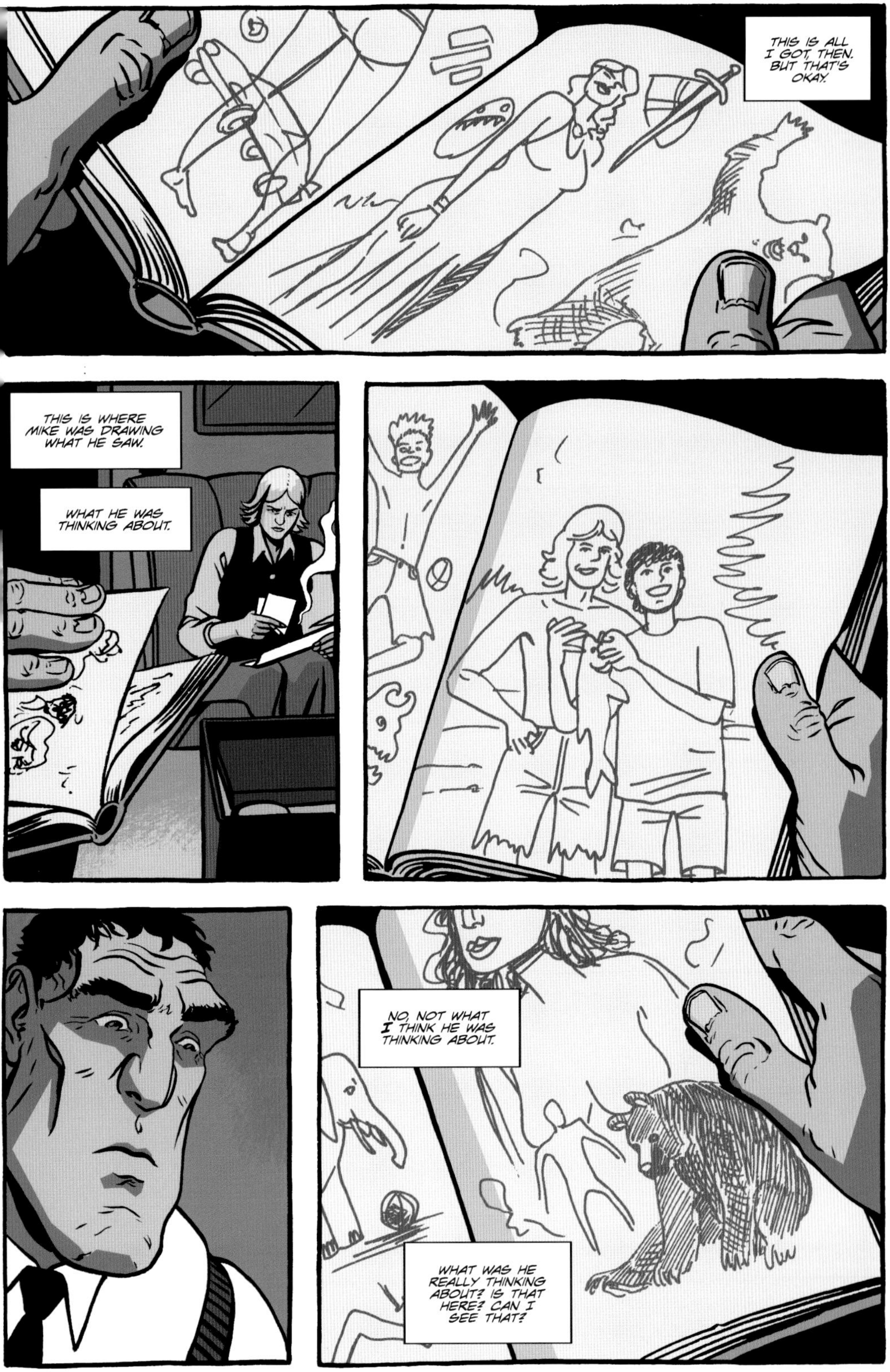
THIS IS ALL I GOT, THEN. BUT THAT'S OKAY.
THIS IS WHERE MIKE WAS DRAWING WHAT HE SAW.
WHAT HE WAS THINKING ABOUT.
NO, NOT WHAT I THINK HE WAS THINKING ABOUT.
WHAT WAS HE REALLY THINKING ABOUT? IS THAT HERE? CAN I SEE THAT?

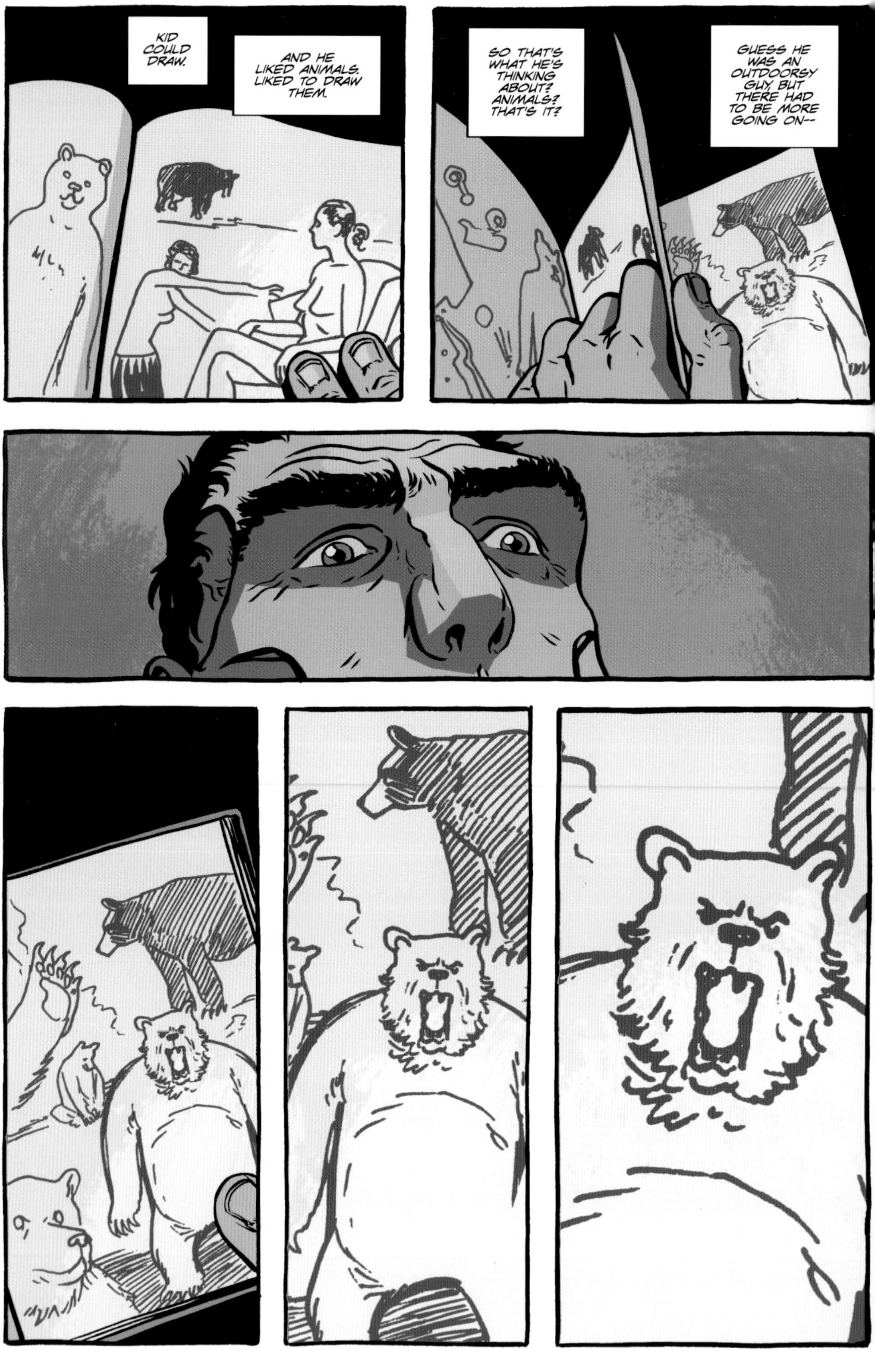
KID COULD DRAW.
AND HE LIKED ANIMALS. LIKED TO DRAW THEM.
SO THAT'S WHAT HE'S THINKING ABOUT? ANIMALS? THAT'S IT?
GUESS HE WAS AN OUTDOORSY GUY, BUT THERE HAD TO BE MORE GOING ON--

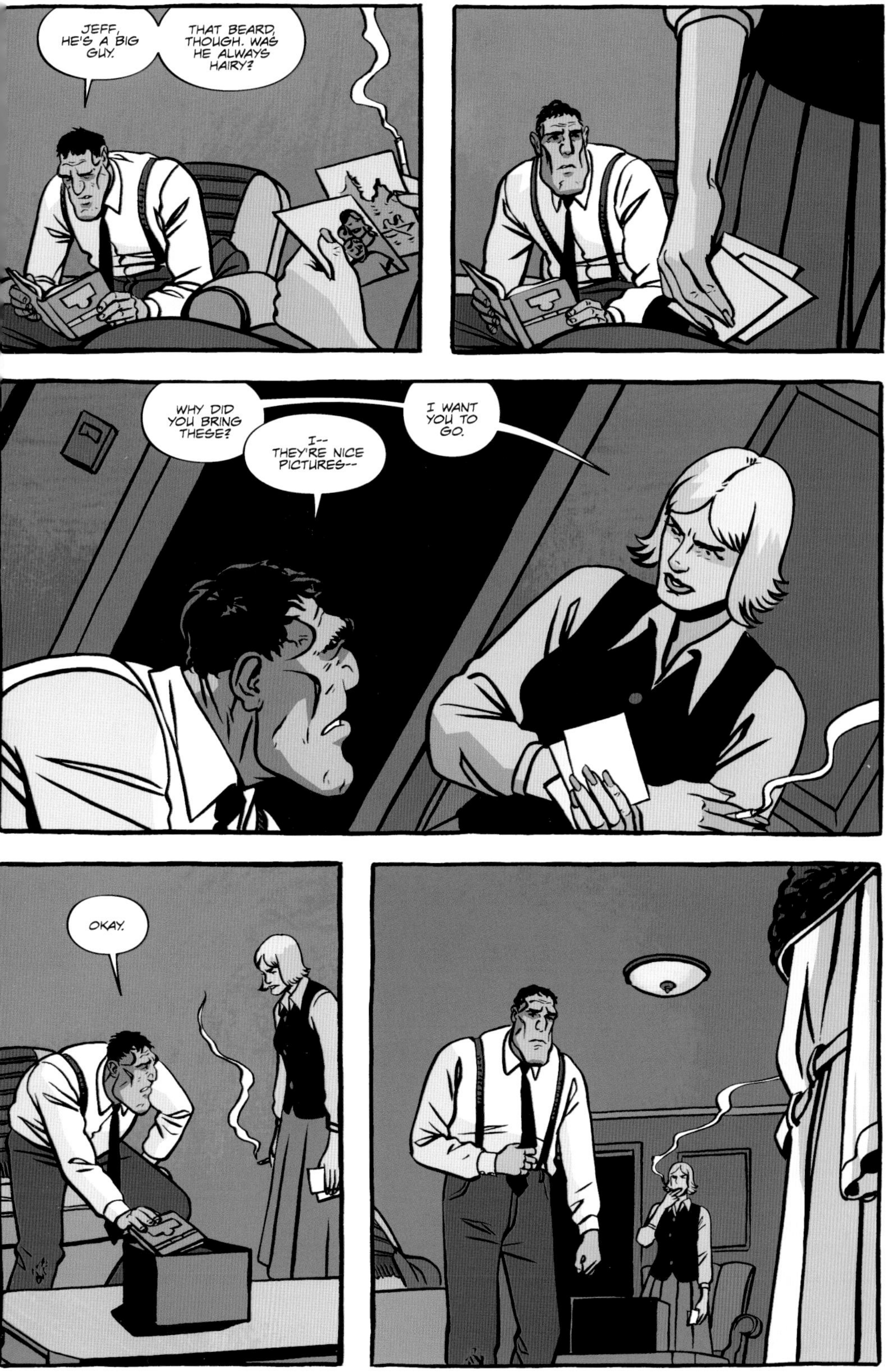
JEFF, HE'S A BIG GUY.
THAT BEARD, THOUGH. WAS HE ALWAYS HAIRY?
WHY DID YOU BRING THESE?
I-- THEY'RE NICE PICTURES--
I WANT YOU TO GO.
OKAY.

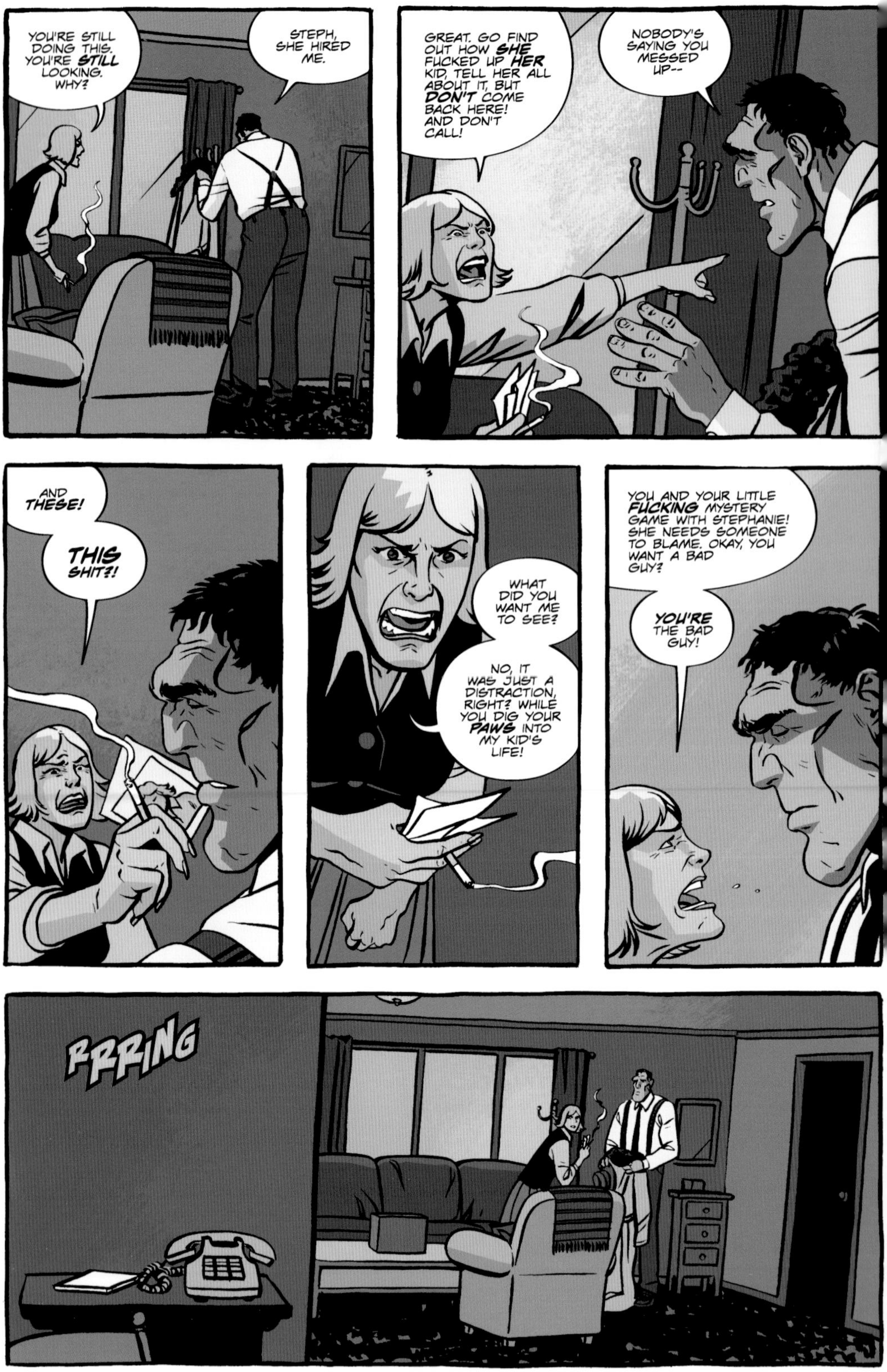
YOU'RE STILL DOING THIS. YOU'RE STILL LOOKING. WHY?
STEPH, SHE HIRED ME.
GREAT. GO FIND OUT HOW SHE FUCKED UP HER KID, TELL HER ALL ABOUT IT, BUT DON'T COME BACK HERE! AND DON'T CALL!
NOBODY'S SAYING YOU MESSED UP--
AND THESE!
THIS SHIT?!
WHAT DID YOU WANT ME TO SEE?
NO, IT WAS JUST A DISTRACTION, RIGHT? WHILE YOU DIG YOUR PAWS INTO MY KID'S LIFE!
YOU AND YOUR LITTLE FUCKING MYSTERY GAME WITH STEPHANIE! SHE NEEDS SOMEONE TO BLAME. OKAY, YOU WANT A BAD GUY?
YOU'RE THE BAD GUY!
RRRING

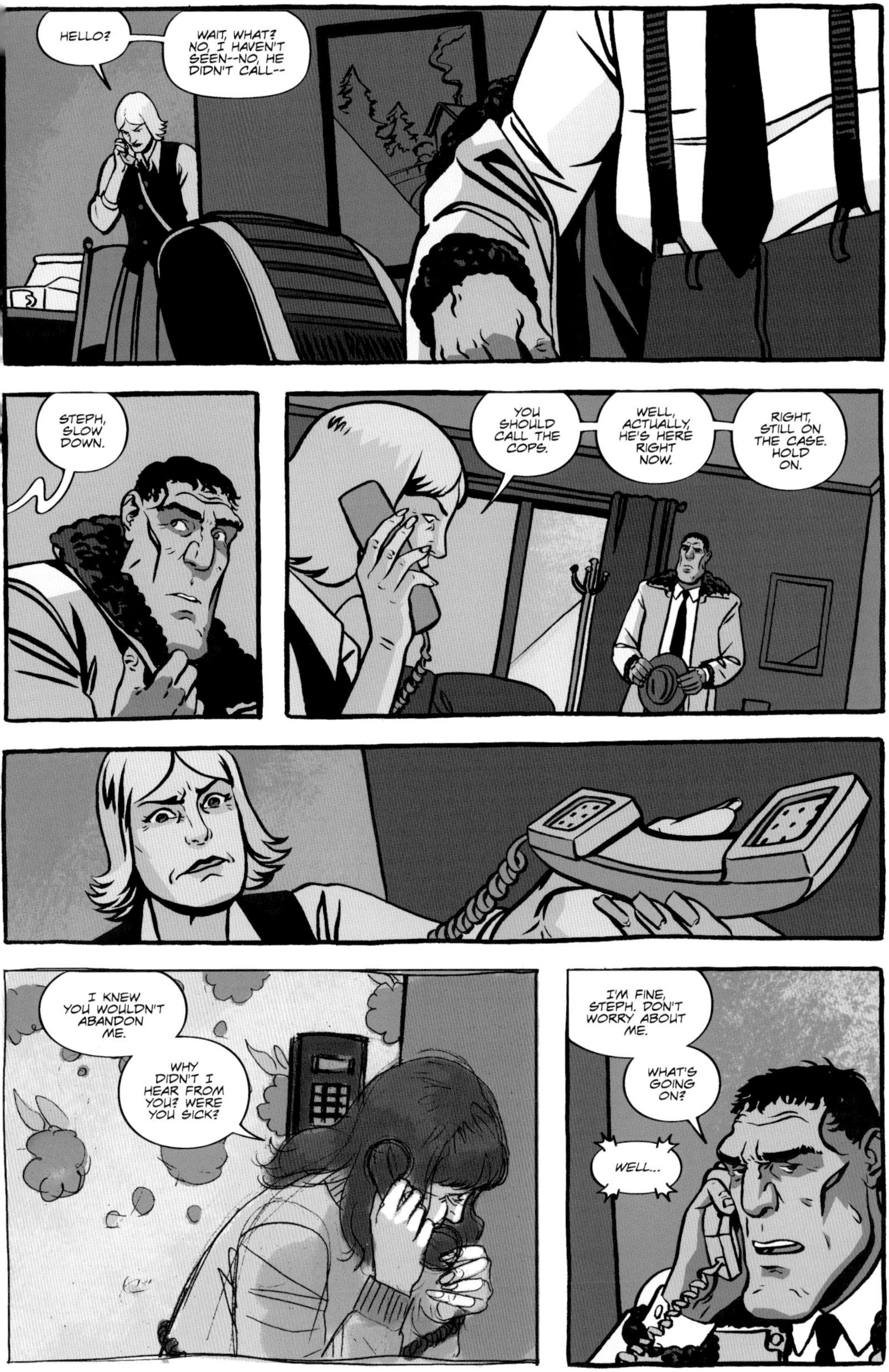
HELLO?
WAIT, WHAT? NO, I HAVEN'T SEEN--NO, HE DIDN'T CALL--
STEPH, SLOW DOWN.
YOU SHOULD CALL THE COPS.
WELL, ACTUALLY, HE'S HERE RIGHT NOW.
RIGHT, STILL ON THE CASE. HOLD ON.
I KNEW YOU WOULDN'T ABANDON ME.
WHY DIDN'T I HEAR FROM YOU? WERE YOU SICK?
I'M FINE, STEPH. DON'T WORRY ABOUT ME.
WHAT'S GOING ON?
WELL...

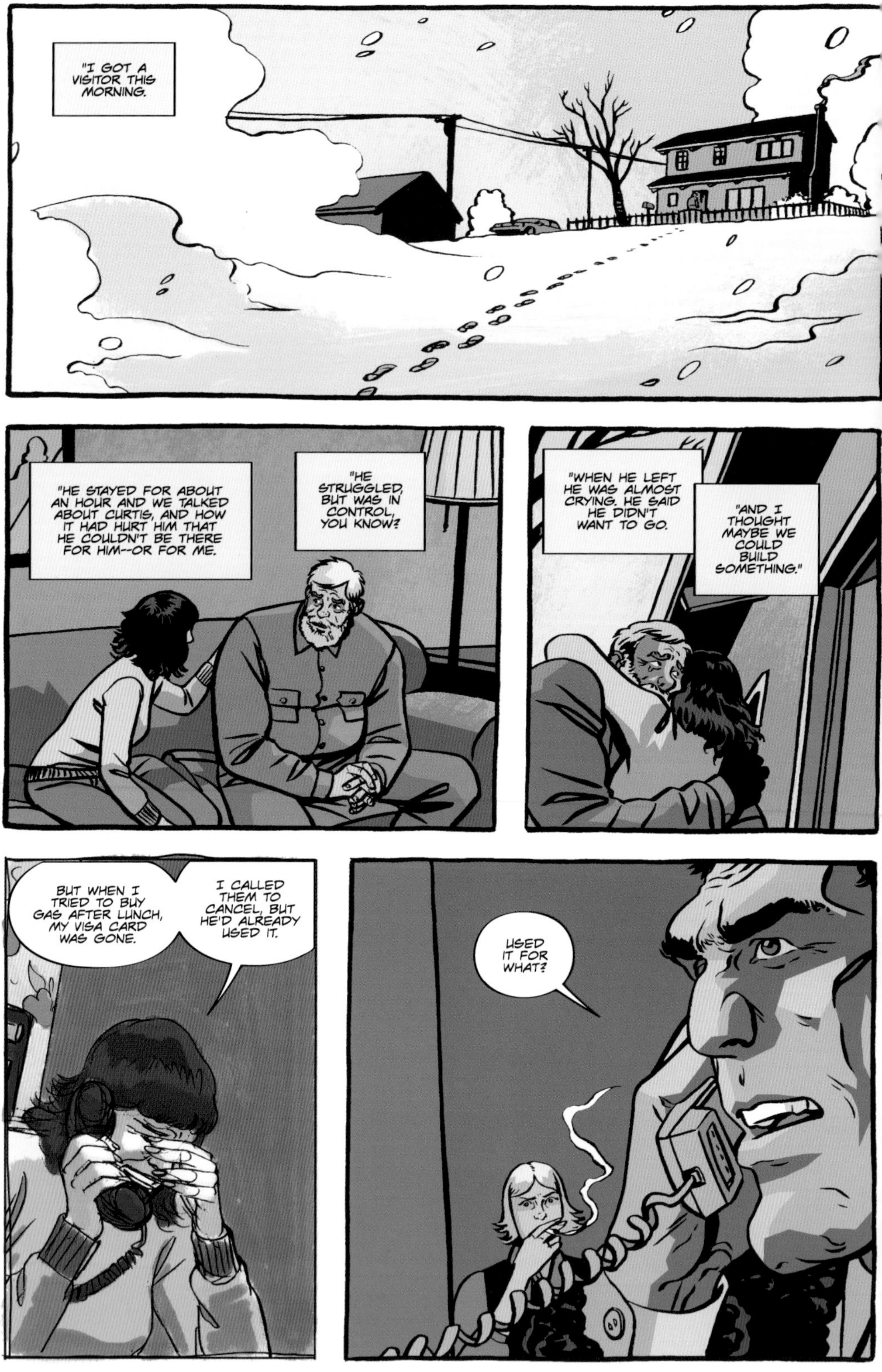
"I GOT A VISITOR THIS MORNING.
"HE STAYED FOR ABOUT AN HOUR AND WE TALKED ABOUT CURTIS, AND HOW IT HAD HURT HIM THAT HE COULDN'T BE THERE FOR HIM--OR FOR ME.
"HE STRUGGLED, BUT WAS IN CONTROL, YOU KNOW?
"WHEN HE LEFT HE WAS ALMOST CRYING. HE SAID HE DIDN'T WANT TO GO.
"AND I THOUGHT MAYBE WE COULD BUILD SOMETHING."
BUT WHEN I TRIED TO BUY GAS AFTER LUNCH, MY VISA CARD WAS GONE.
I CALLED THEM TO CANCEL, BUT HE'D ALREADY USED IT.
USED IT FOR WHAT?

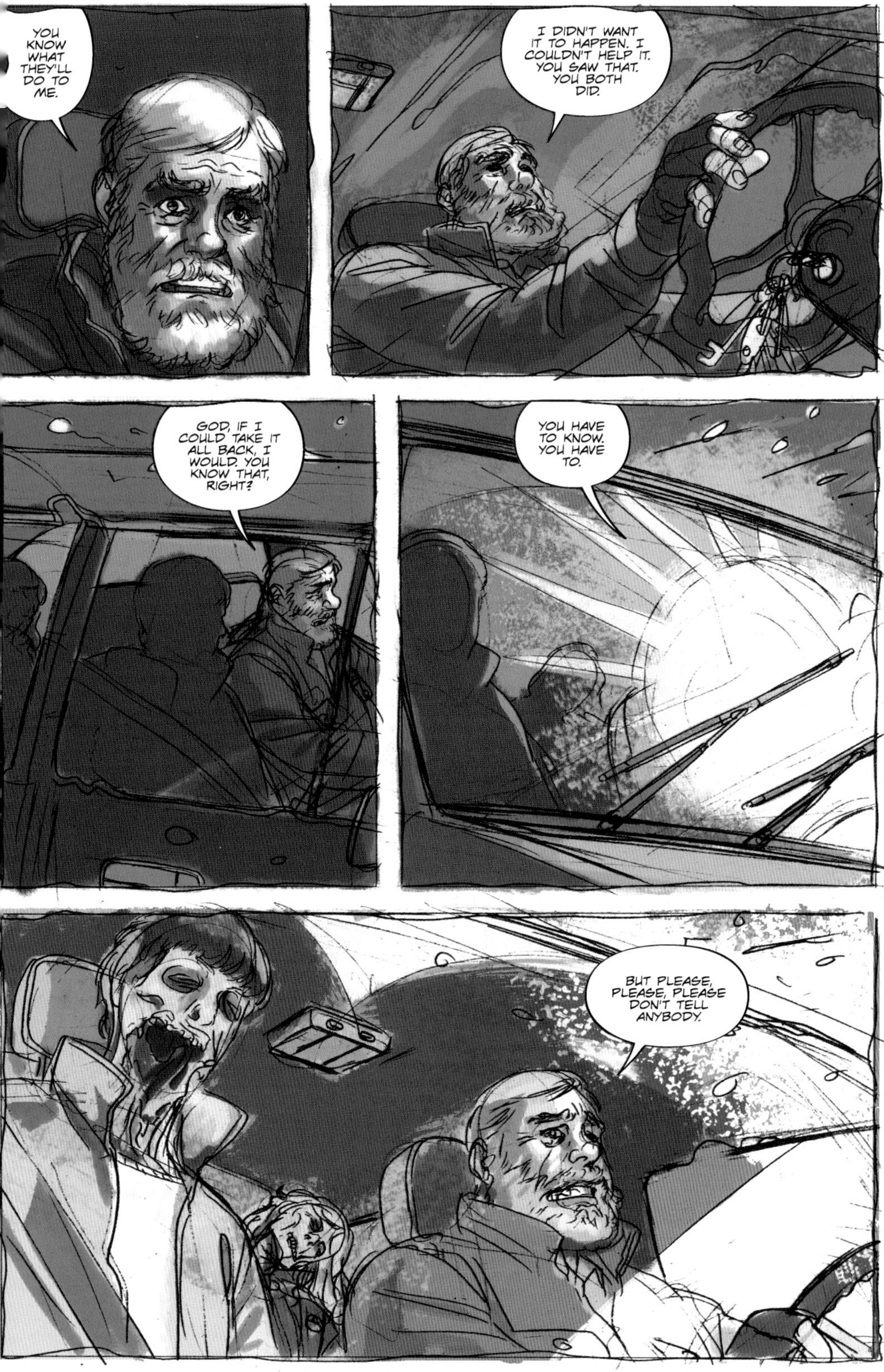
YOU KNOW WHAT THEY'LL DO TO ME.
I DIDN'T WANT IT TO HAPPEN. I COULDN'T HELP IT. YOU SAW THAT. YOU BOTH DID.
GOD, IF I COULD TAKE IT ALL BACK, I WOULD. YOU KNOW THAT, RIGHT?
YOU HAVE TO KNOW. YOU HAVE TO.
BUT PLEASE, PLEASE, PLEASE DON'T TELL ANYBODY.

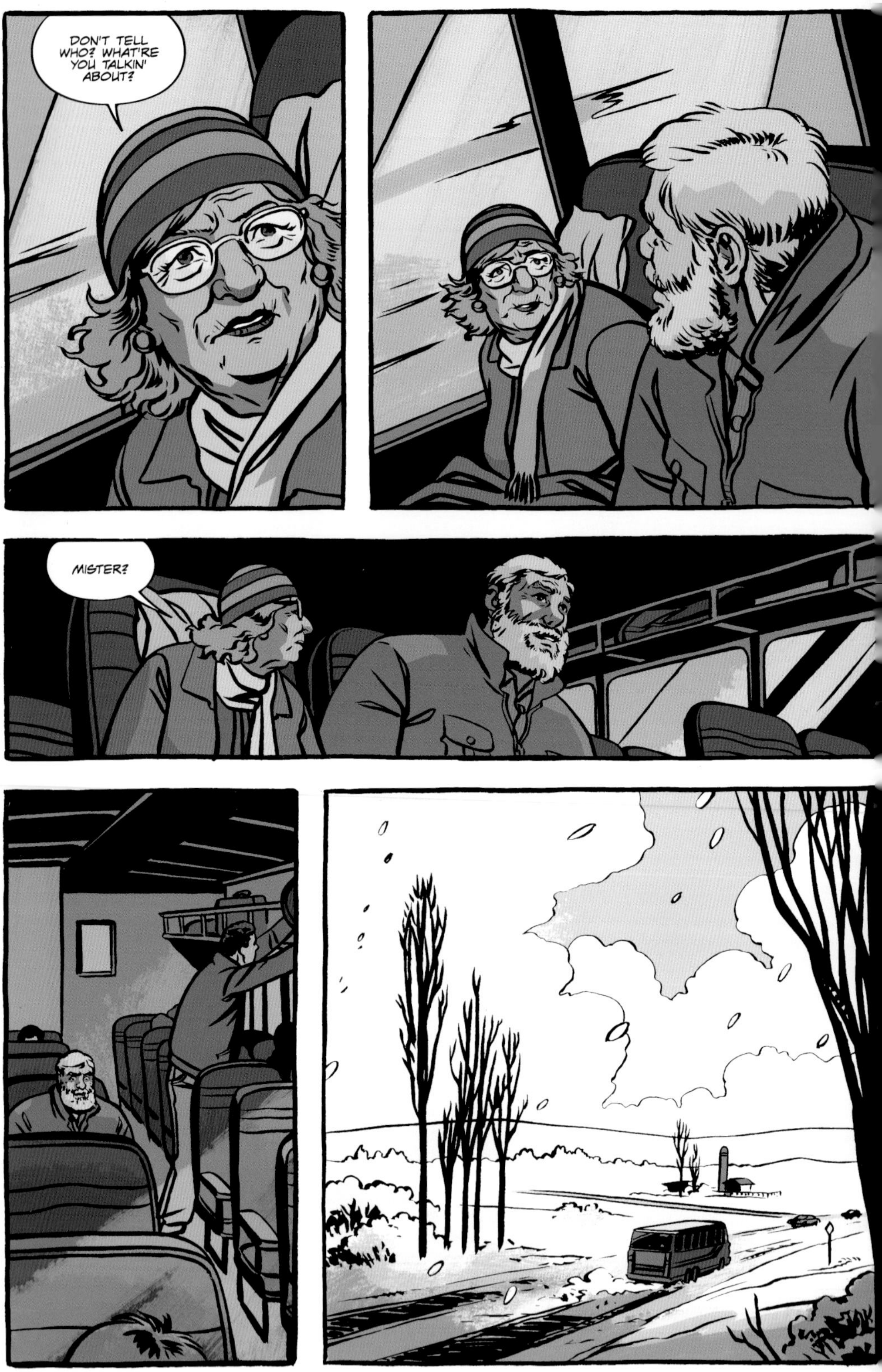
DON'T TELL WHO? WHAT'RE YOU TALKIN' ABOUT?
MISTER?

— CHAPTER FOUR —

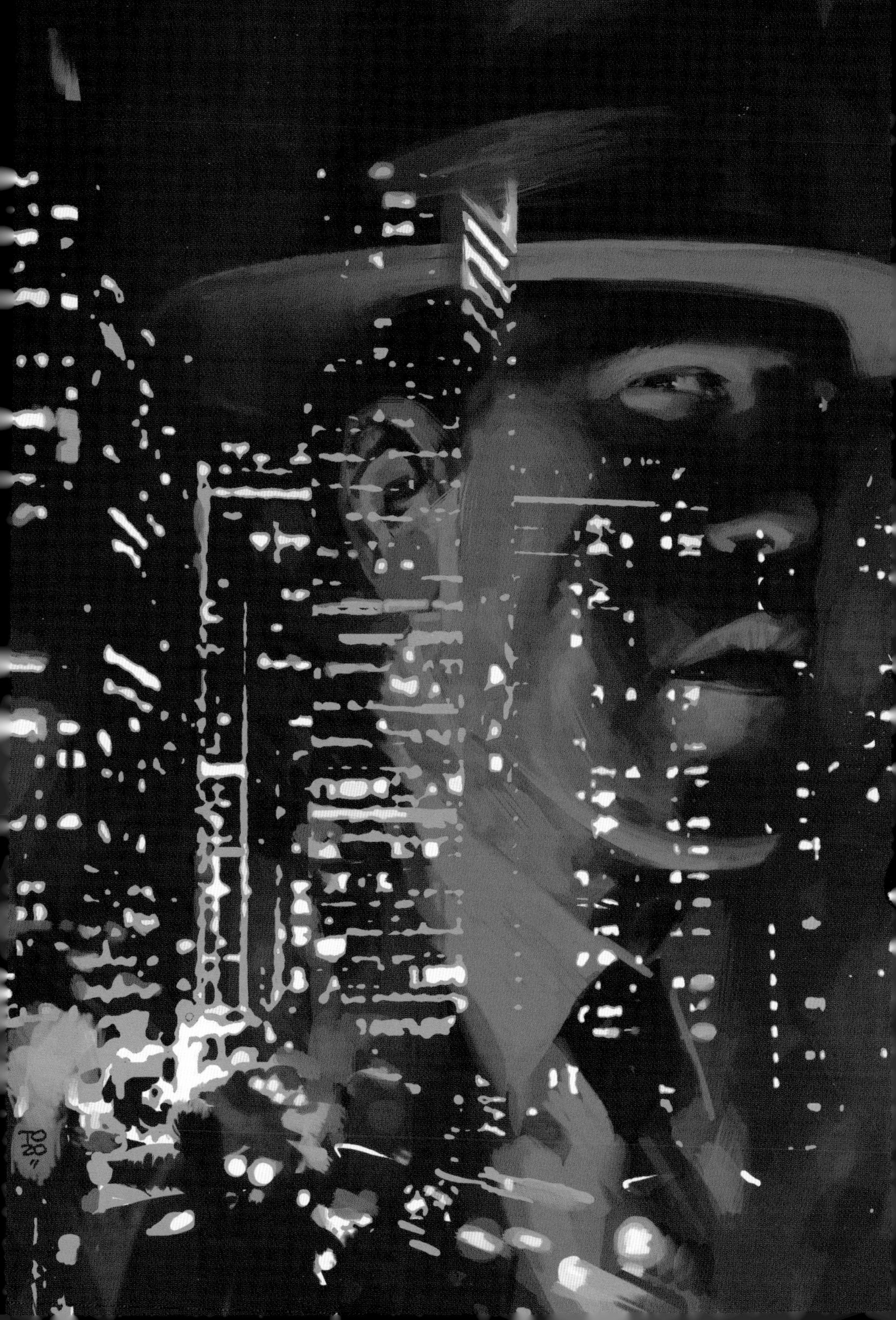

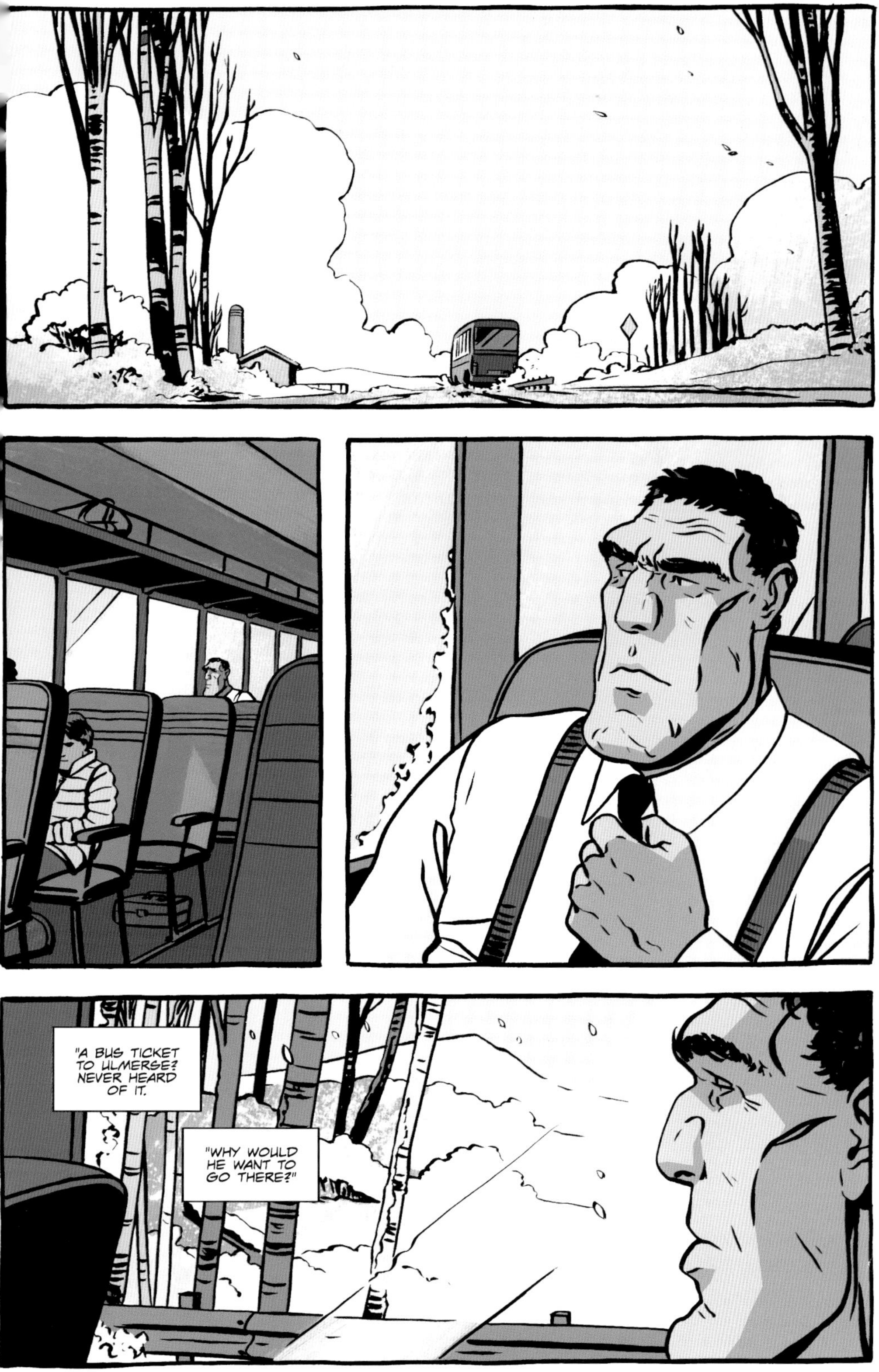
"A BUS TICKET TO ULMERSE? NEVER HEARD OF IT.
"WHY WOULD HE WANT TO GO THERE?"

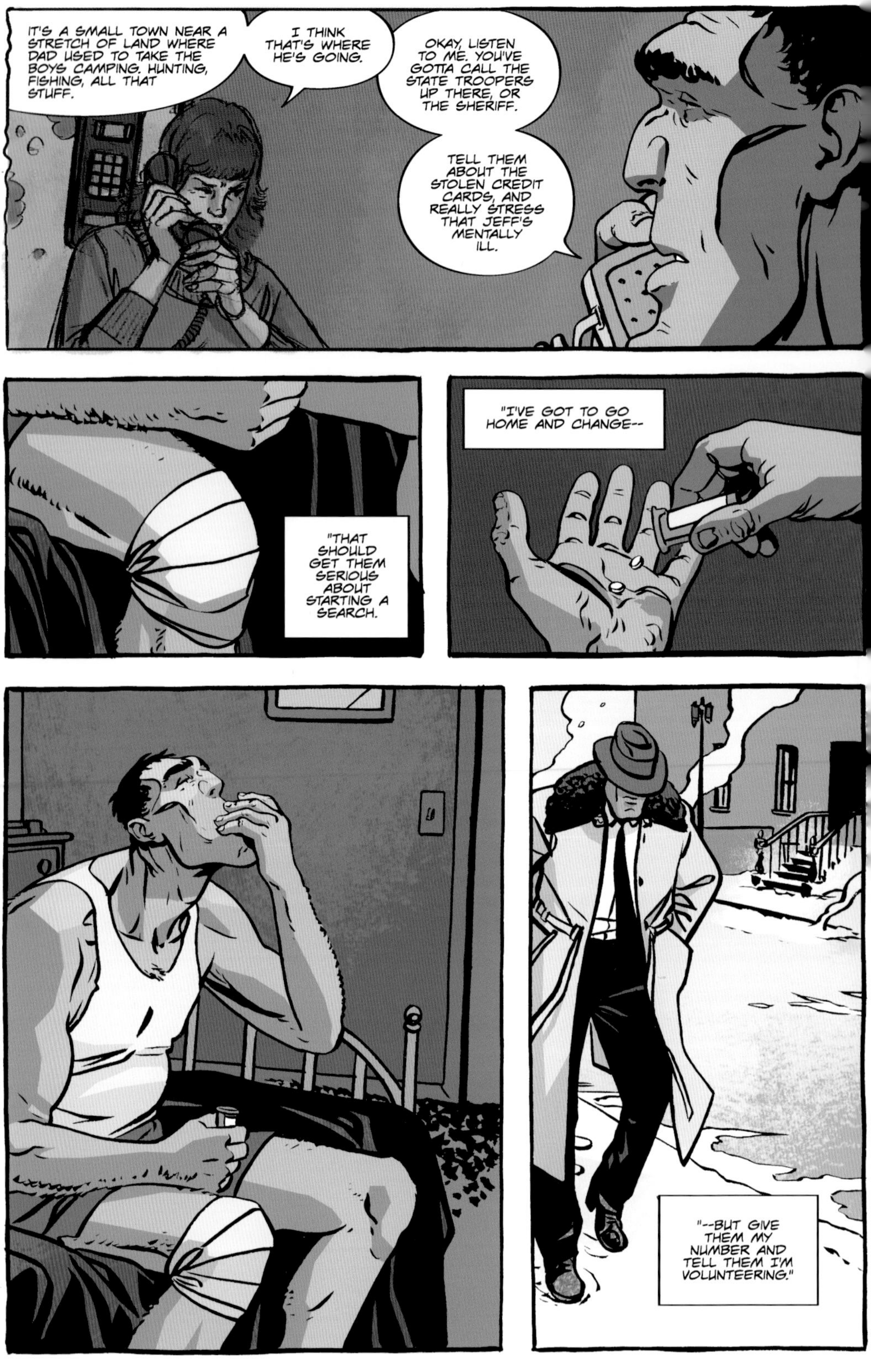
IT'S A SMALL TOWN NEAR A STRETCH OF LAND WHERE DAD USED TO TAKE THE BOYS CAMPING. HUNTING, FISHING, ALL THAT STUFF.
I THINK THAT'S WHERE HE'S GOING.
OKAY, LISTEN TO ME. YOU'VE GOTTA CALL THE STATE TROOPERS UP THERE, OR THE SHERIFF.
TELL THEM ABOUT THE STOLEN CREDIT CARDS, AND REALLY STRESS THAT JEFF'S MENTALLY ILL.
"THAT SHOULD GET THEM SERIOUS ABOUT STARTING A SEARCH.
"I'VE GOT TO GO HOME AND CHANGE--
"--BUT GIVE THEM MY NUMBER AND TELL THEM I'M VOLUNTEERING."

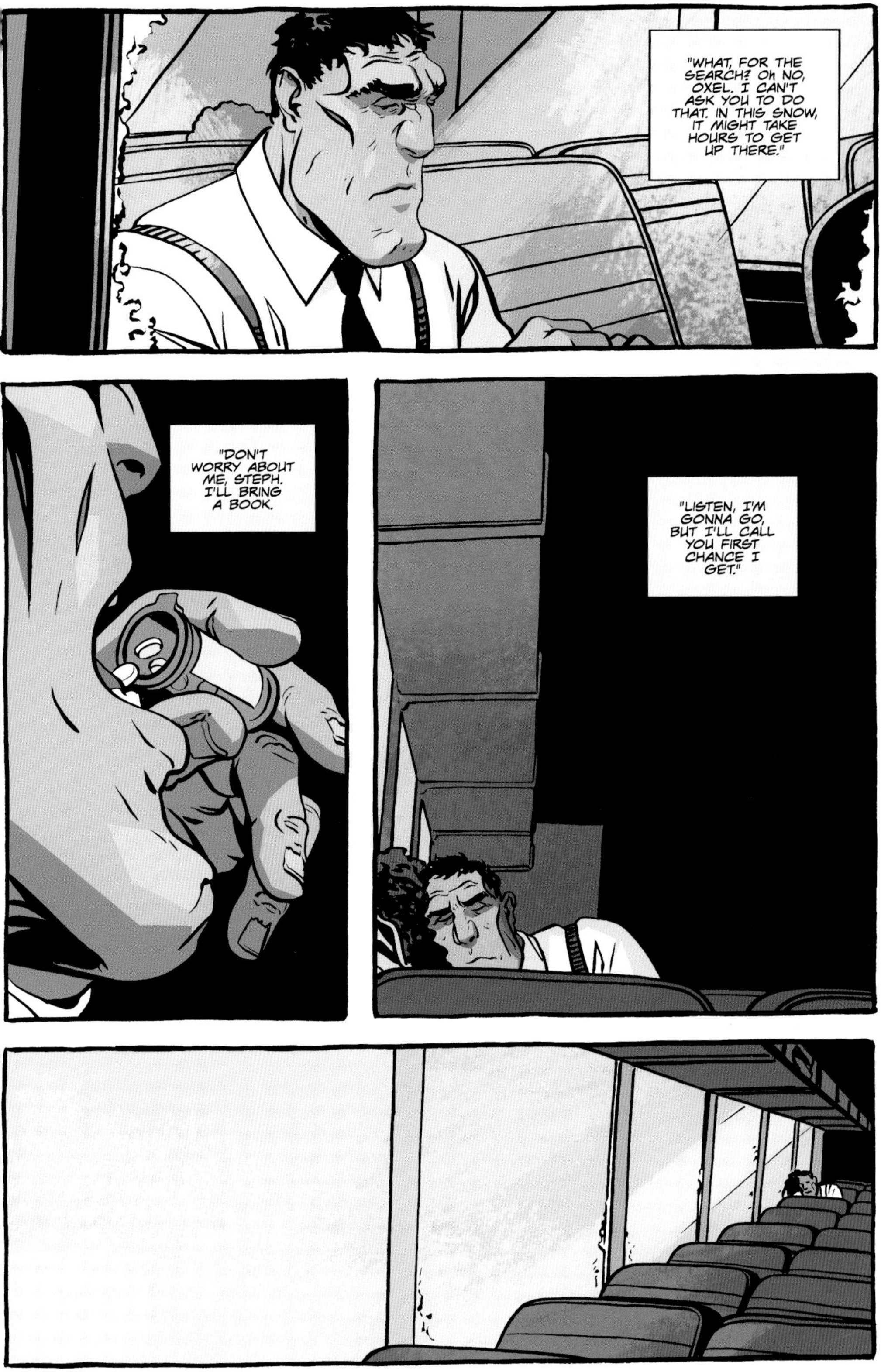
"WHAT, FOR THE SEARCH? Oh NO, OXEL. I CAN'T ASK YOU TO DO THAT. IN THIS SNOW, IT MIGHT TAKE HOURS TO GET UP THERE."
"DON'T WORRY ABOUT ME, STEPH. I'LL BRING A BOOK.
"LISTEN, I'M GONNA GO, BUT I'LL CALL YOU FIRST CHANCE I GET."

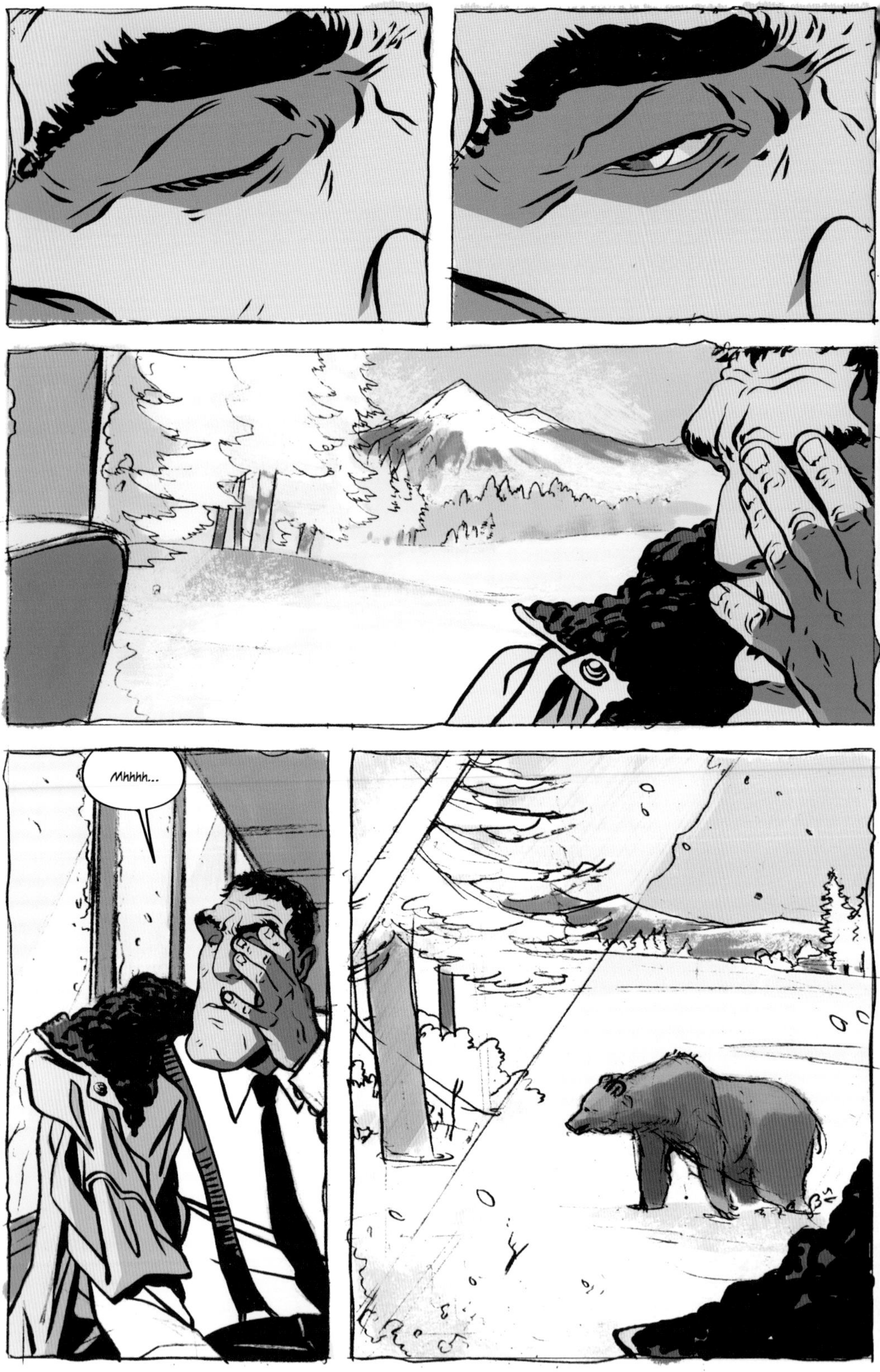
Mhhhh...

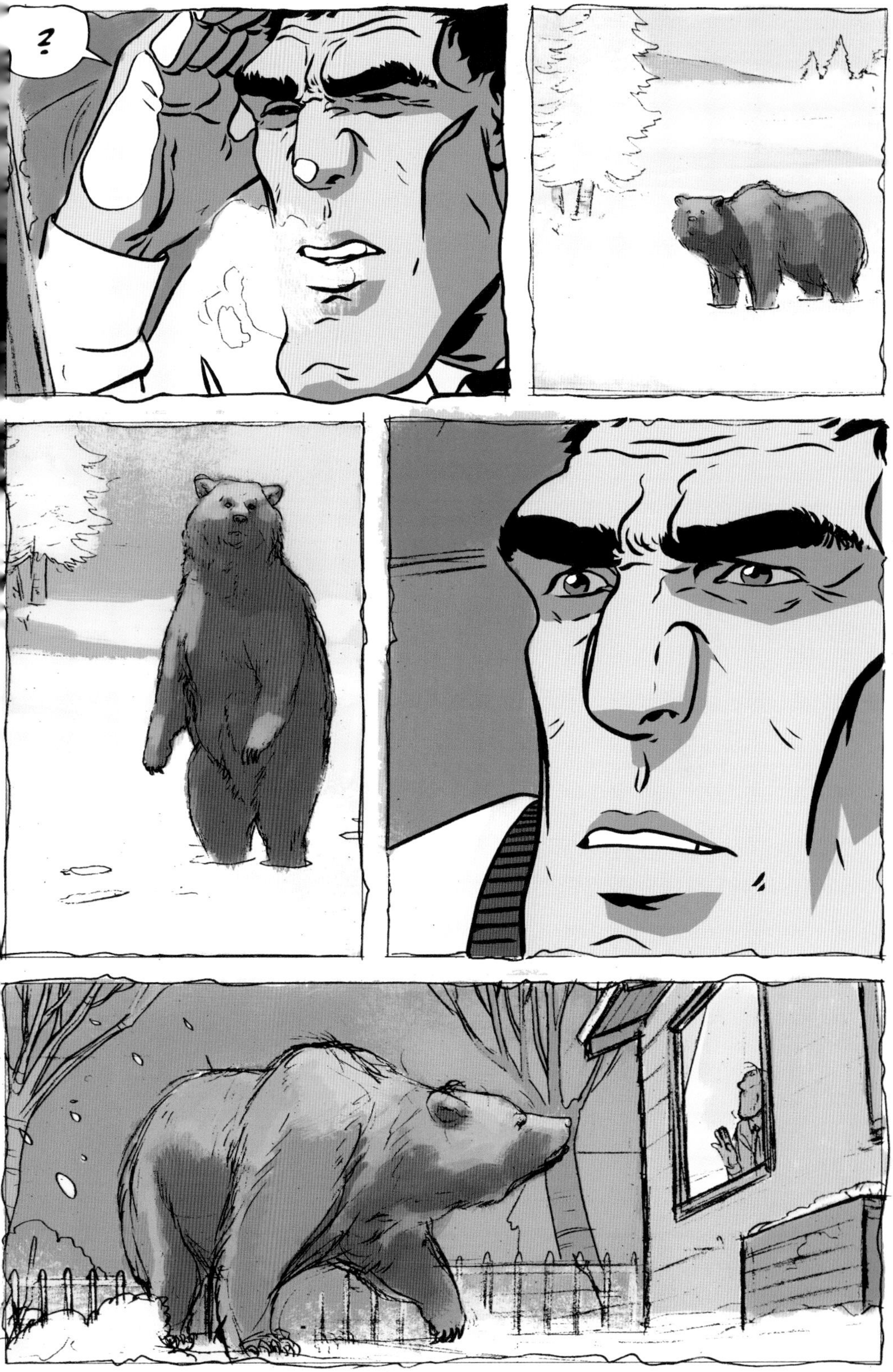
?

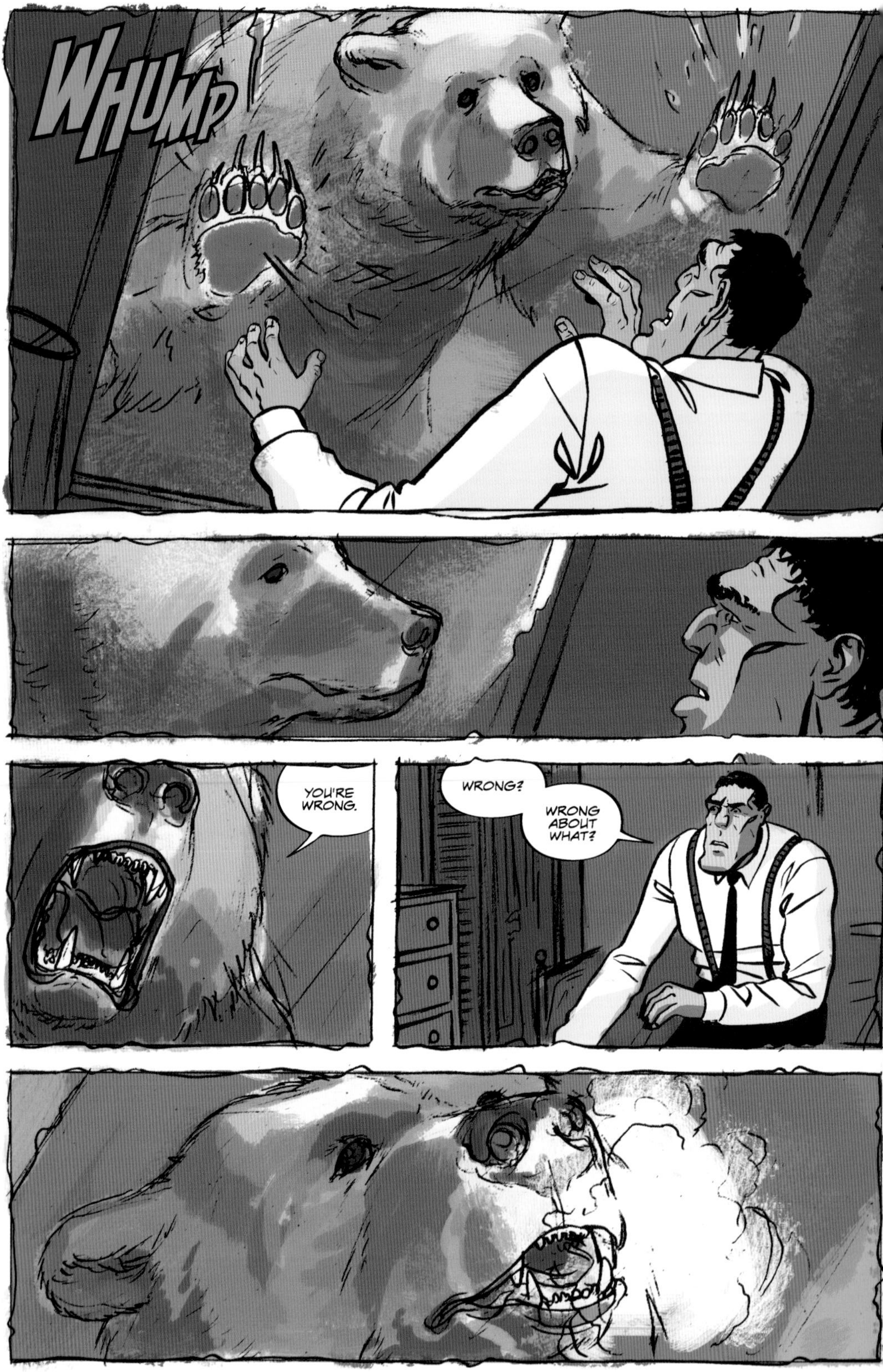
WHUMP
YOU'RE WRONG.
WRONG?
WRONG ABOUT WHAT?

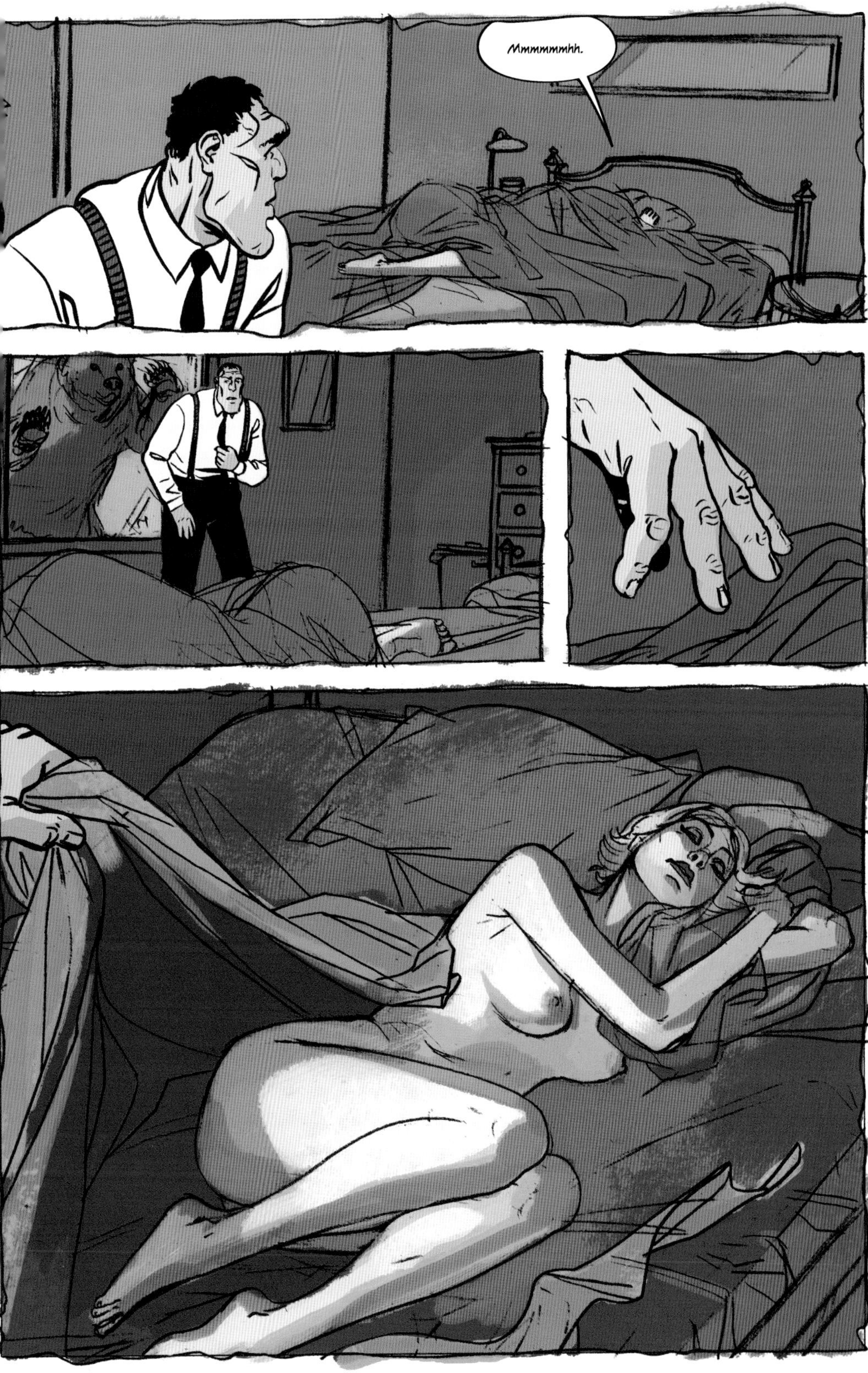
Mmmmmmhh.

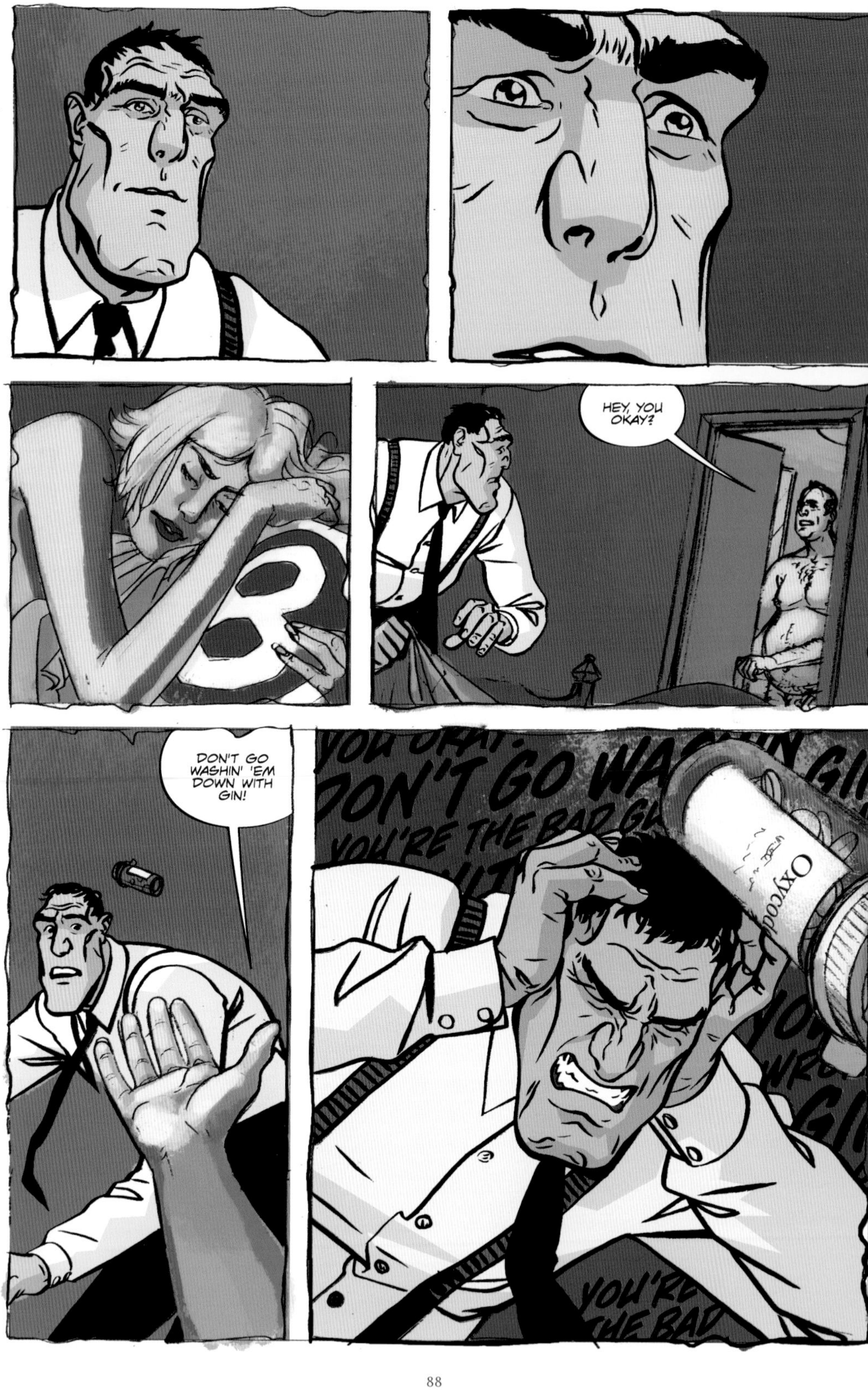
HEY, YOU OKAY?
DON'T GO WASHIN' 'EM DOWN WITH GIN!
YOU OKAY.
DON'T GO WASHIN' GI
YOU'RE THE BAD GU
YOU'RE THE BAD
Oxycod

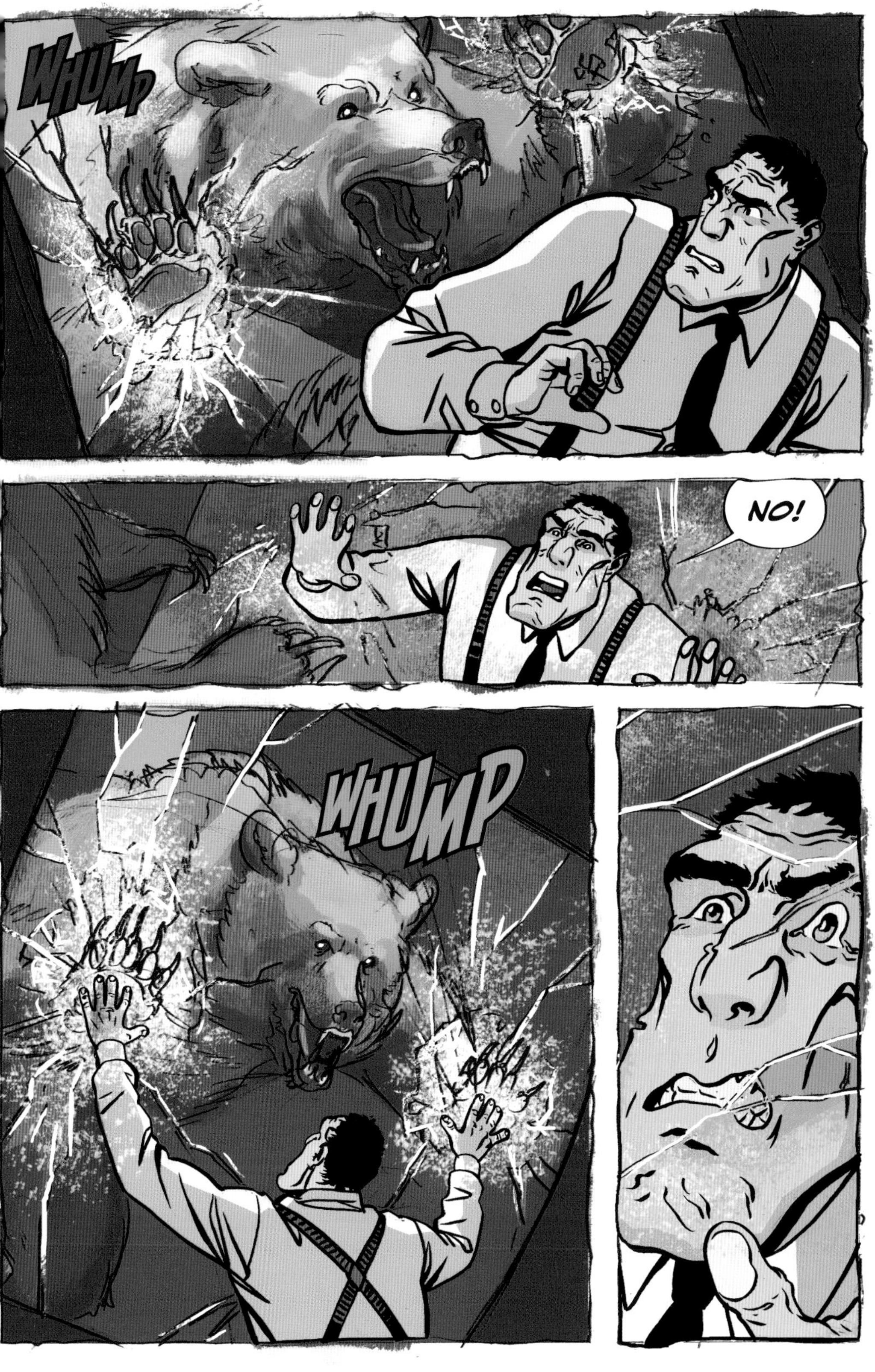
WHUMP
NO!
WHUMP

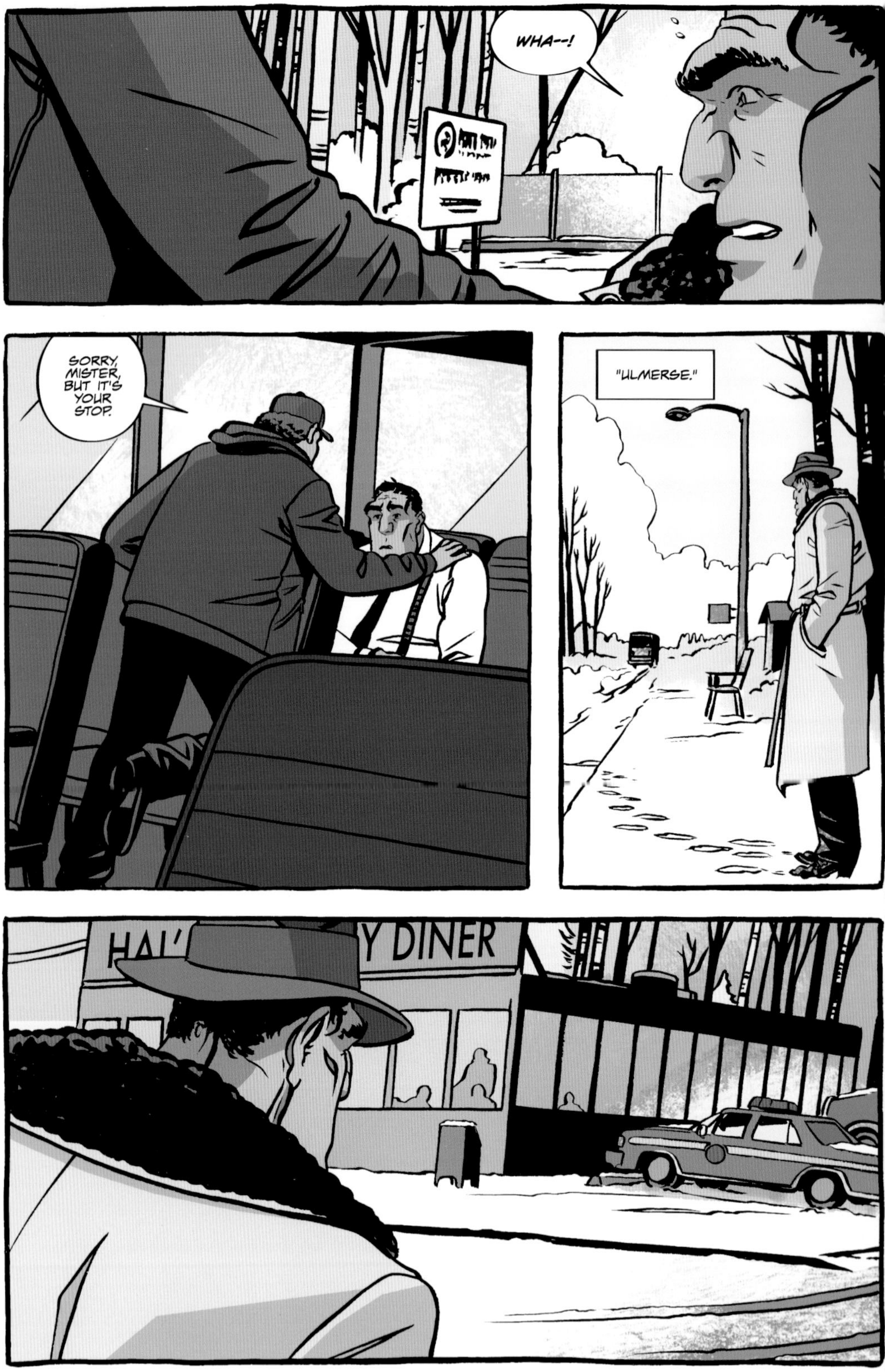
WHA--!
SORRY, MISTER, BUT IT'S YOUR STOP.
"ULMERSE."
Y DINER

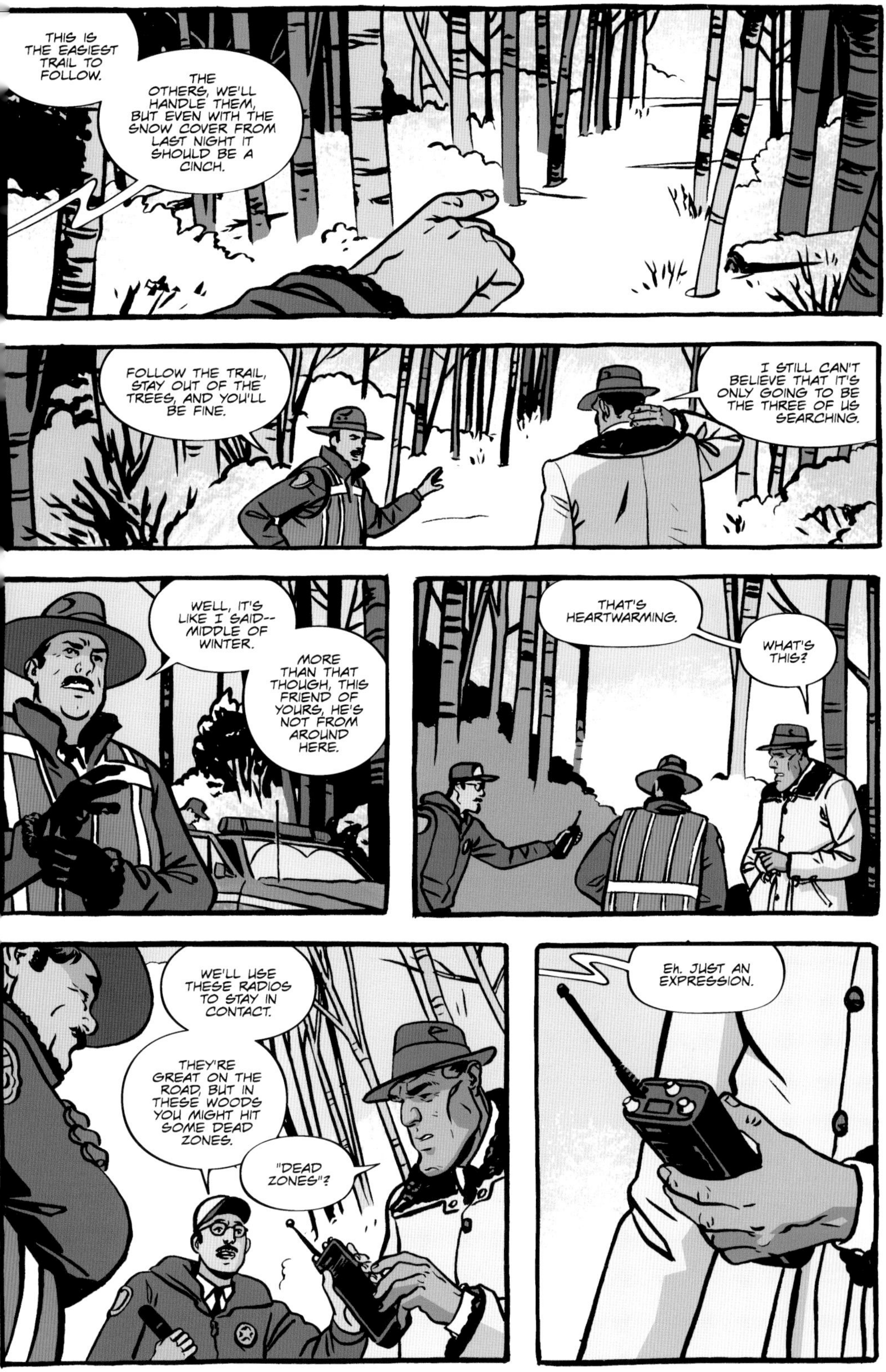
THIS IS THE EASIEST TRAIL TO FOLLOW.
THE OTHERS, WE'LL HANDLE THEM, BUT EVEN WITH THE SNOW COVER FROM LAST NIGHT IT SHOULD BE A CINCH.
FOLLOW THE TRAIL, STAY OUT OF THE TREES, AND YOU'LL BE FINE.
I STILL CAN'T BELIEVE THAT IT'S ONLY GOING TO BE THE THREE OF US SEARCHING.
WELL, IT'S LIKE I SAID-- MIDDLE OF WINTER.
MORE THAN THAT THOUGH, THIS FRIEND OF YOURS, HE'S NOT FROM AROUND HERE.
THAT'S HEARTWARMING.
WHAT'S THIS?
WE'LL USE THESE RADIOS TO STAY IN CONTACT.
THEY'RE GREAT ON THE ROAD, BUT IN THESE WOODS YOU MIGHT HIT SOME DEAD ZONES.
"DEAD ZONES"?
Eh. JUST AN EXPRESSION.

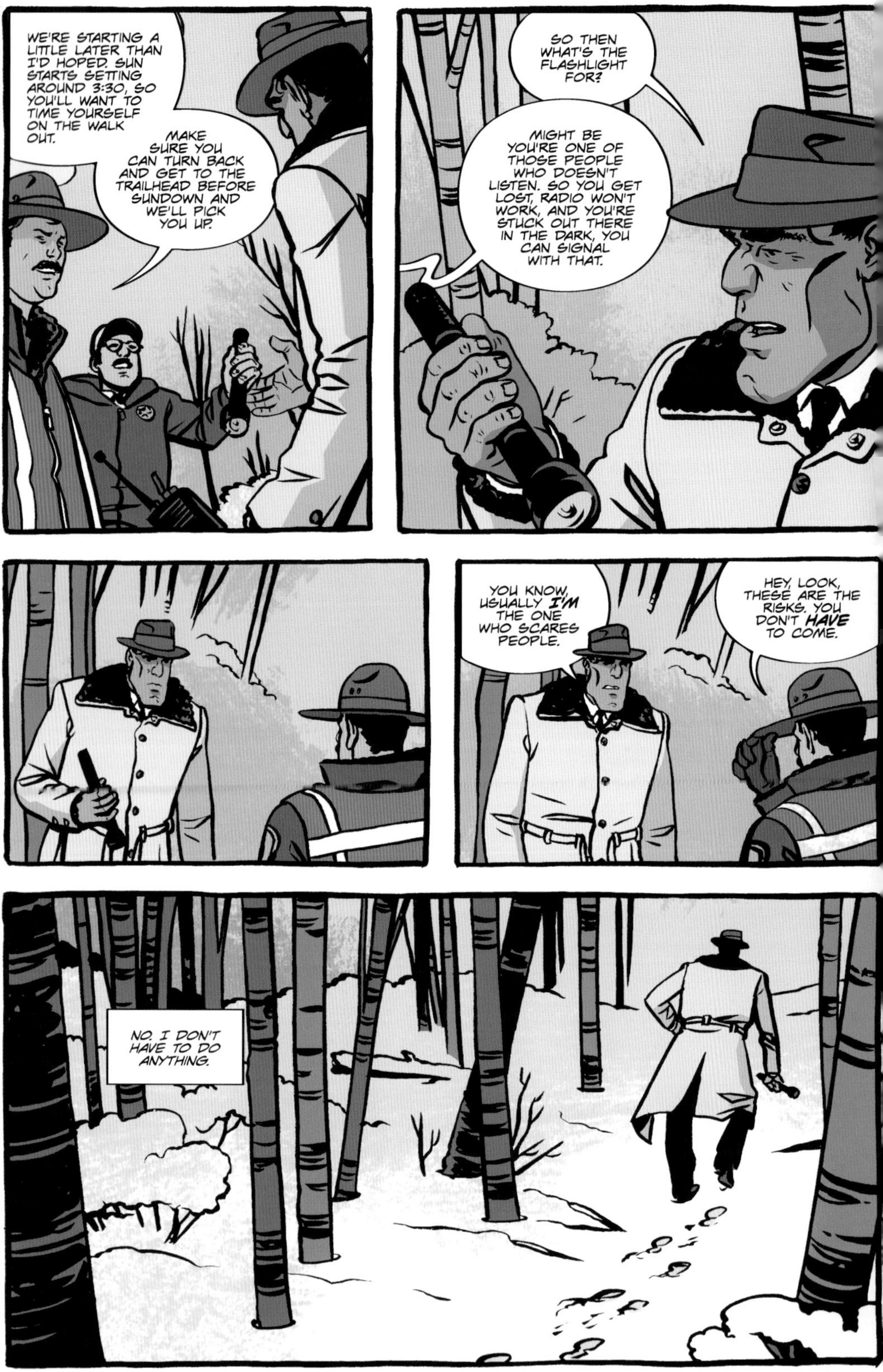
WE'RE STARTING A LITTLE LATER THAN I'D HOPED. SUN STARTS SETTING AROUND 3:30, SO YOU'LL WANT TO TIME YOURSELF ON THE WALK OUT.
MAKE SURE YOU CAN TURN BACK AND GET TO THE TRAILHEAD BEFORE SUNDOWN AND WE'LL PICK YOU UP.
SO THEN WHAT'S THE FLASHLIGHT FOR?
MIGHT BE YOU'RE ONE OF THOSE PEOPLE WHO DOESN'T LISTEN. SO YOU GET LOST, RADIO WON'T WORK, AND YOU'RE STUCK OUT THERE IN THE DARK, YOU CAN SIGNAL WITH THAT.
YOU KNOW, USUALLY I'M THE ONE WHO SCARES PEOPLE.
HEY, LOOK, THESE ARE THE RISKS. YOU DON'T HAVE TO COME.
NO. I DON'T HAVE TO DO ANYTHING.

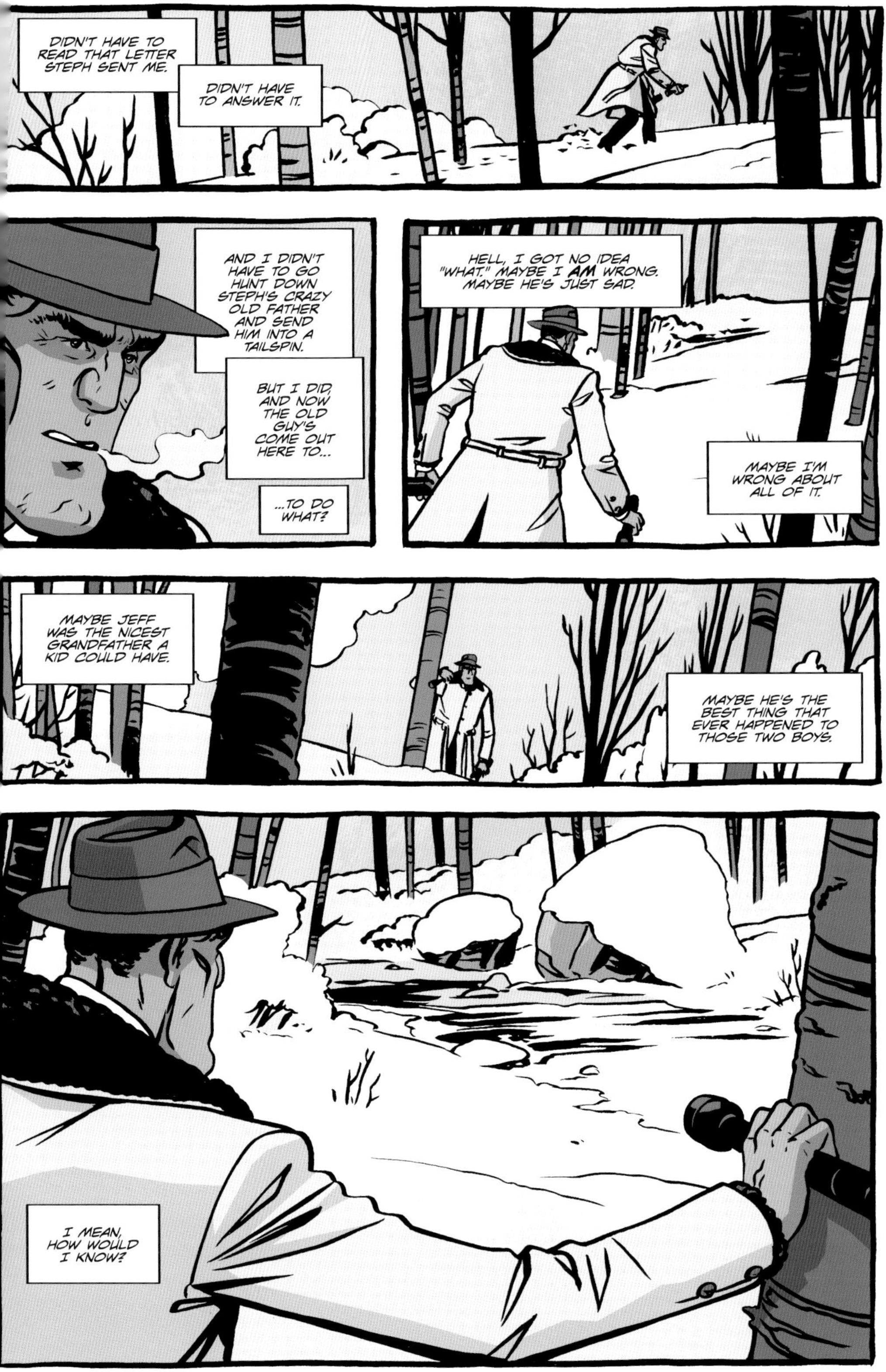
DIDN'T HAVE TO READ THAT LETTER STEPH SENT ME.
DIDN'T HAVE TO ANSWER IT.
AND I DIDN'T HAVE TO GO HUNT DOWN STEPH'S CRAZY OLD FATHER AND SEND HIM INTO A TAILSPIN.
BUT I DID, AND NOW THE OLD GUY'S COME OUT HERE TO...
...TO DO WHAT?
HELL, I GOT NO IDEA "WHAT." MAYBE I AM WRONG. MAYBE HE'S JUST SAD.
MAYBE I'M WRONG ABOUT ALL OF IT.
MAYBE JEFF WAS THE NICEST GRANDFATHER A KID COULD HAVE.
MAYBE HE'S THE BEST THING THAT EVER HAPPENED TO THOSE TWO BOYS.
I MEAN, HOW WOULD I KNOW?

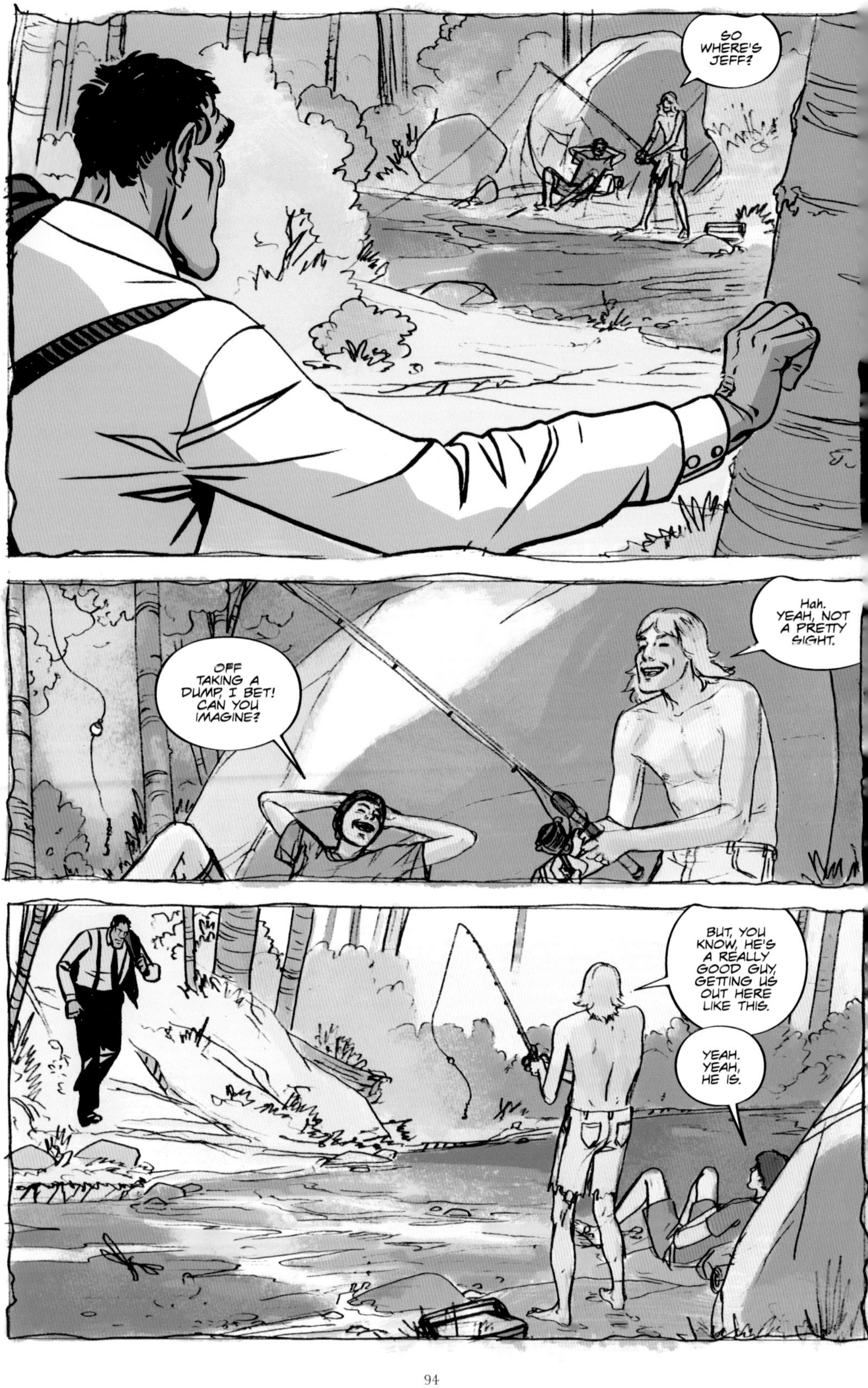
SO WHERE'S JEFF?
OFF TAKING A DUMP, I BET! CAN YOU IMAGINE?
Hah. YEAH, NOT A PRETTY SIGHT.
BUT, YOU KNOW, HE'S A REALLY GOOD GUY, GETTING US OUT HERE LIKE THIS.
YEAH. YEAH, HE IS.

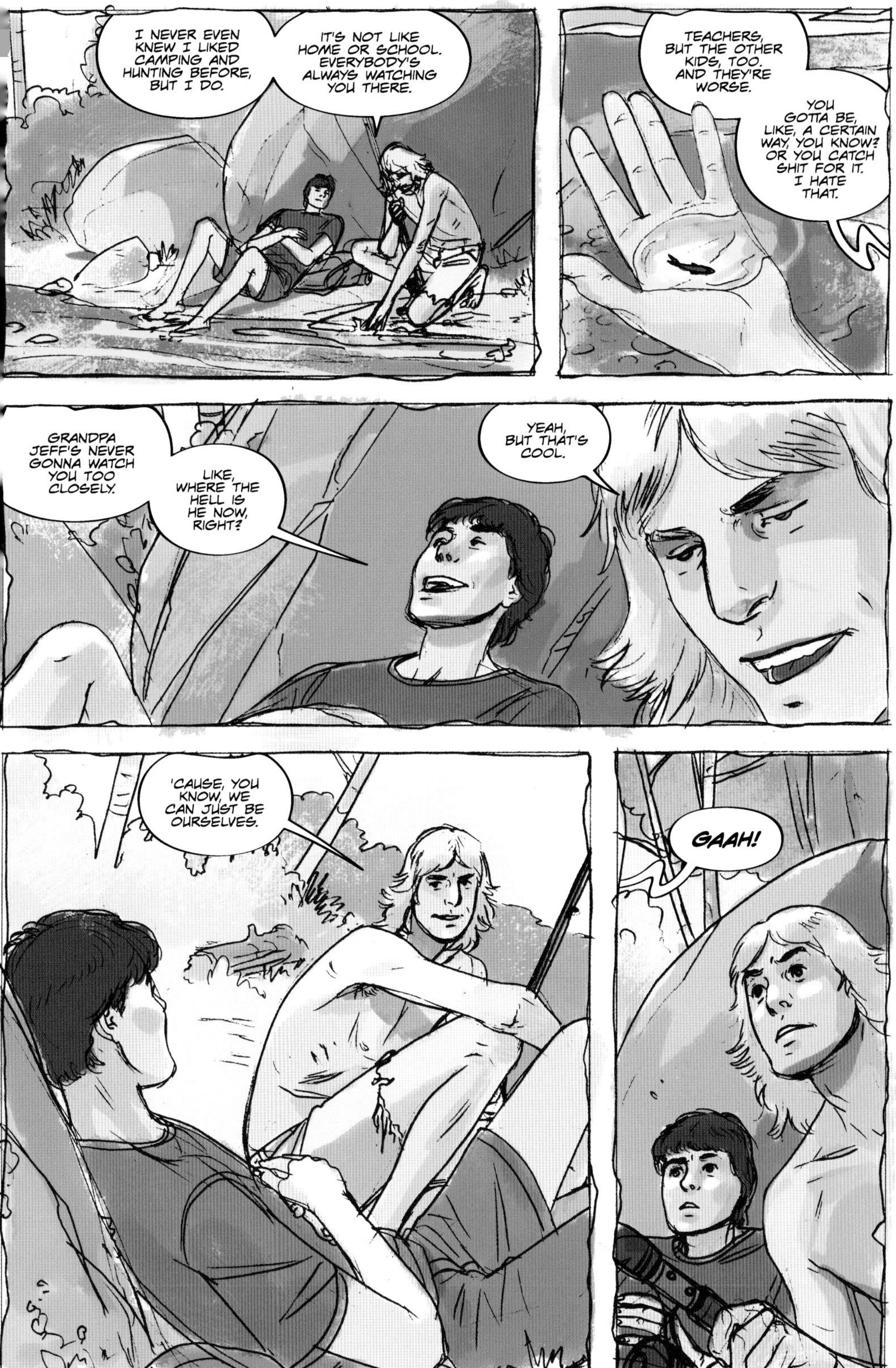
I NEVER EVEN KNEW I LIKED CAMPING AND HUNTING BEFORE, BUT I DO.
IT'S NOT LIKE HOME OR SCHOOL. EVERYBODY'S ALWAYS WATCHING YOU THERE.
TEACHERS, BUT THE OTHER KIDS, TOO. AND THEY'RE WORSE.
YOU GOTTA BE, LIKE, A CERTAIN WAY, YOU KNOW? OR YOU CATCH SHIT FOR IT. I HATE THAT.
GRANDPA JEFF'S NEVER GONNA WATCH YOU TOO CLOSELY.
LIKE, WHERE THE HELL IS HE NOW, RIGHT?
YEAH, BUT THAT'S COOL.
'CAUSE, YOU KNOW, WE CAN JUST BE OURSELVES.
GAAH!

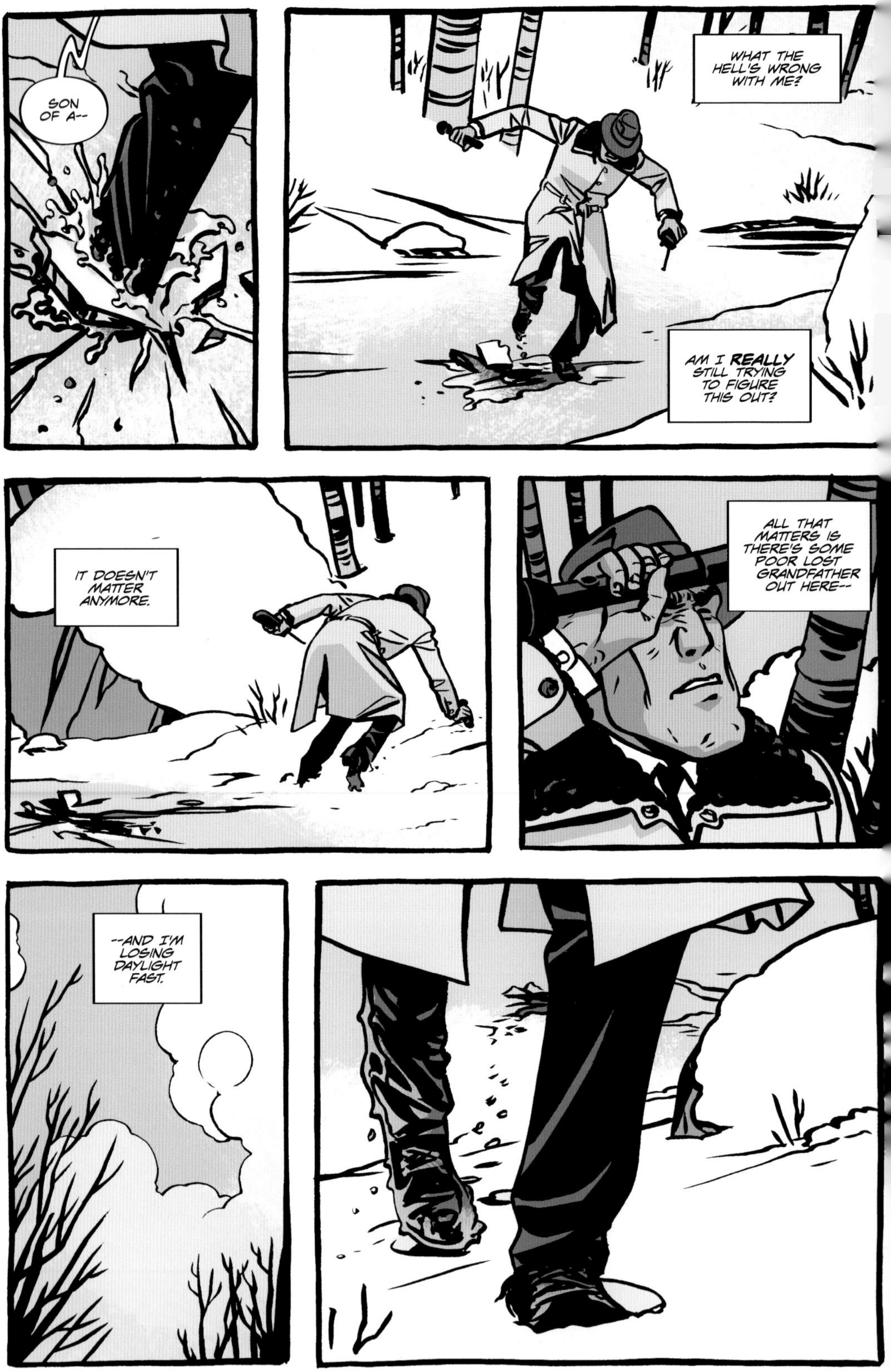
SON OF A--
WHAT THE HELL'S WRONG WITH ME?
AM I **REALLY** STILL TRYING TO FIGURE THIS OUT?
IT DOESN'T MATTER ANYMORE.
ALL THAT MATTERS IS THERE'S SOME POOR LOST GRANDFATHER OUT HERE--
--AND I'M LOSING DAYLIGHT FAST.

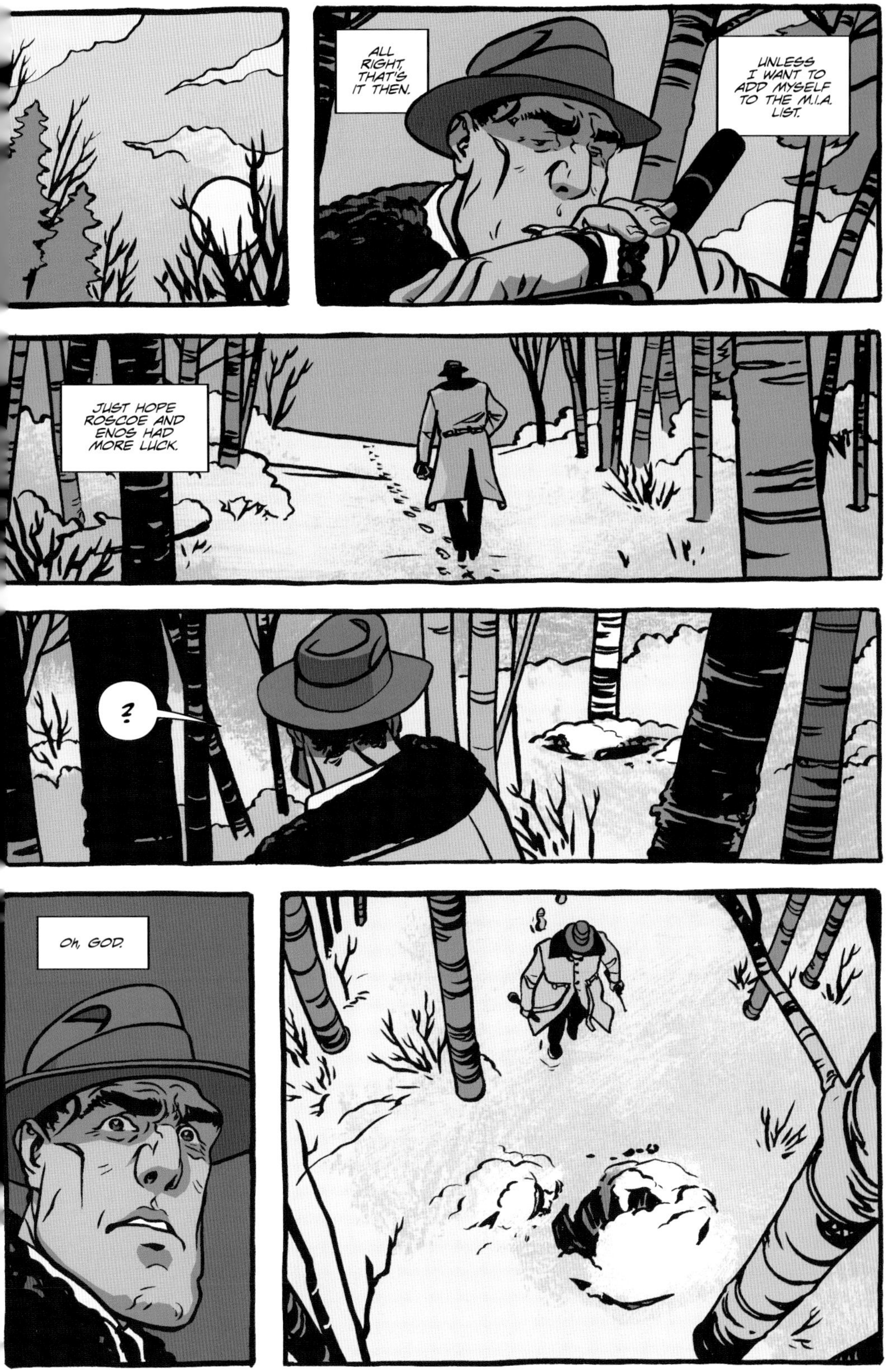
ALL RIGHT, THAT'S IT THEN.
UNLESS I WANT TO ADD MYSELF TO THE M.I.A. LIST.
JUST HOPE ROSCOE AND ENOS HAD MORE LUCK.
?
Oh, GOD.

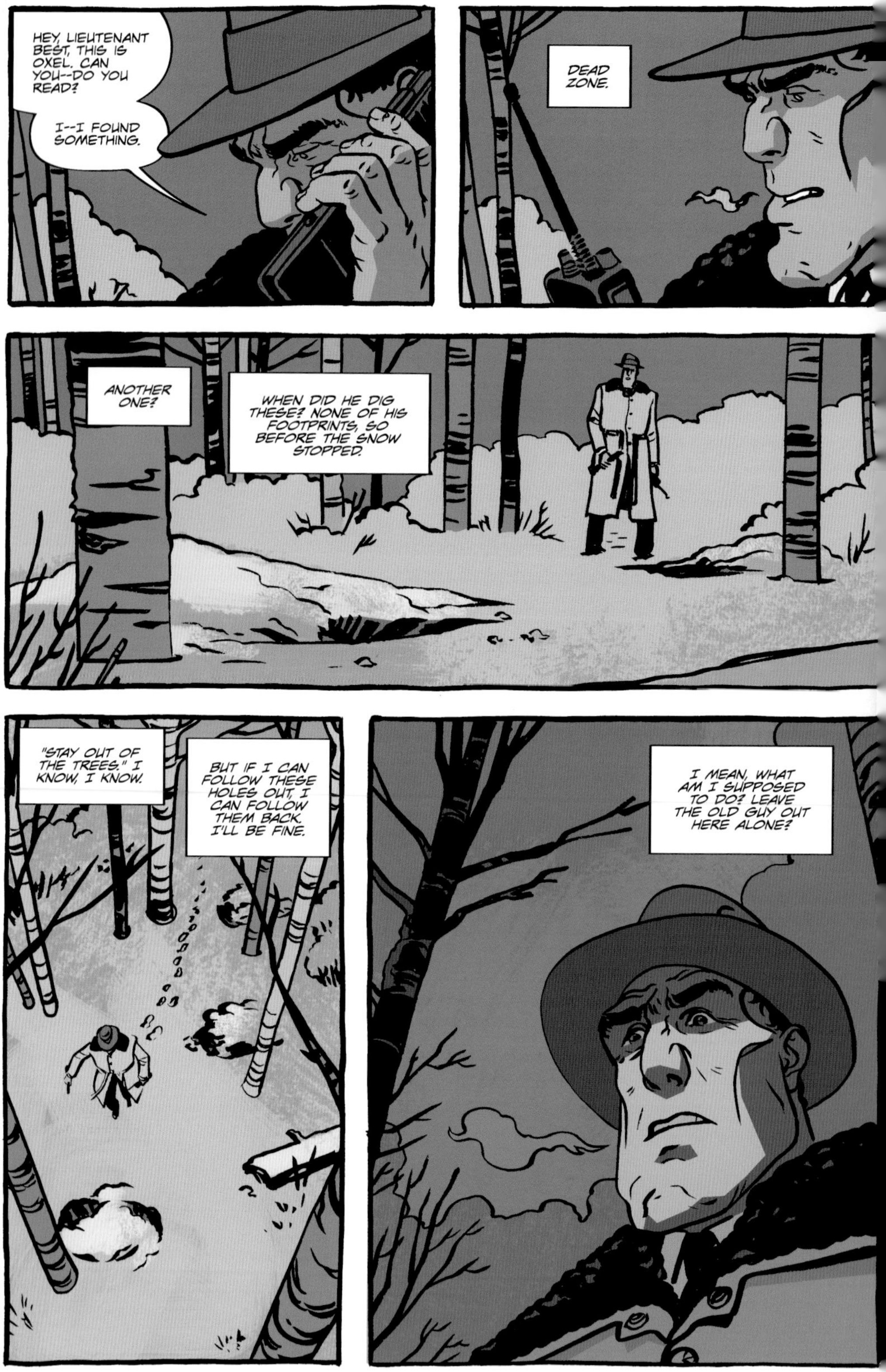
HEY, LIEUTENANT BEST, THIS IS OXEL. CAN YOU--DO YOU READ?
I--I FOUND SOMETHING.
DEAD ZONE.
ANOTHER ONE?
WHEN DID HE DIG THESE? NONE OF HIS FOOTPRINTS, SO BEFORE THE SNOW STOPPED.
"STAY OUT OF THE TREES." I KNOW, I KNOW.
BUT IF I CAN FOLLOW THESE HOLES OUT, I CAN FOLLOW THEM BACK. I'LL BE FINE.
I MEAN, WHAT AM I SUPPOSED TO DO? LEAVE THE OLD GUY OUT HERE ALONE?

NO.
PLEASE,
NO.

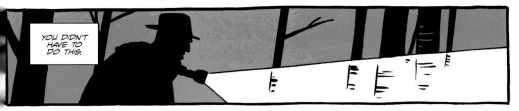

YOU DIDN'T
HAVE TO
DO THIS.

NOT ANY
OF IT.

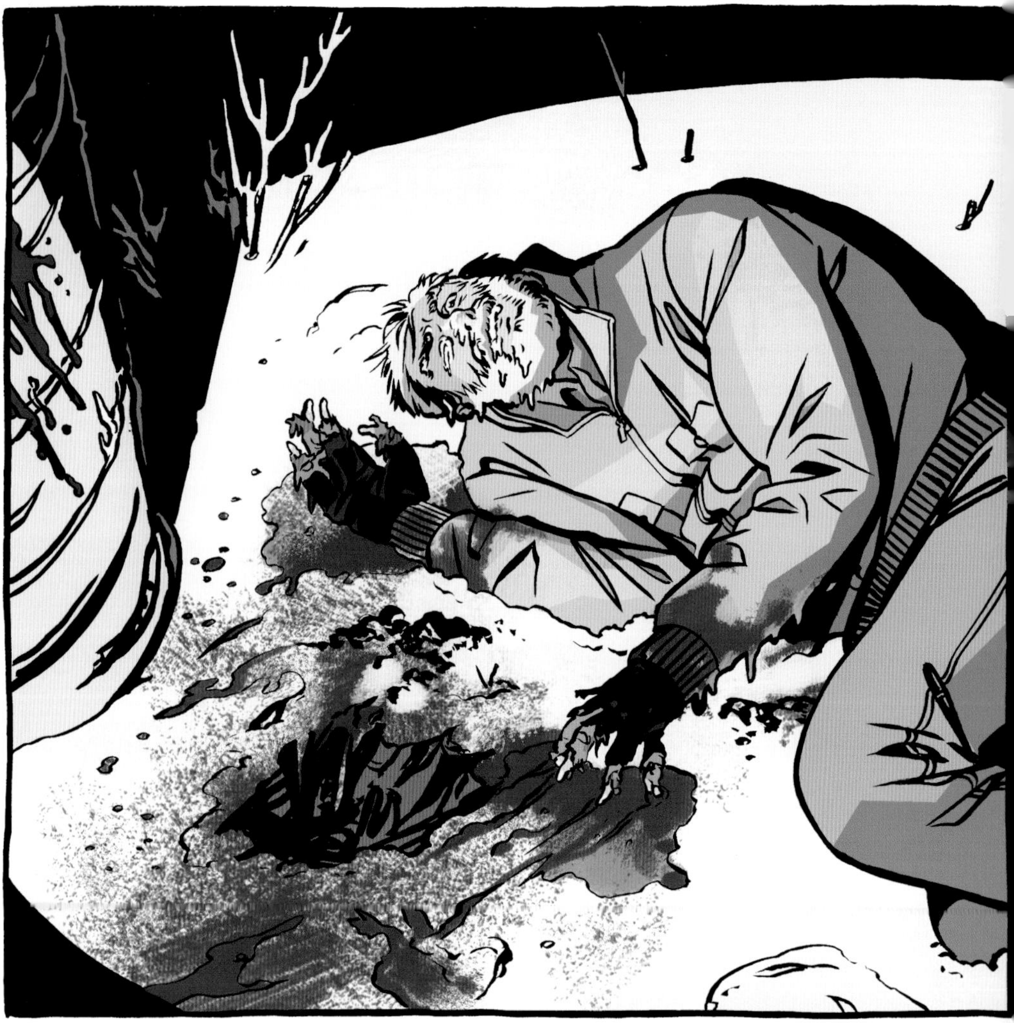

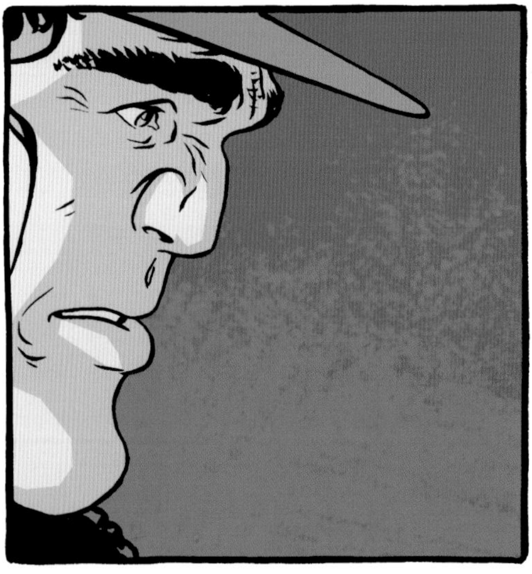

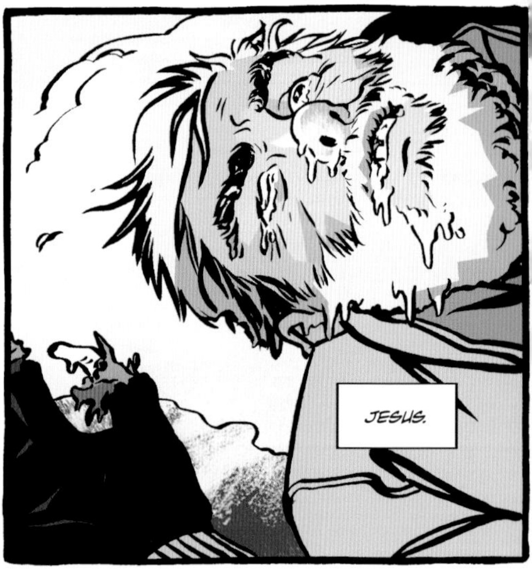
JESUS.

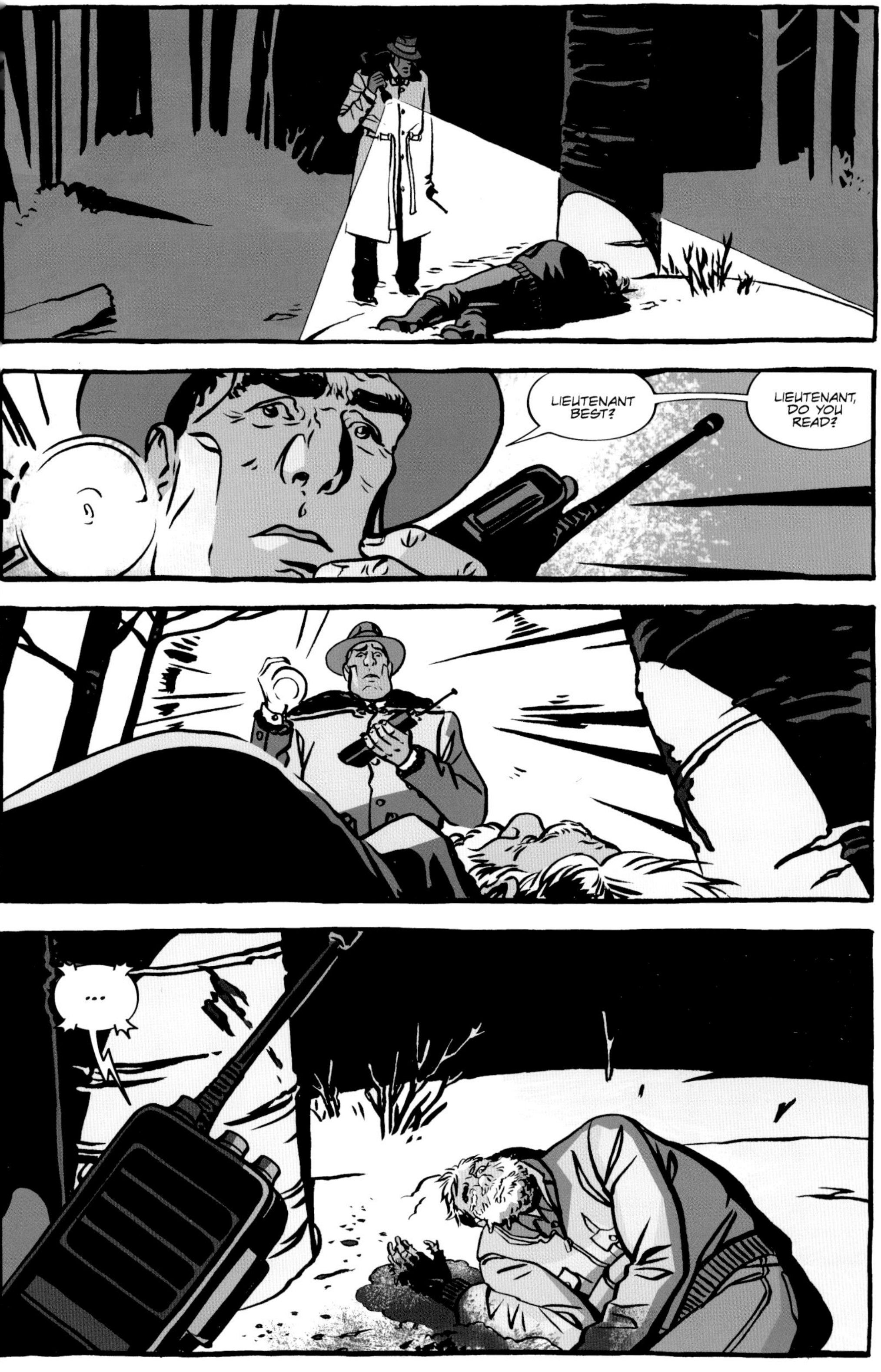
LIEUTENANT BEST?
LIEUTENANT, DO YOU READ?
...

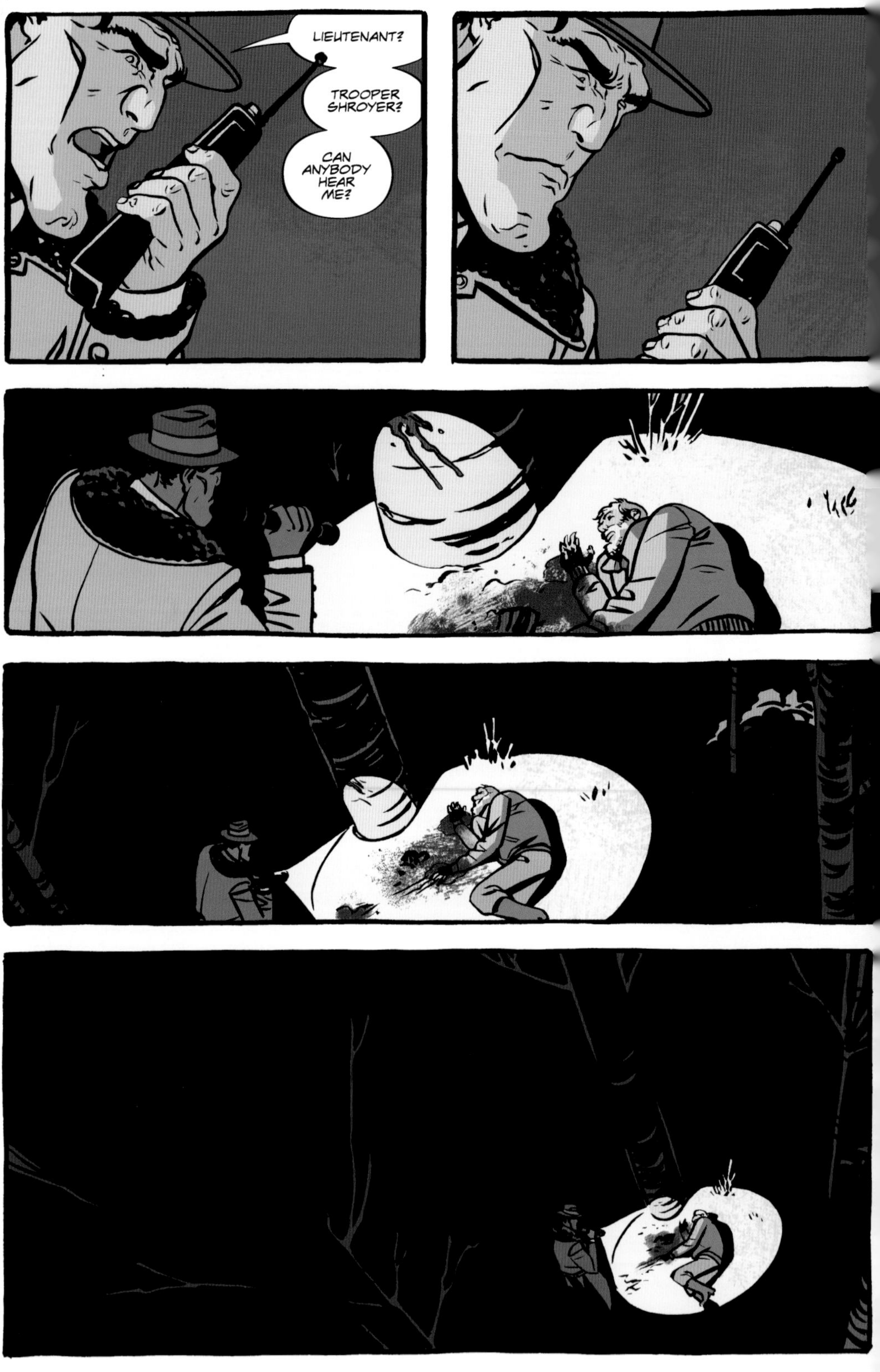
LIEUTENANT?
TROOPER SHROYER?
CAN ANYBODY HEAR ME?

— CHAPTER FIVE —

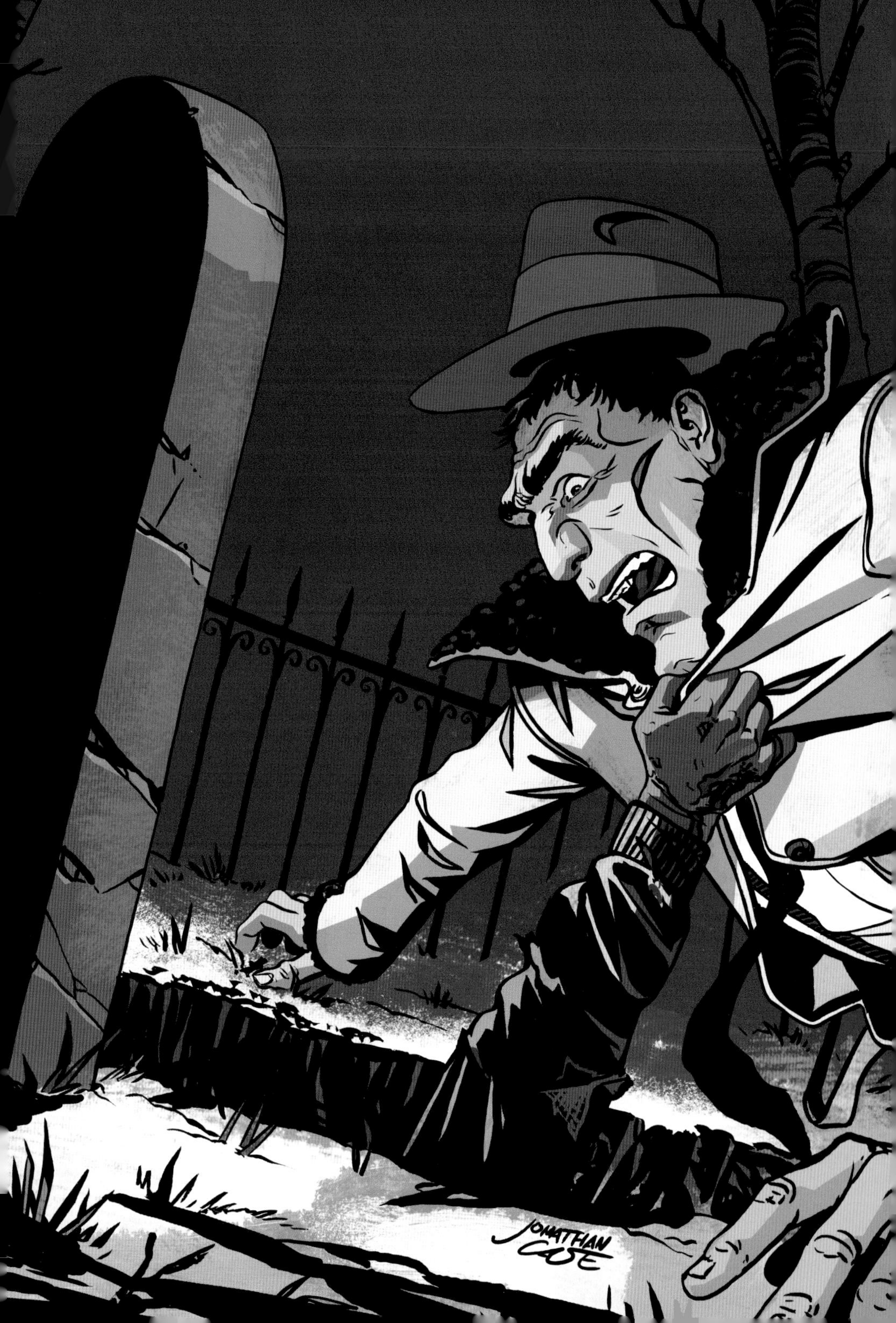
JONATHAN CASE

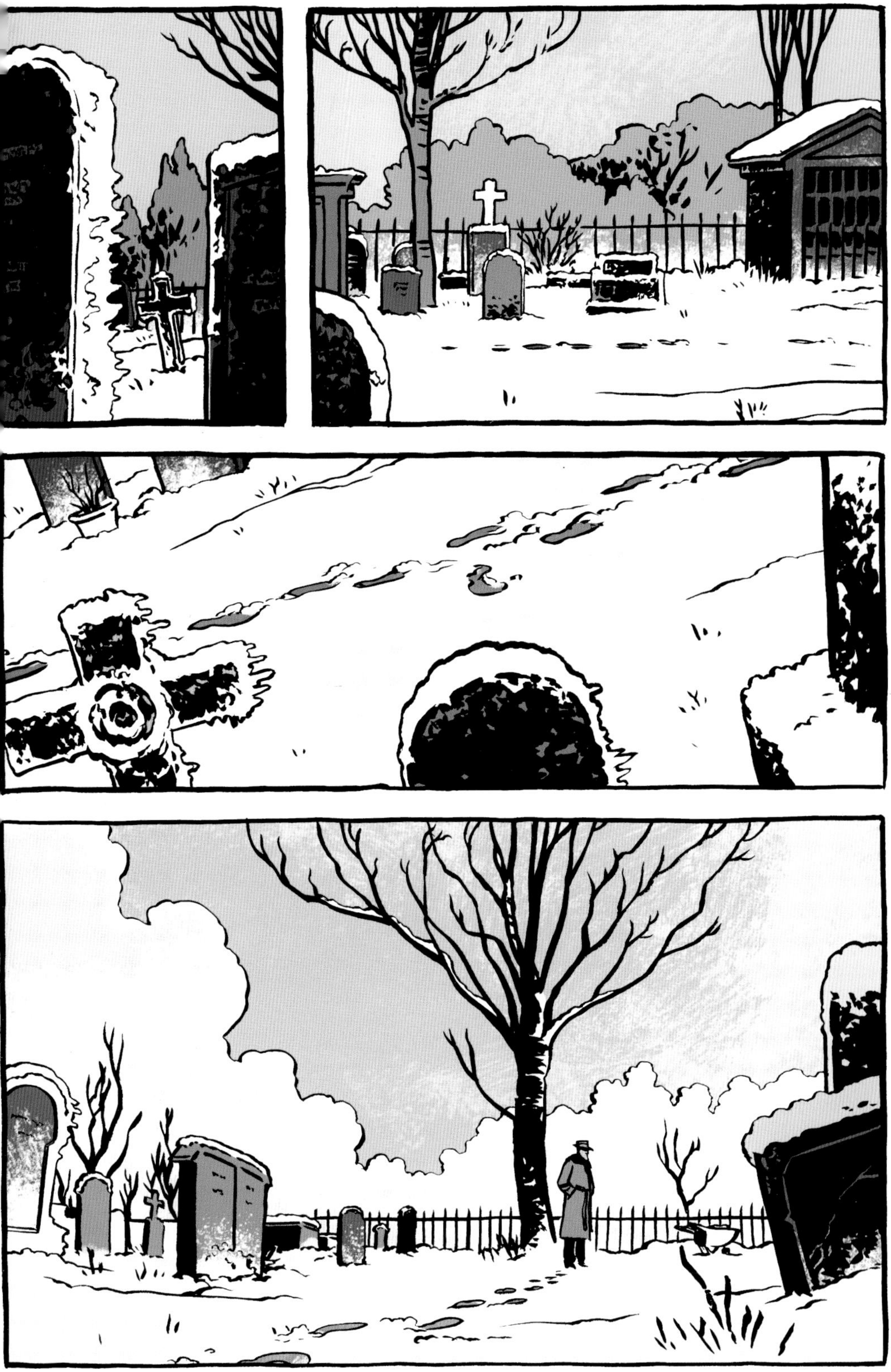

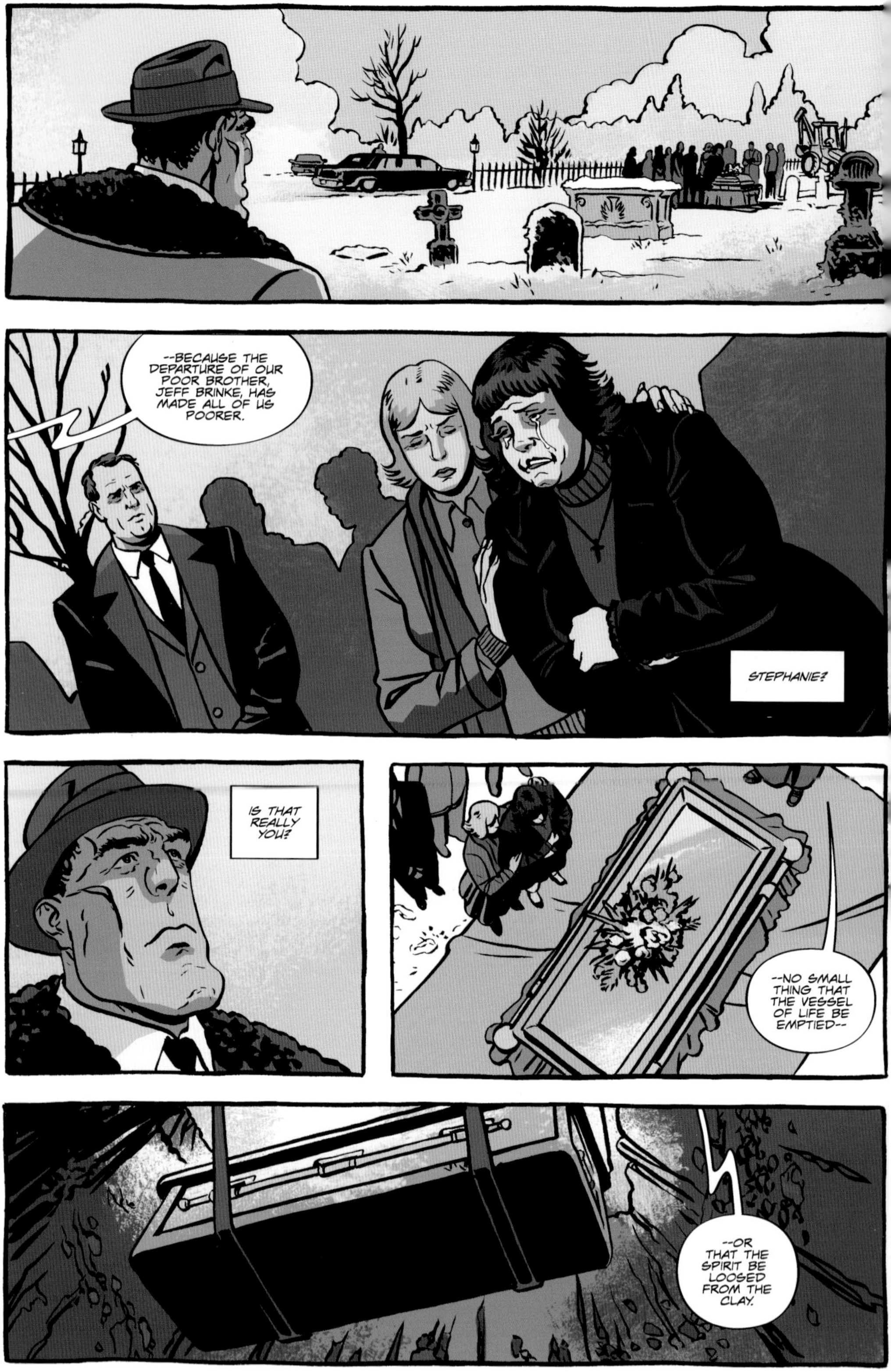
--BECAUSE THE DEPARTURE OF OUR POOR BROTHER, JEFF BRINKE, HAS MADE ALL OF US POORER.
STEPHANIE?
IS THAT REALLY YOU?
--NO SMALL THING THAT THE VESSEL OF LIFE BE EMPTIED--
--OR THAT THE SPIRIT BE LOOSED FROM THE CLAY.

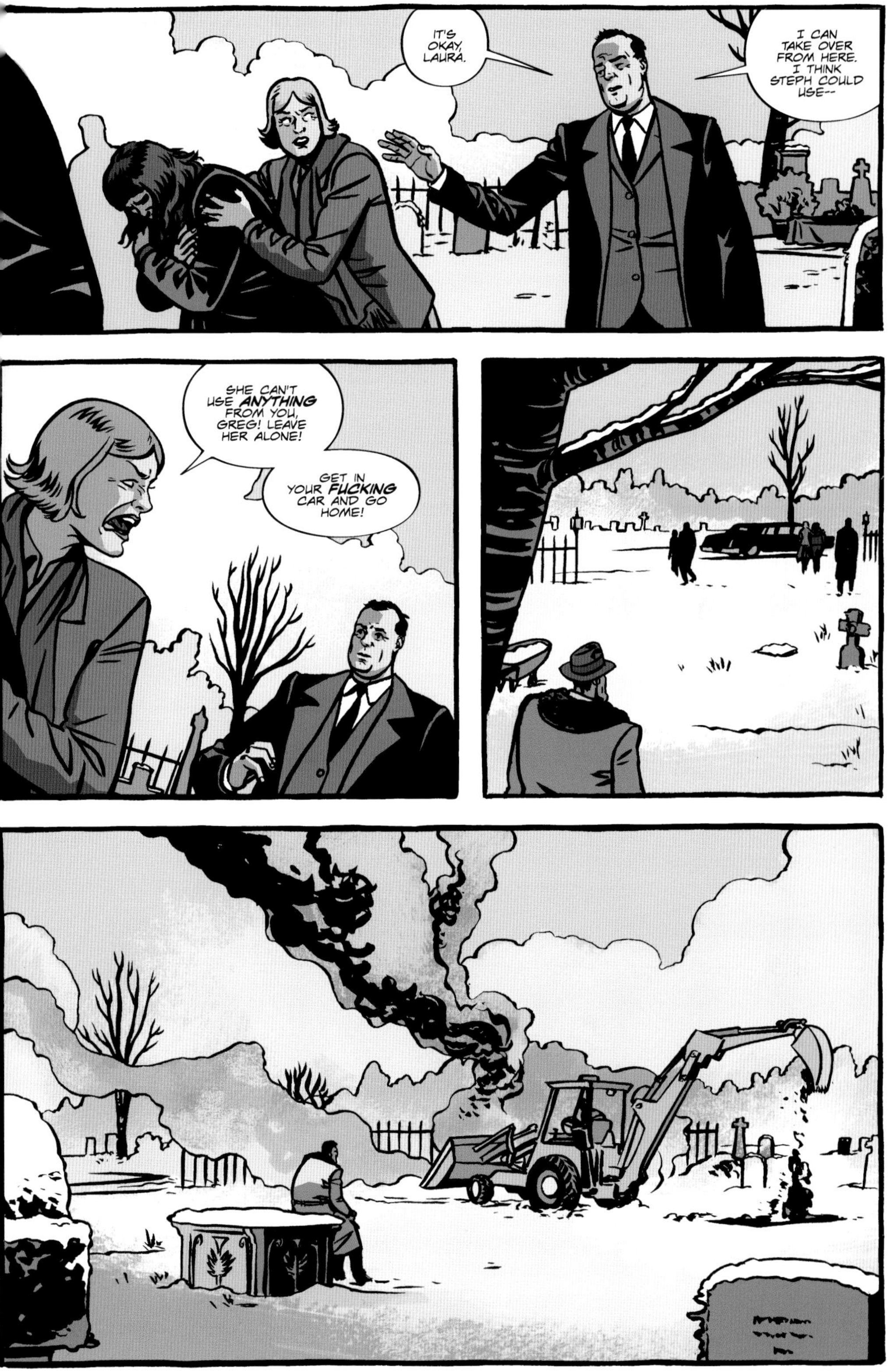
IT'S OKAY, LAURA.
I CAN TAKE OVER FROM HERE. I THINK STEPH COULD USE--
SHE CAN'T USE ANYTHING FROM YOU, GREG! LEAVE HER ALONE!
GET IN YOUR FUCKING CAR AND GO HOME!

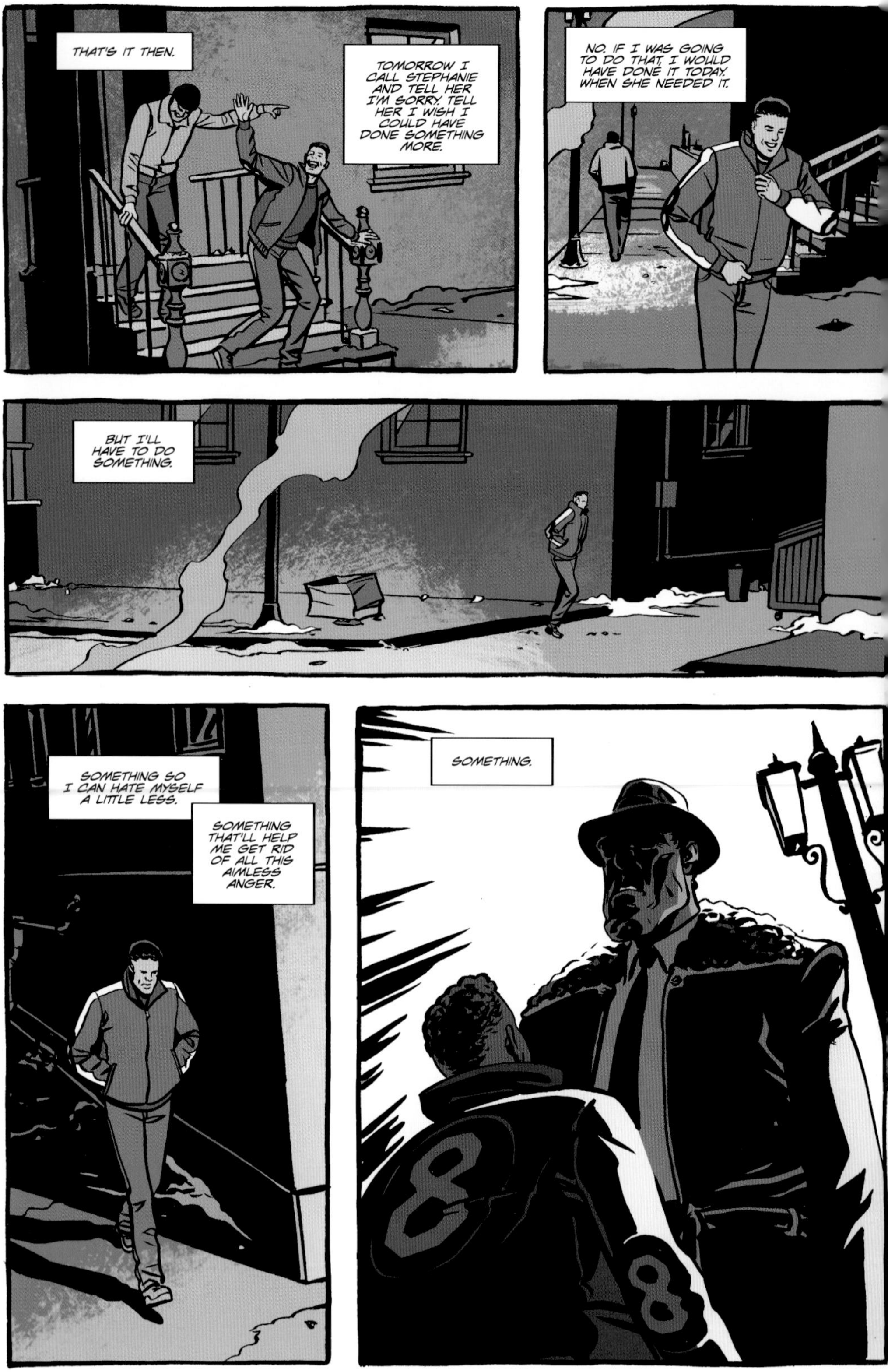
THAT'S IT THEN.
TOMORROW I CALL STEPHANIE AND TELL HER I'M SORRY. TELL HER I WISH I COULD HAVE DONE SOMETHING MORE.
NO. IF I WAS GOING TO DO THAT, I WOULD HAVE DONE IT TODAY. WHEN SHE NEEDED IT.
BUT I'LL HAVE TO DO SOMETHING.
SOMETHING SO I CAN HATE MYSELF A LITTLE LESS.
SOMETHING THAT'LL HELP ME GET RID OF ALL THIS AIMLESS ANGER.
SOMETHING.

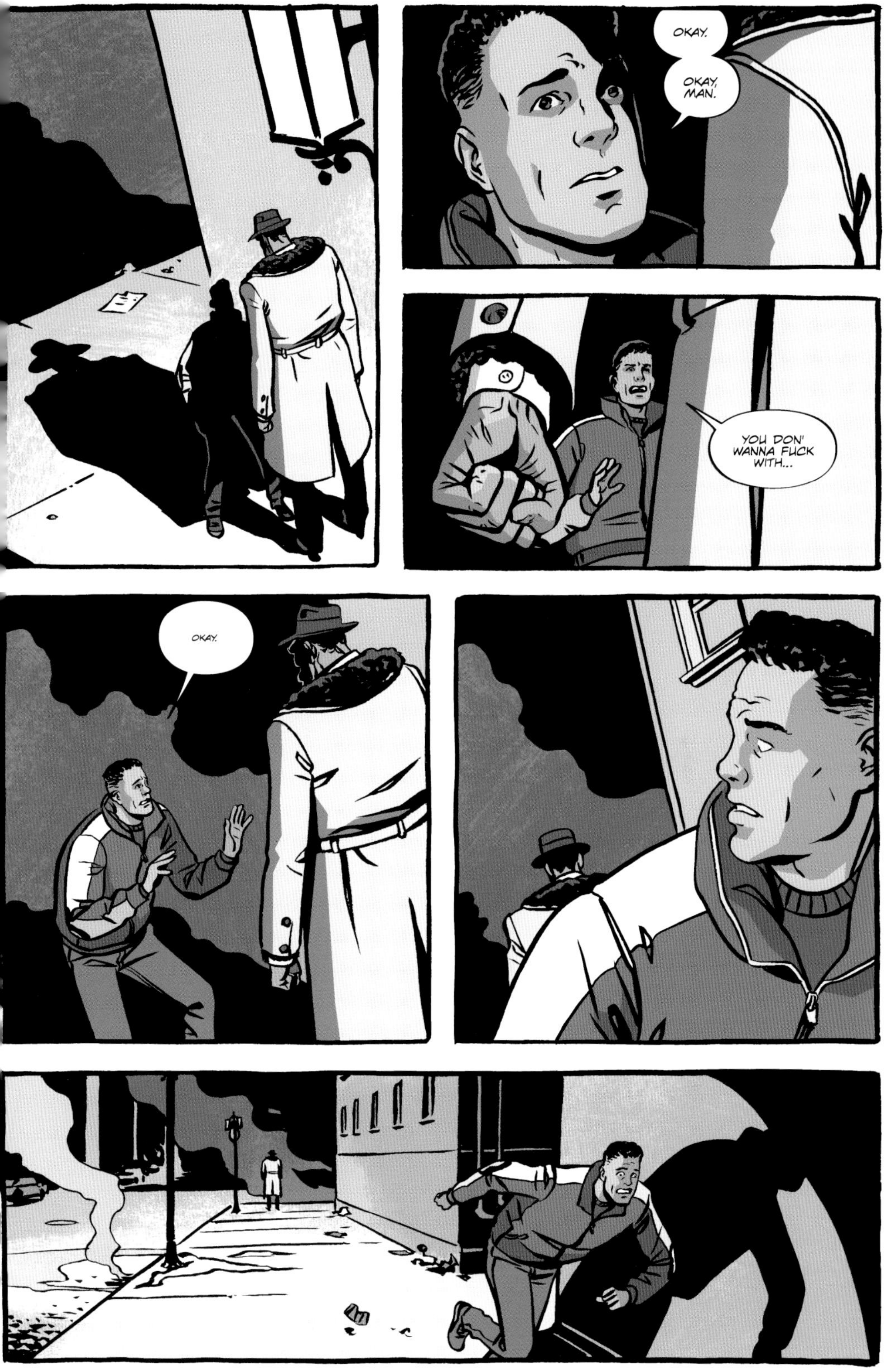
OKAY.
OKAY, MAN.
YOU DON' WANNA FUCK WITH...
OKAY.

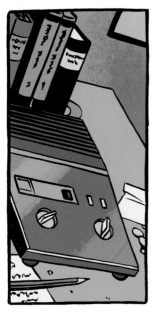

HELLO, MR...MR. KARN-HUS?

THIS IS ESTHER FROM THE ORCHARD STREET HOMELESS SHELTER. YOU WERE LOOKING FOR JEFF BRINKE LAST WEEK AND LEFT YOUR CARD WITH CAROL.

MR. BRINKE HASN'T SHOWN UP SINCE THEN, MORE THAN A WEEK, BUT HIS CART'S STILL HERE--FULL OF HIS BELONGINGS--AND WELL, WE NEED THE SPACE.

"WE DON'T HAVE A FAMILY CONTACT FOR HIM, AND NORMALLY WE'D JUST DUMP IT, BUT THEN I FOUND YOUR CARD AND--"

IT'S A FACT OF THE JOB. EVERY WINTER WE LOSE A FEW. USUALLY, YOU'RE NEVER SURE WHAT HAPPENED.

I LIKED JEFF, THOUGH. MORE THAN MOST. SAD.

YOU KNOW, YOU CAN JUST GIVE ME HIS DAUGHTER'S NUMBER AND I CAN CALL HER.

IT'S OKAY. SHE'S BEEN THROUGH ENOUGH FOR A WHILE...

I UNDERSTAND.

THAT'S REALLY NICE OF YOU.

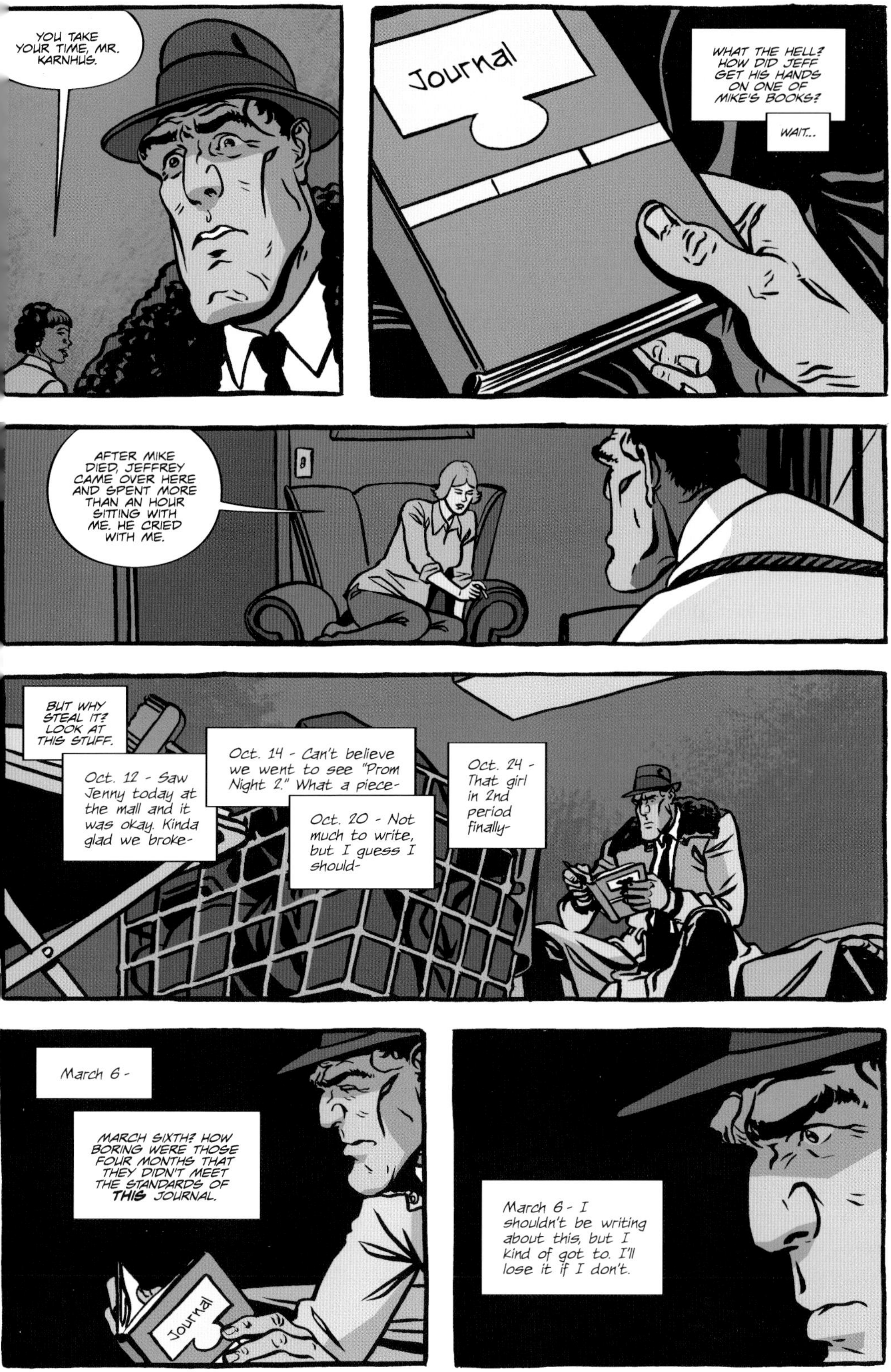
YOU TAKE YOUR TIME, MR. KARNHUS.
Journal
WHAT THE HELL? HOW DID JEFF GET HIS HANDS ON ONE OF MIKE'S BOOKS?
WAIT...
AFTER MIKE DIED, JEFFREY CAME OVER HERE AND SPENT MORE THAN AN HOUR SITTING WITH ME. HE CRIED WITH ME.
BUT WHY STEAL IT? LOOK AT THIS STUFF.
Oct. 12 - Saw Jenny today at the mall and it was okay. Kinda glad we broke-
Oct. 14 - Can't believe we went to see "Prom Night 2." What a piece-
Oct. 20 - Not much to write, but I guess I should-
Oct. 24 - That girl in 2nd period finally-
March 6 -
MARCH SIXTH? HOW BORING WERE THOSE FOUR MONTHS THAT THEY DIDN'T MEET THE STANDARDS OF THIS JOURNAL.
Journal
March 6 - I shouldn't be writing about this, but I kind of got to. I'll lose it if I don't.

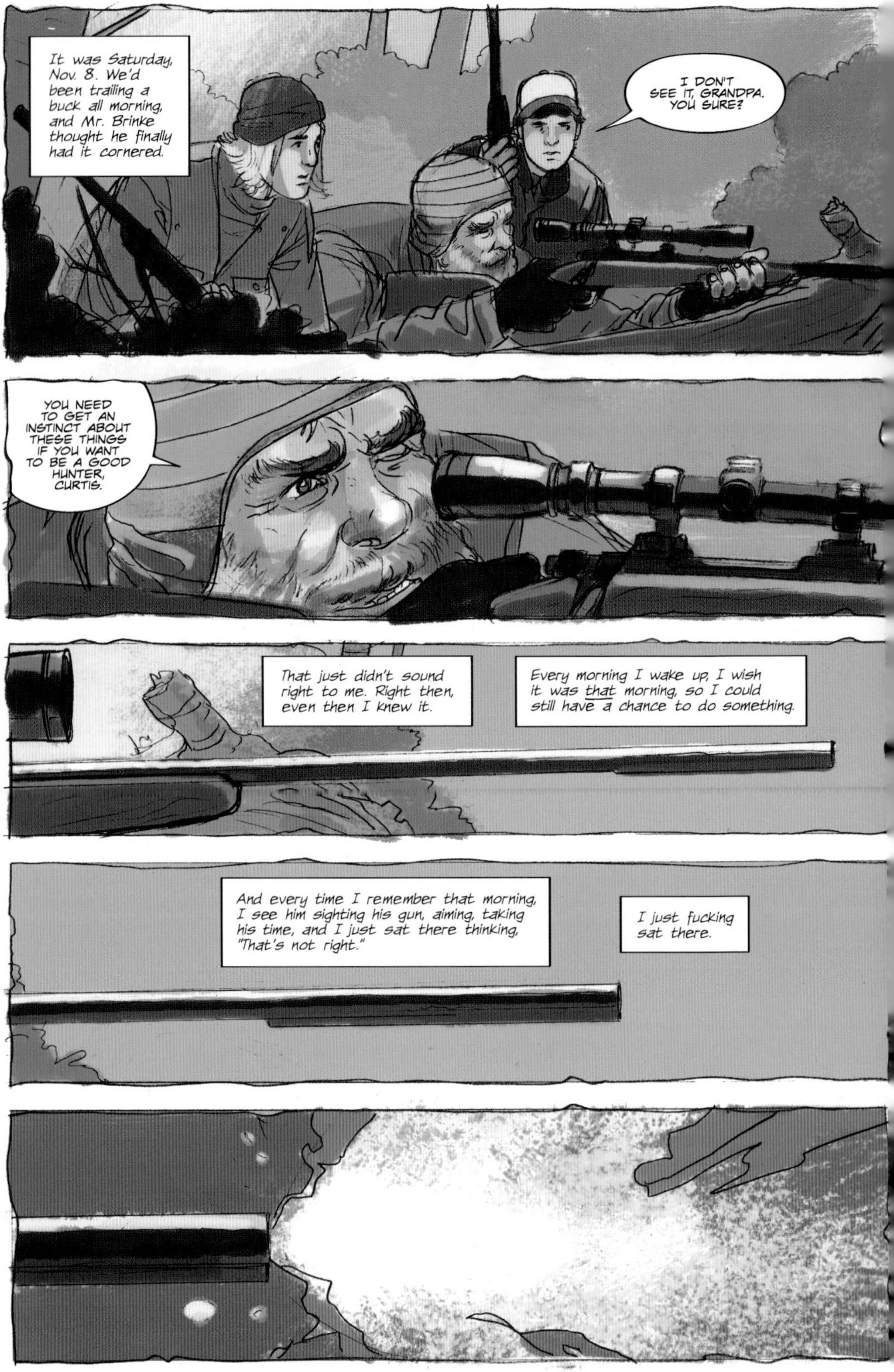

It was Saturday, Nov. 8. We'd been trailing a buck all morning, and Mr. Brinke thought he finally had it cornered.
I DON'T SEE IT, GRANDPA. YOU SURE?
YOU NEED TO GET AN INSTINCT ABOUT THESE THINGS IF YOU WANT TO BE A GOOD HUNTER, CURTIS.
That just didn't sound right to me. Right then, even then I knew it.
Every morning I wake up, I wish it was that morning, so I could still have a chance to do something.
And every time I remember that morning, I see him sighting his gun, aiming, taking his time, and I just sat there thinking, "That's not right."
I just fucking sat there.

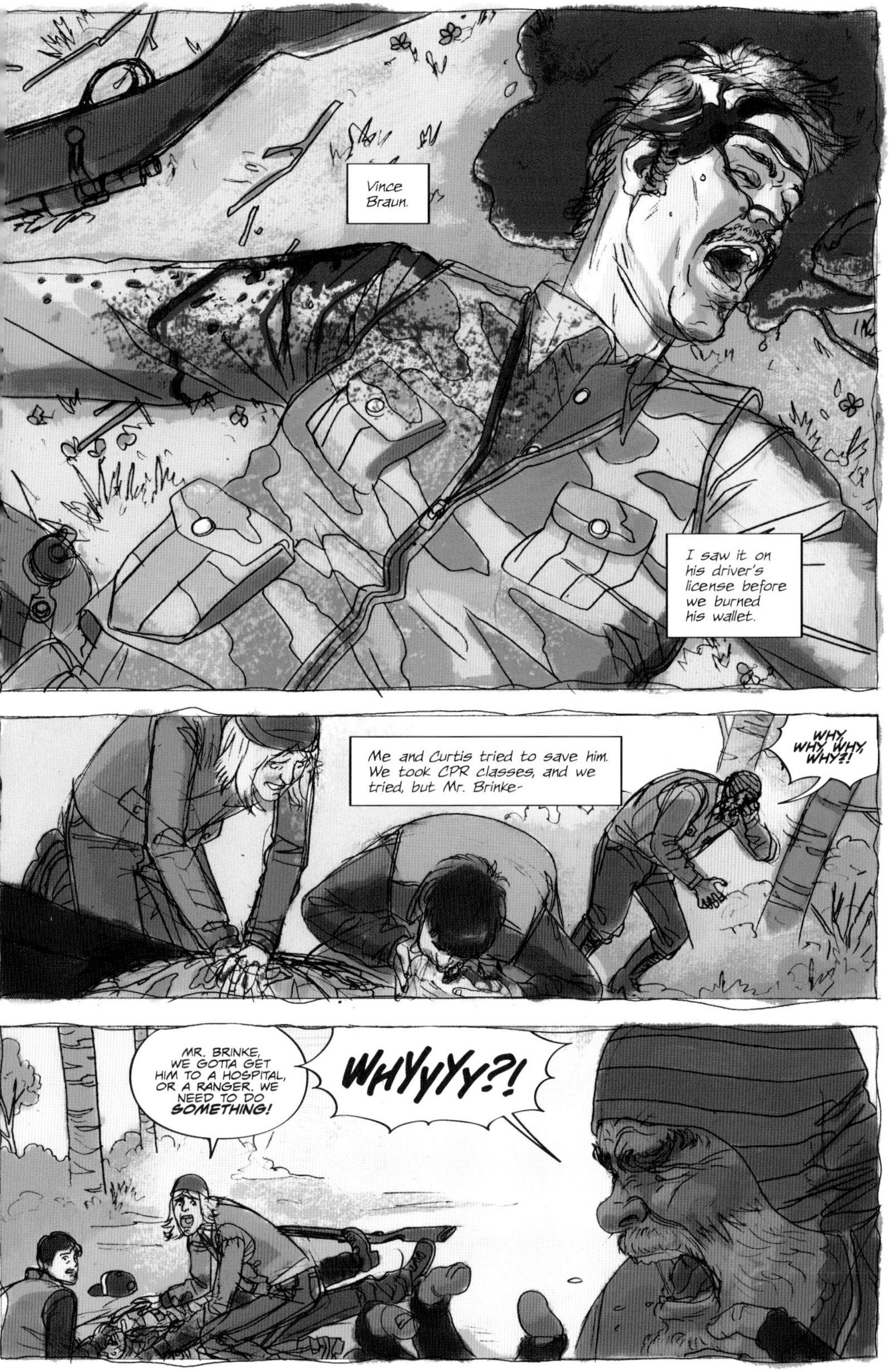

Vince Braun.
I saw it on his driver's license before we burned his wallet.
Me and Curtis tried to save him. We took CPR classes, and we tried, but Mr. Brinke-
WHY, WHY, WHY, WHY?!
MR. BRINKE, WE GOTTA GET HIM TO A HOSPITAL, OR A RANGER. WE NEED TO DO SOMETHING!
WHYyYy?!

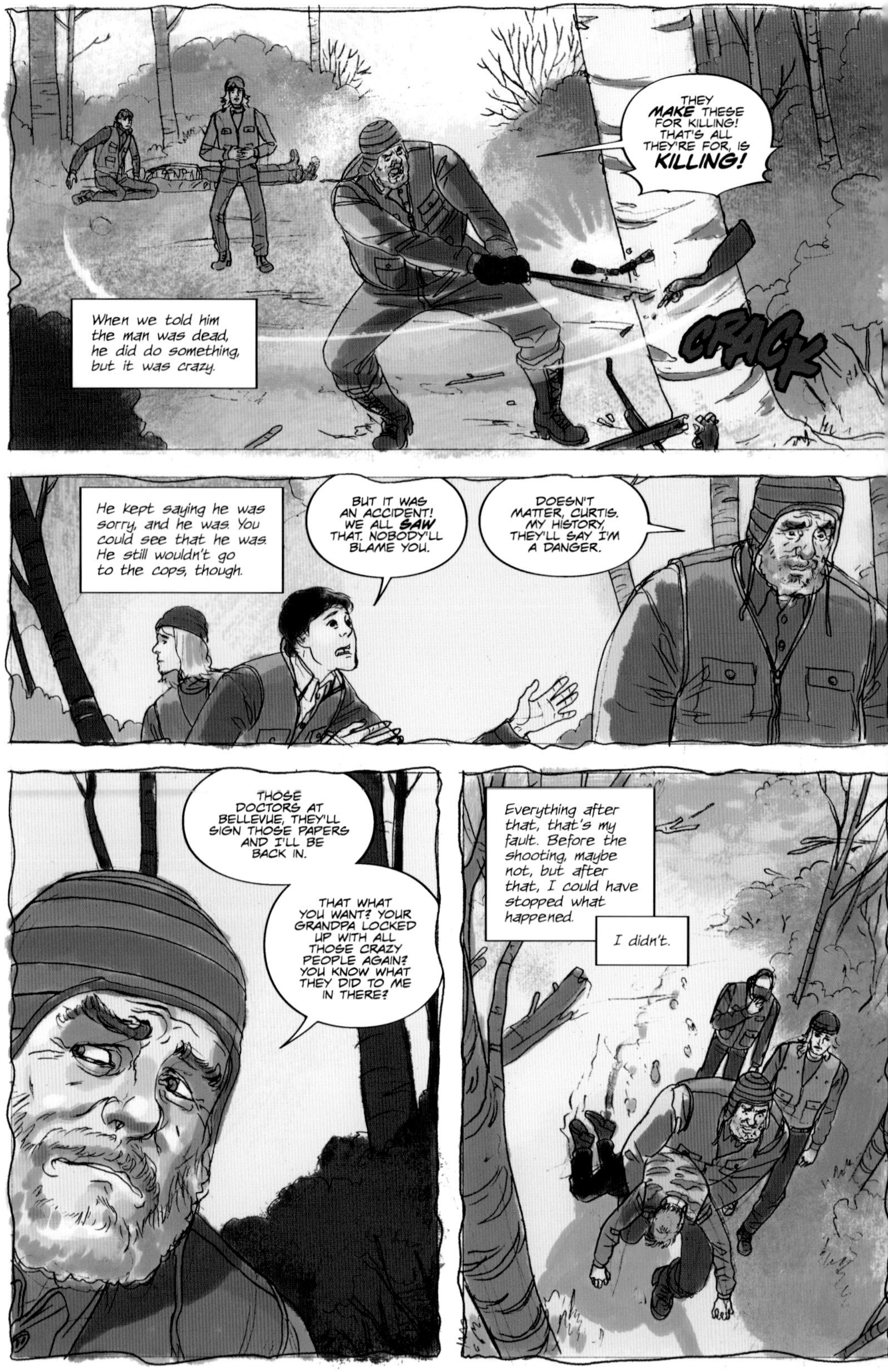
THEY MAKE THESE FOR KILLING! THAT'S ALL THEY'RE FOR, IS KILLING!
When we told him the man was dead, he did do something, but it was crazy.
CRACK
He kept saying he was sorry, and he was. You could see that he was. He still wouldn't go to the cops, though.
BUT IT WAS AN ACCIDENT! WE ALL SAW THAT. NOBODY'LL BLAME YOU.
DOESN'T MATTER, CURTIS. MY HISTORY, THEY'LL SAY I'M A DANGER.
THOSE DOCTORS AT BELLEVUE, THEY'LL SIGN THOSE PAPERS AND I'LL BE BACK IN.
THAT WHAT YOU WANT? YOUR GRANDPA LOCKED UP WITH ALL THOSE CRAZY PEOPLE AGAIN? YOU KNOW WHAT THEY DID TO ME IN THERE?
Everything after that, that's my fault. Before the shooting, maybe not, but after that, I could have stopped what happened.
I didn't.

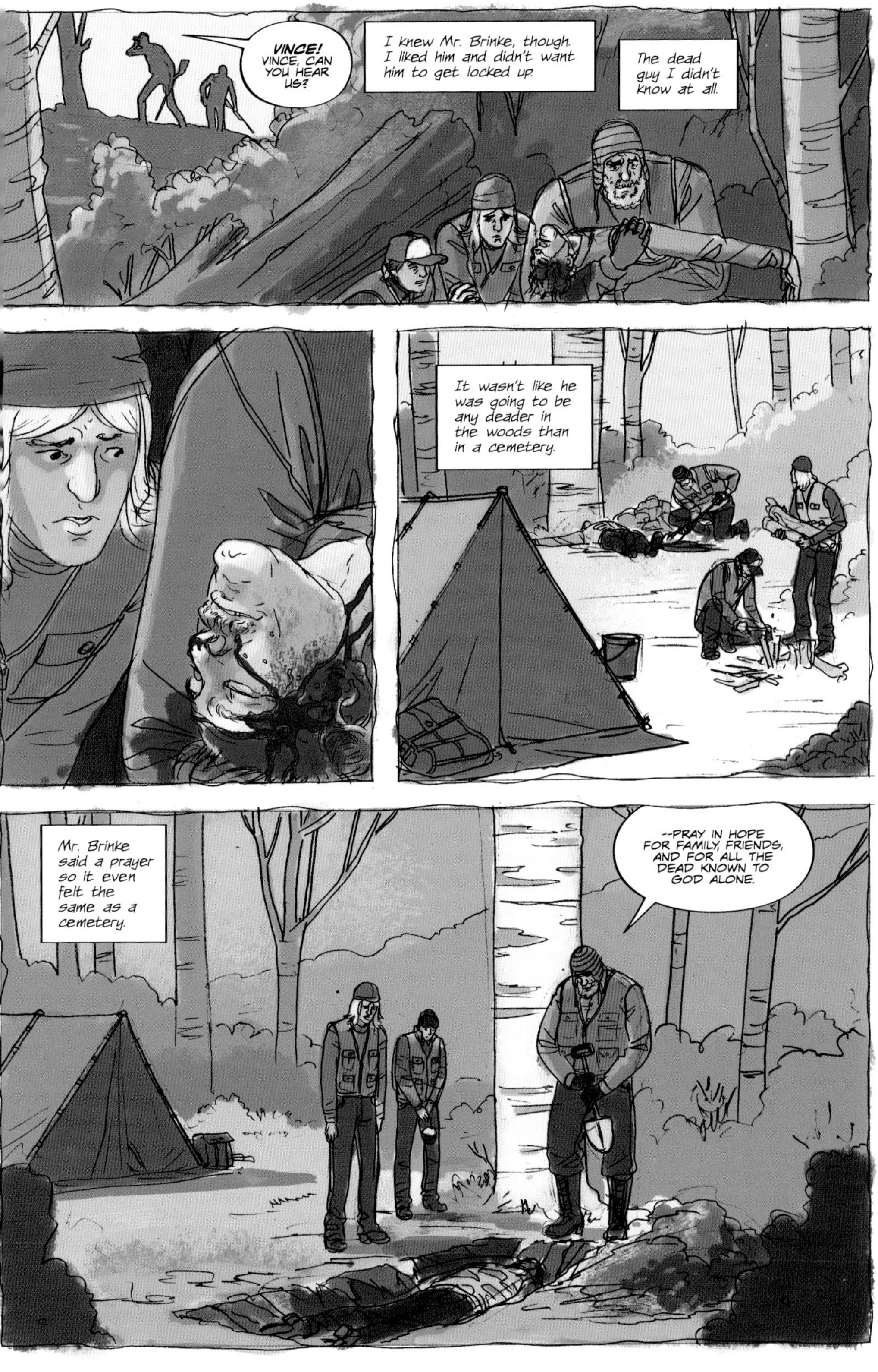
VINCE! VINCE, CAN YOU HEAR US?
I knew Mr. Brinke, though. I liked him and didn't want him to get locked up.
The dead guy I didn't know at all.
It wasn't like he was going to be any deader in the woods than in a cemetery.
Mr. Brinke said a prayer so it even felt the same as a cemetery.
--PRAY IN HOPE FOR FAMILY, FRIENDS, AND FOR ALL THE DEAD KNOWN TO GOD ALONE.

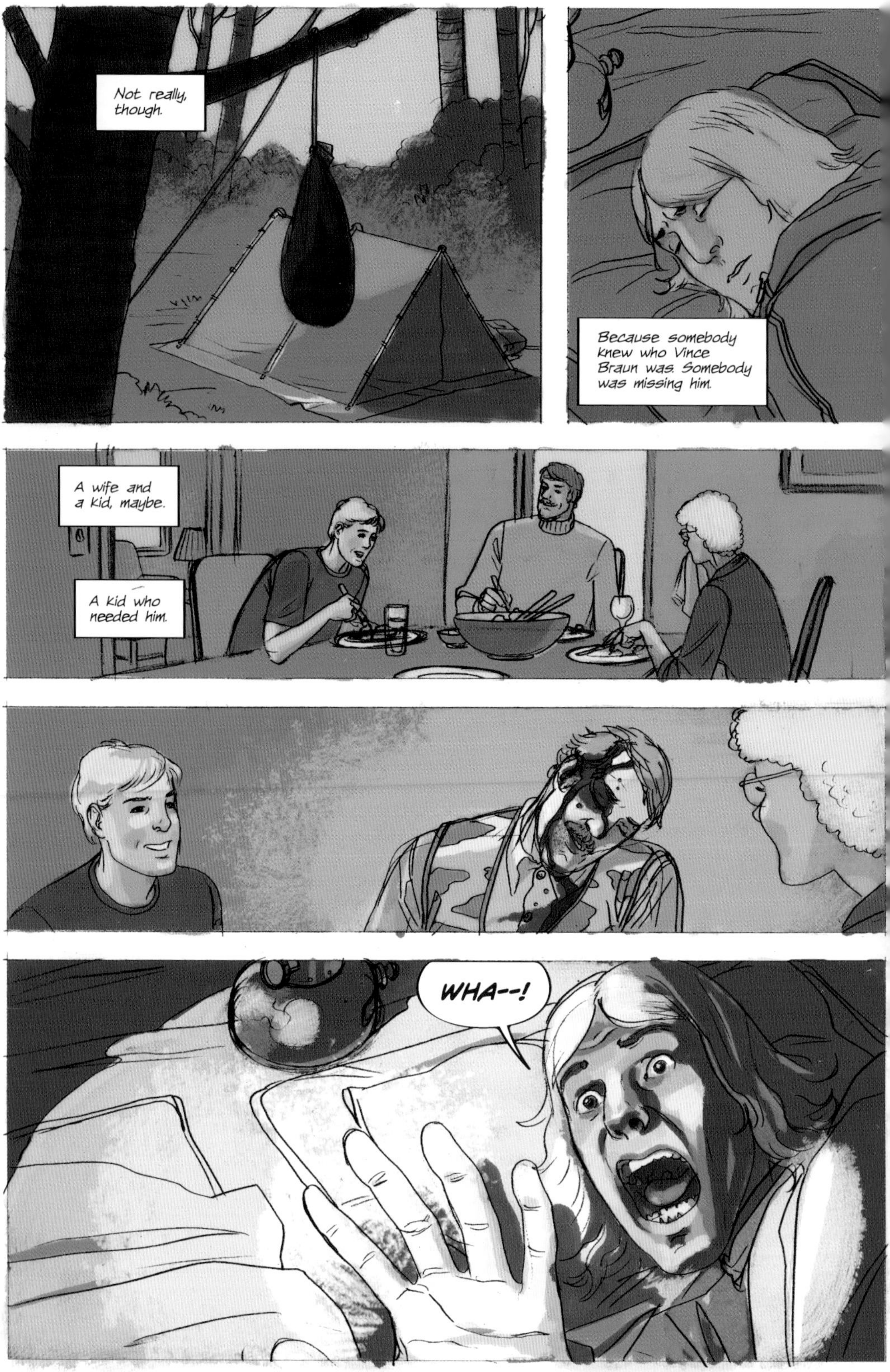
Not really, though.
Because somebody knew who Vince Braun was. Somebody was missing him.
A wife and a kid, maybe.
A kid who needed him.
WHA--!

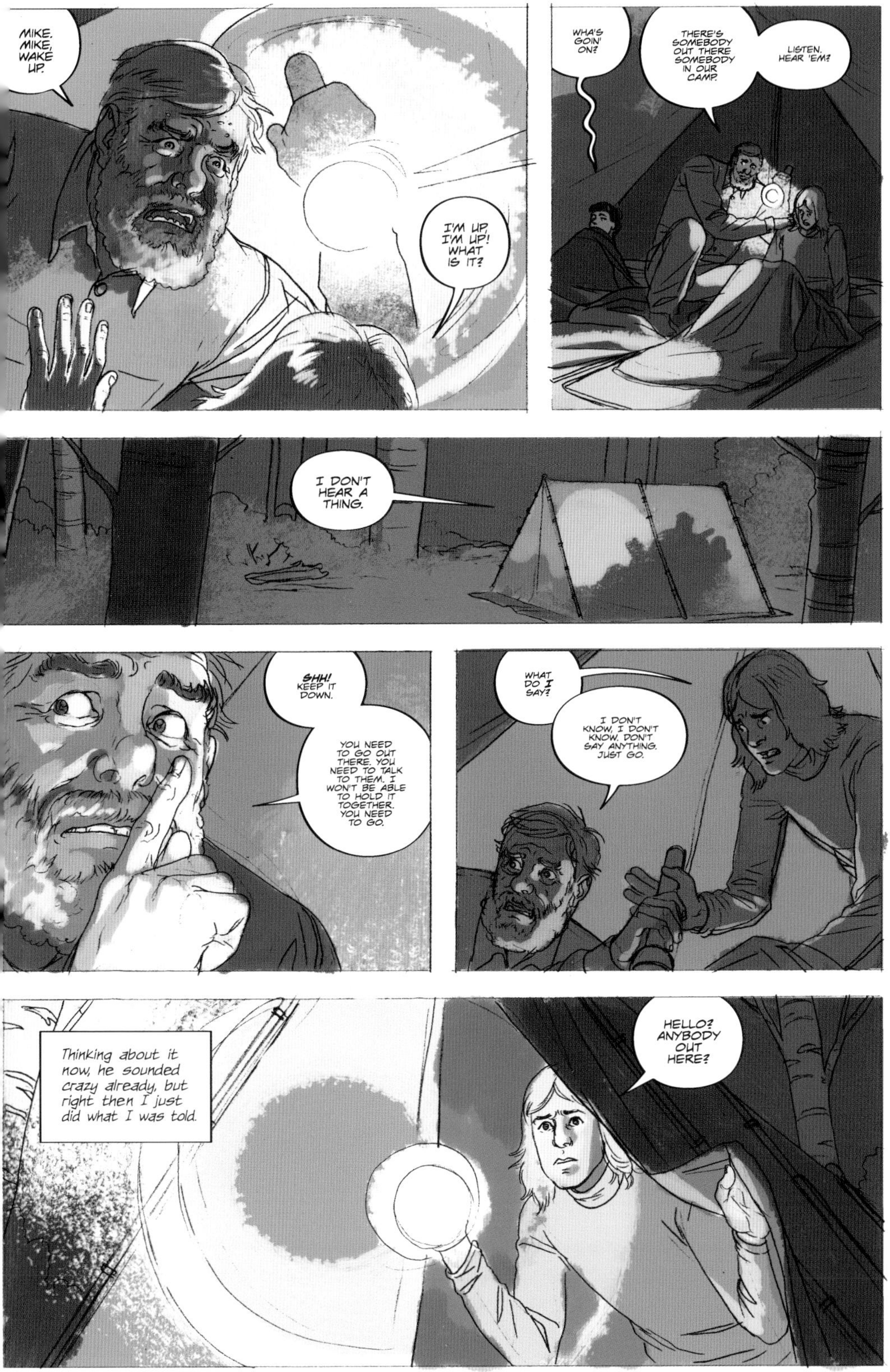
MIKE. MIKE, WAKE UP.
I'M UP, I'M UP! WHAT IS IT?
WHA'S GOIN' ON?
THERE'S SOMEBODY OUT THERE SOMEBODY IN OUR CAMP.
LISTEN. HEAR 'EM?
I DON'T HEAR A THING.
SHH! KEEP IT DOWN.
YOU NEED TO GO OUT THERE. YOU NEED TO TALK TO THEM. I WON'T BE ABLE TO HOLD IT TOGETHER. YOU NEED TO GO.
WHAT DO I SAY?
I DON'T KNOW, I DON'T KNOW. DON'T SAY ANYTHING. JUST GO.
Thinking about it now, he sounded crazy already, but right then I just did what I was told.
HELLO? ANYBODY OUT HERE?

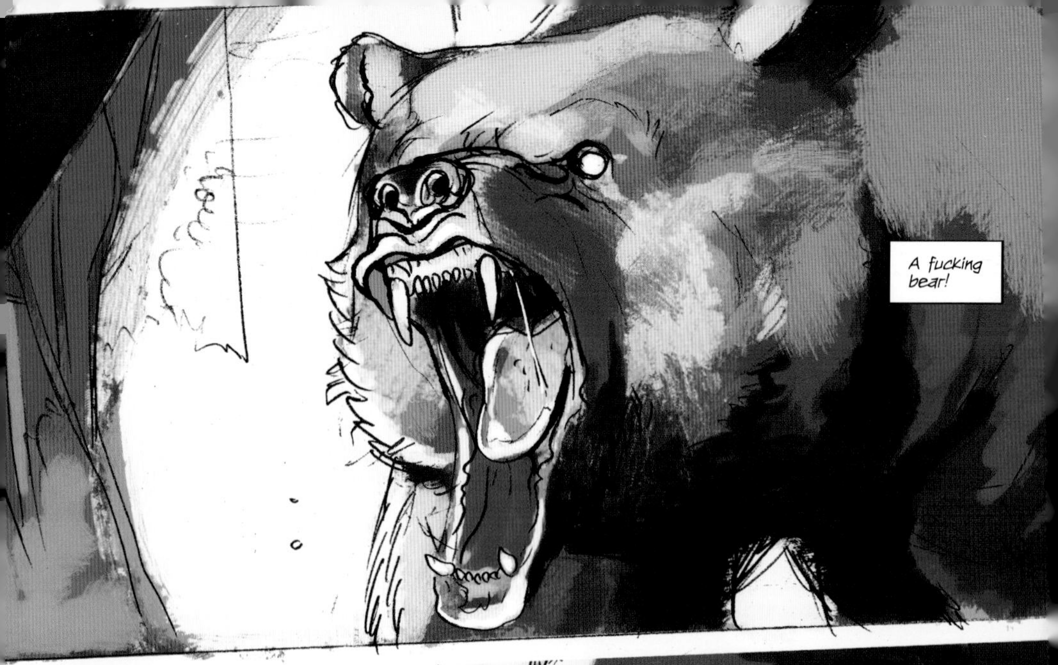
A fucking bear!

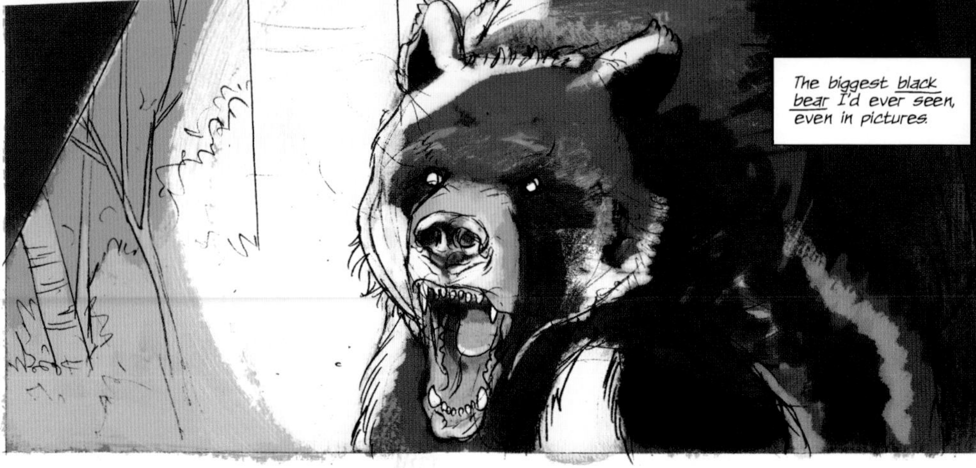
The biggest black bear I'd ever seen, even in pictures.

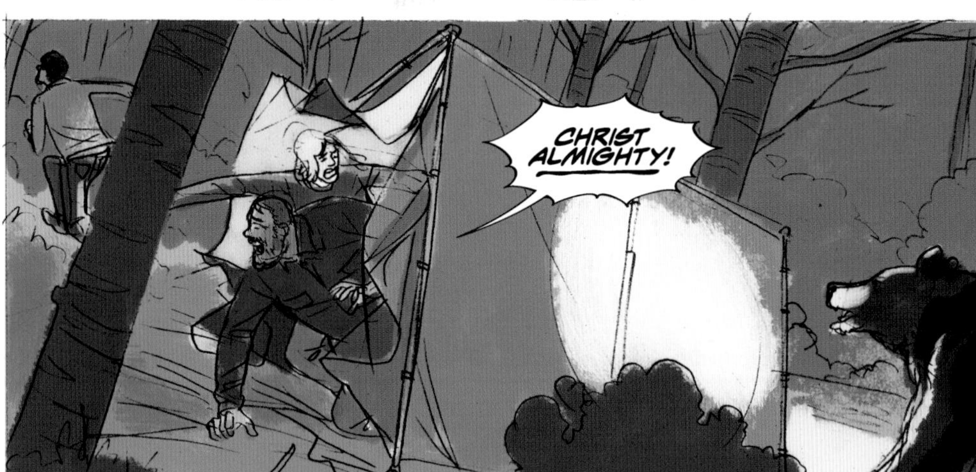
CHRIST ALMIGHTY!

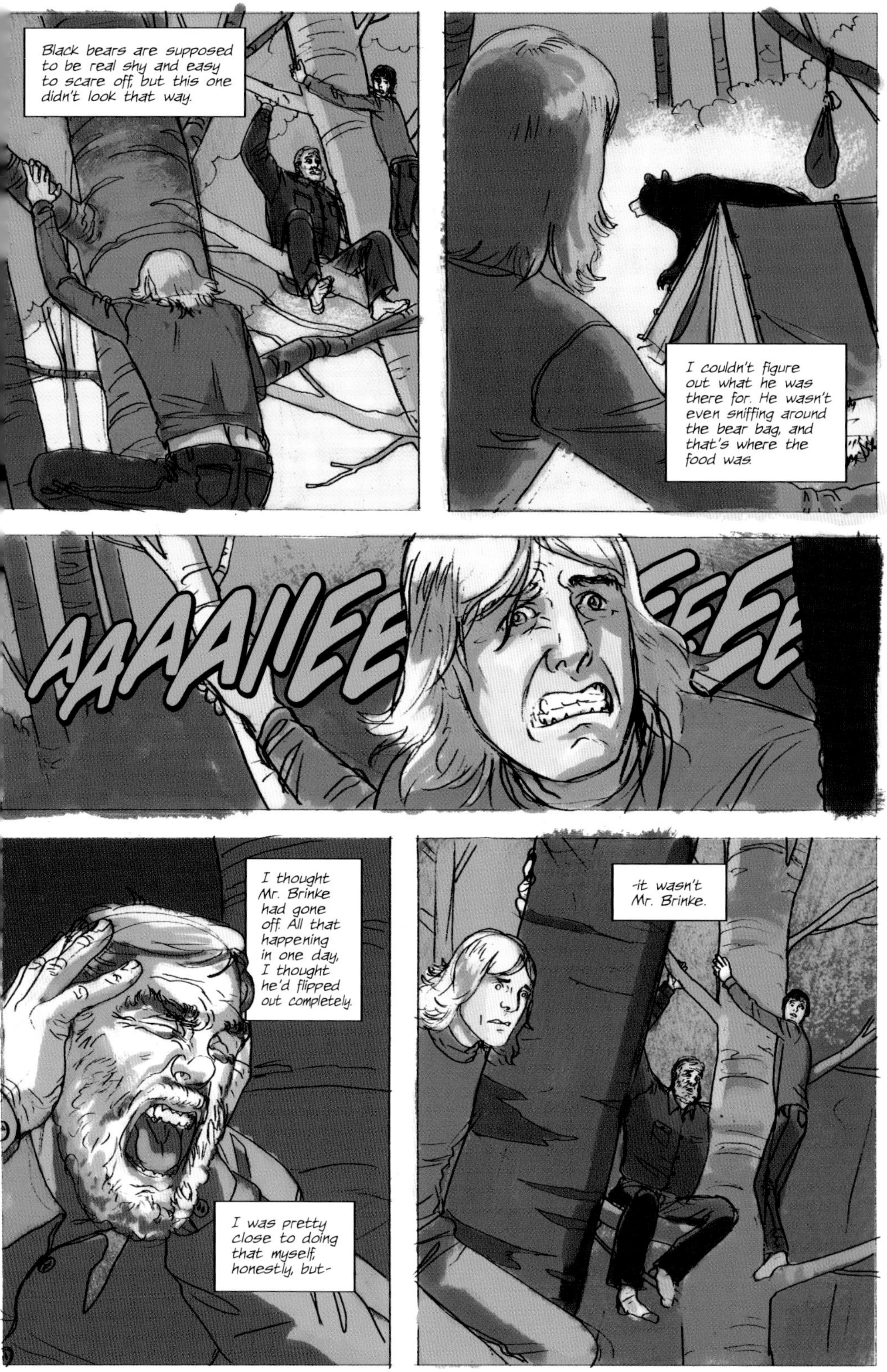
Black bears are supposed to be real shy and easy to scare off, but this one didn't look that way.
I couldn't figure out what he was there for. He wasn't even sniffing around the bear bag, and that's where the food was.
AAAAIIEEEEEE
I thought Mr. Brinke had gone off. All that happening in one day, I thought he'd flipped out completely.
I was pretty close to doing that myself, honestly, but-
-it wasn't Mr. Brinke.

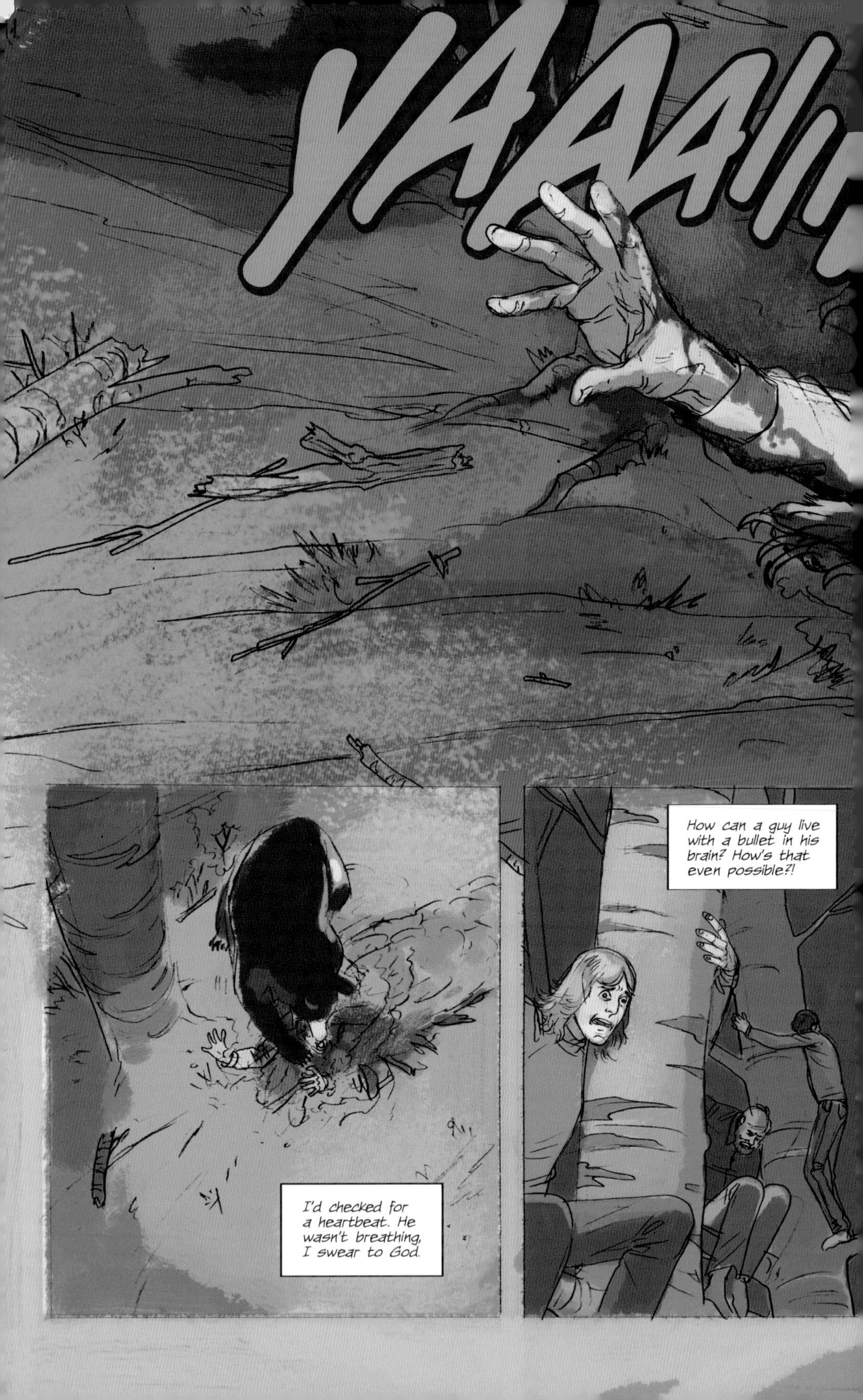
YAAAII!
I'd checked for a heartbeat. He wasn't breathing, I swear to God.
How can a guy live with a bullet in his brain? How's that even possible?!

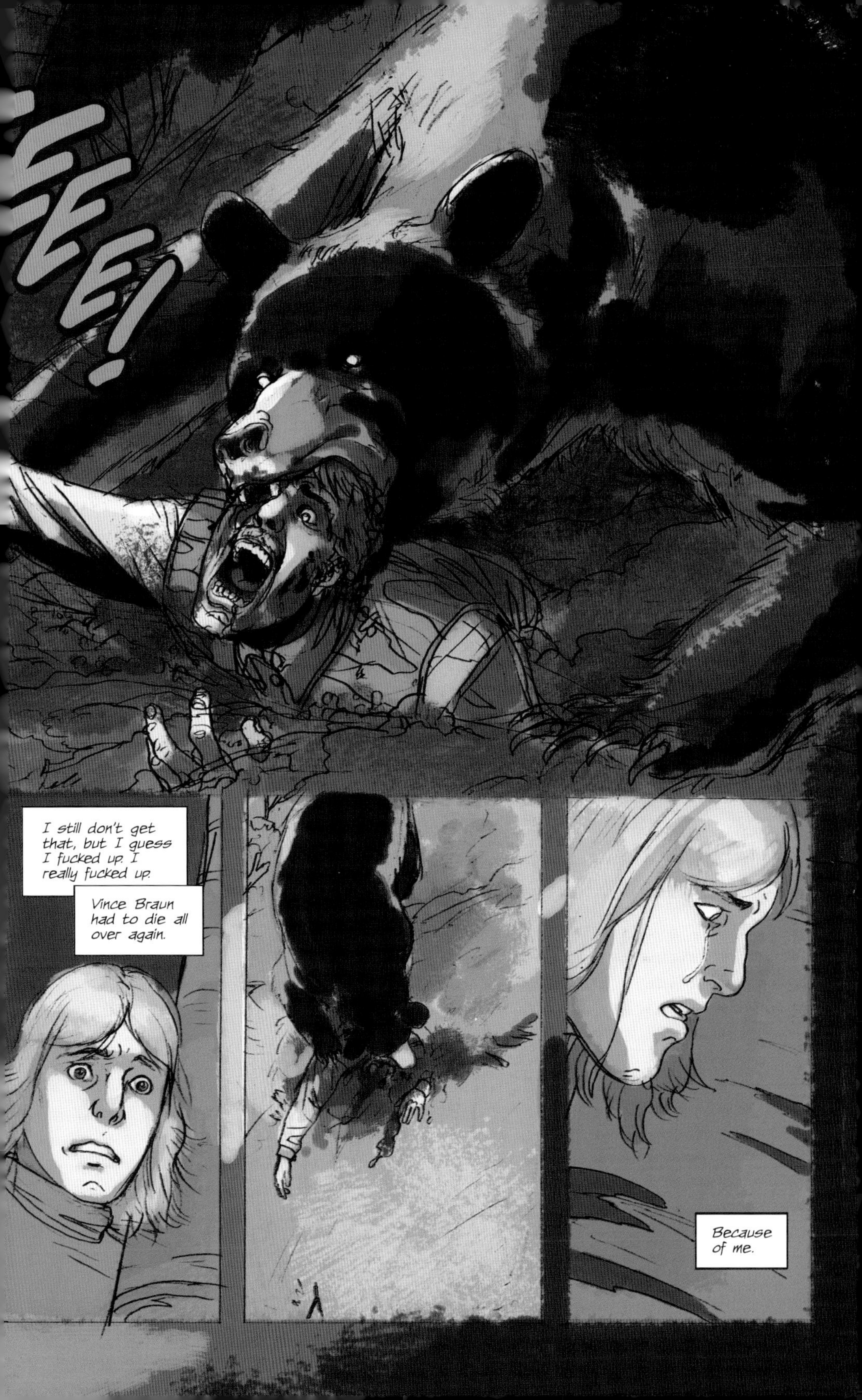
I still don't get that, but I guess I fucked up. I really fucked up.
Vince Braun had to die all over again.
Because of me.

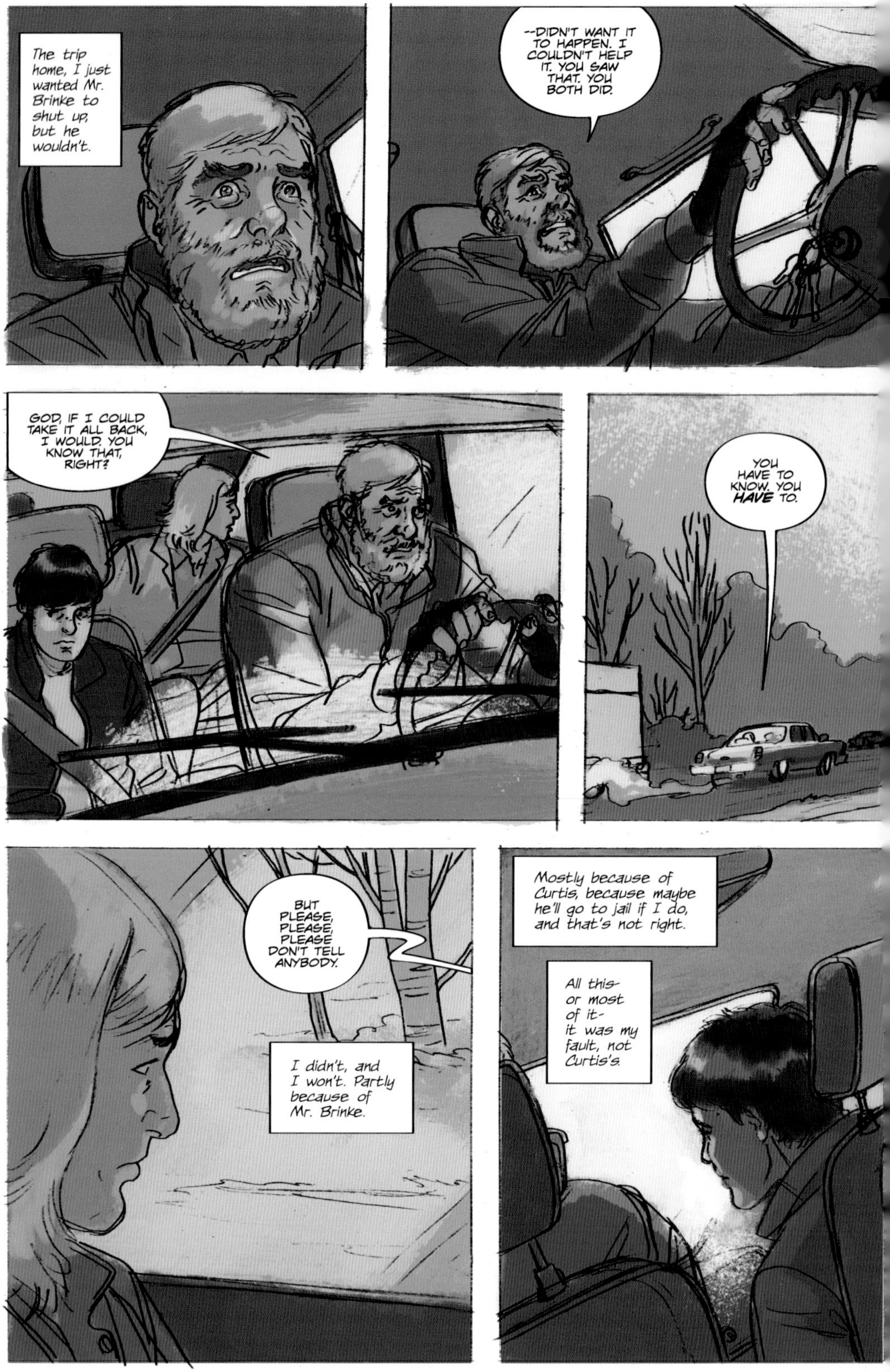
The trip home, I just wanted Mr. Brinke to shut up, but he wouldn't.
--DIDN'T WANT IT TO HAPPEN. I COULDN'T HELP IT. YOU SAW THAT. YOU BOTH DID.
GOD, IF I COULD TAKE IT ALL BACK, I WOULD. YOU KNOW THAT, RIGHT?
YOU HAVE TO KNOW. YOU HAVE TO.
BUT PLEASE, PLEASE, PLEASE DON'T TELL ANYBODY.
I didn't, and I won't. Partly because of Mr. Brinke.
Mostly because of Curtis, because maybe he'll go to jail if I do, and that's not right.
All this- or most of it- it was my fault, not Curtis's.

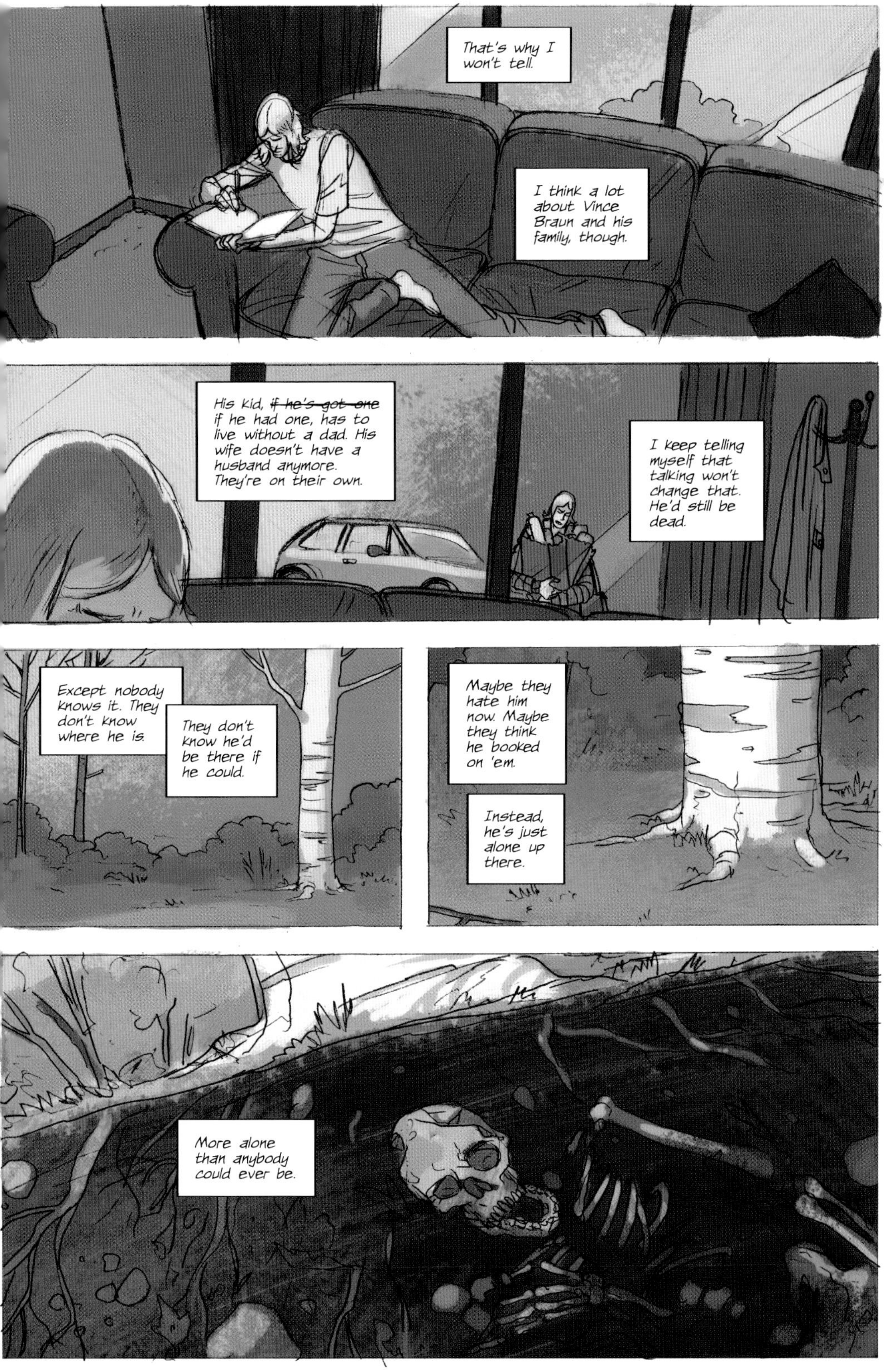
That's why I won't tell.
I think a lot about Vince Braun and his family, though.
His kid, ~~if he's got one~~ if he had one, has to live without a dad. His wife doesn't have a husband anymore. They're on their own.
I keep telling myself that talking won't change that. He'd still be dead.
Except nobody knows it. They don't know where he is.
They don't know he'd be there if he could.
Maybe they hate him now. Maybe they think he booked on 'em.
Instead, he's just alone up there.
More alone than anybody could ever be.

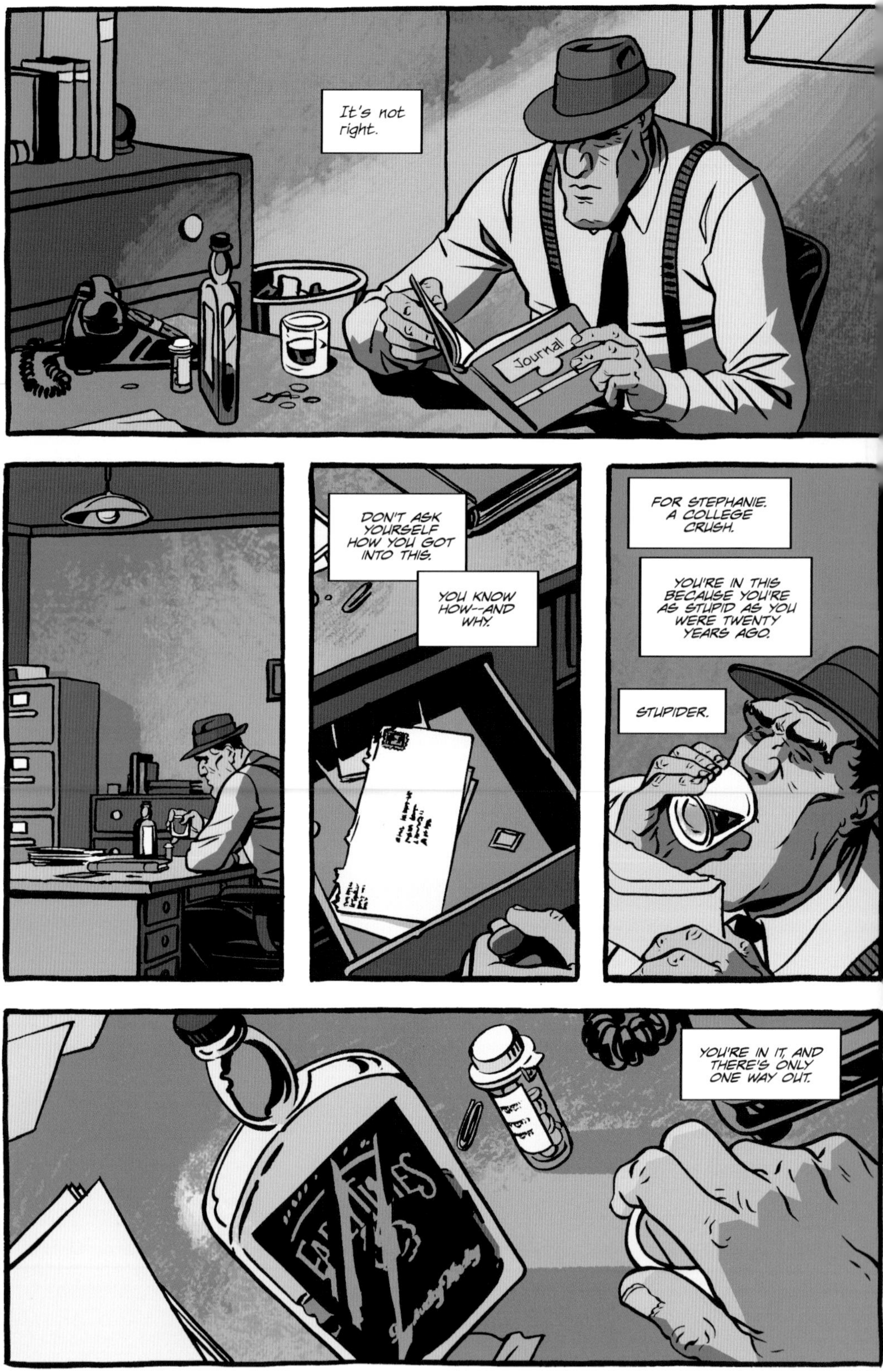
It's not right.
Journal
DON'T ASK YOURSELF HOW YOU GOT INTO THIS.
YOU KNOW HOW--AND WHY.
FOR STEPHANIE. A COLLEGE CRUSH.
YOU'RE IN THIS BECAUSE YOU'RE AS STUPID AS YOU WERE TWENTY YEARS AGO.
STUPIDER.
YOU'RE IN IT, AND THERE'S ONLY ONE WAY OUT.

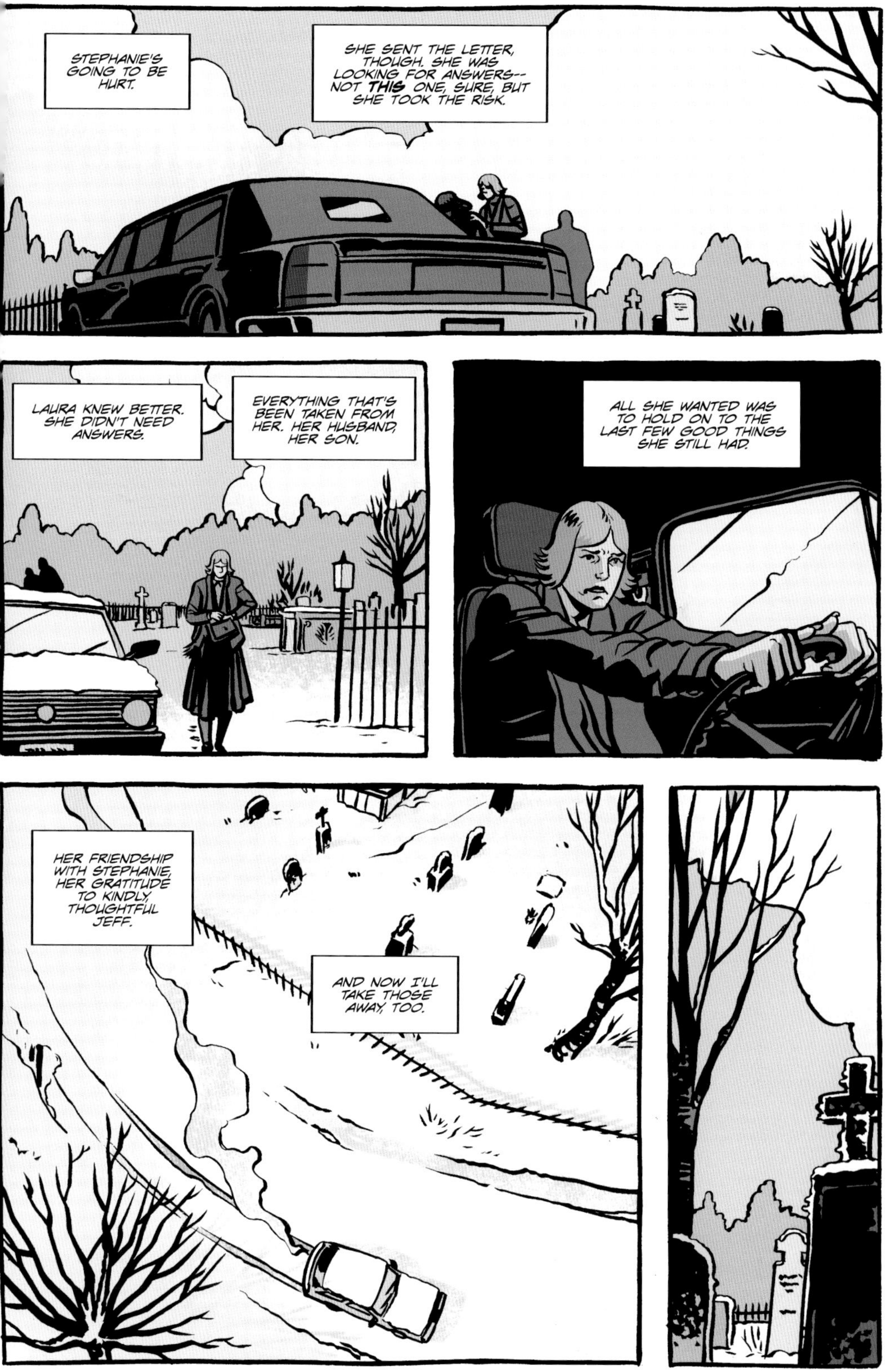
STEPHANIE'S GOING TO BE HURT.
SHE SENT THE LETTER, THOUGH. SHE WAS LOOKING FOR ANSWERS-- NOT THIS ONE, SURE, BUT SHE TOOK THE RISK.
LAURA KNEW BETTER. SHE DIDN'T NEED ANSWERS.
EVERYTHING THAT'S BEEN TAKEN FROM HER. HER HUSBAND, HER SON.
ALL SHE WANTED WAS TO HOLD ON TO THE LAST FEW GOOD THINGS SHE STILL HAD.
HER FRIENDSHIP WITH STEPHANIE, HER GRATITUDE TO KINDLY, THOUGHTFUL JEFF.
AND NOW I'LL TAKE THOSE AWAY, TOO.

THIS LETTER.

THIS GODDAMNED LETTER.

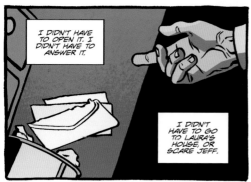

I DIDN'T HAVE TO OPEN IT. I DIDN'T HAVE TO ANSWER IT.

I DIDN'T HAVE TO GO TO LAURA'S HOUSE, OR SCARE JEFF.

HELLO, LIEUTENANT BEST?

I HAVE TO TELL YOU SOMETHING.

THE END

THE CREEP
SKETCHBOOK

CASE: We set Oxel's design pretty quickly. While the initial direction I received was to essentially make him Rondo Hatton, John suggested I explore a different look, in the broader range of acromegaly. I tried to make him ugly, but not so much that I couldn't sympathize with him.

ARCUDI: Getting this right was *major* in my book. Before Jonathan came along, Oxel just looked way too much like Rondo Hatton. It made him (wholly unintentionally) something of a caricature, no matter how well he was drawn. Some readers saw a movie heavy, not a human being. Jonathan was able to really give Oxel his own look, and that made him three-dimensional.

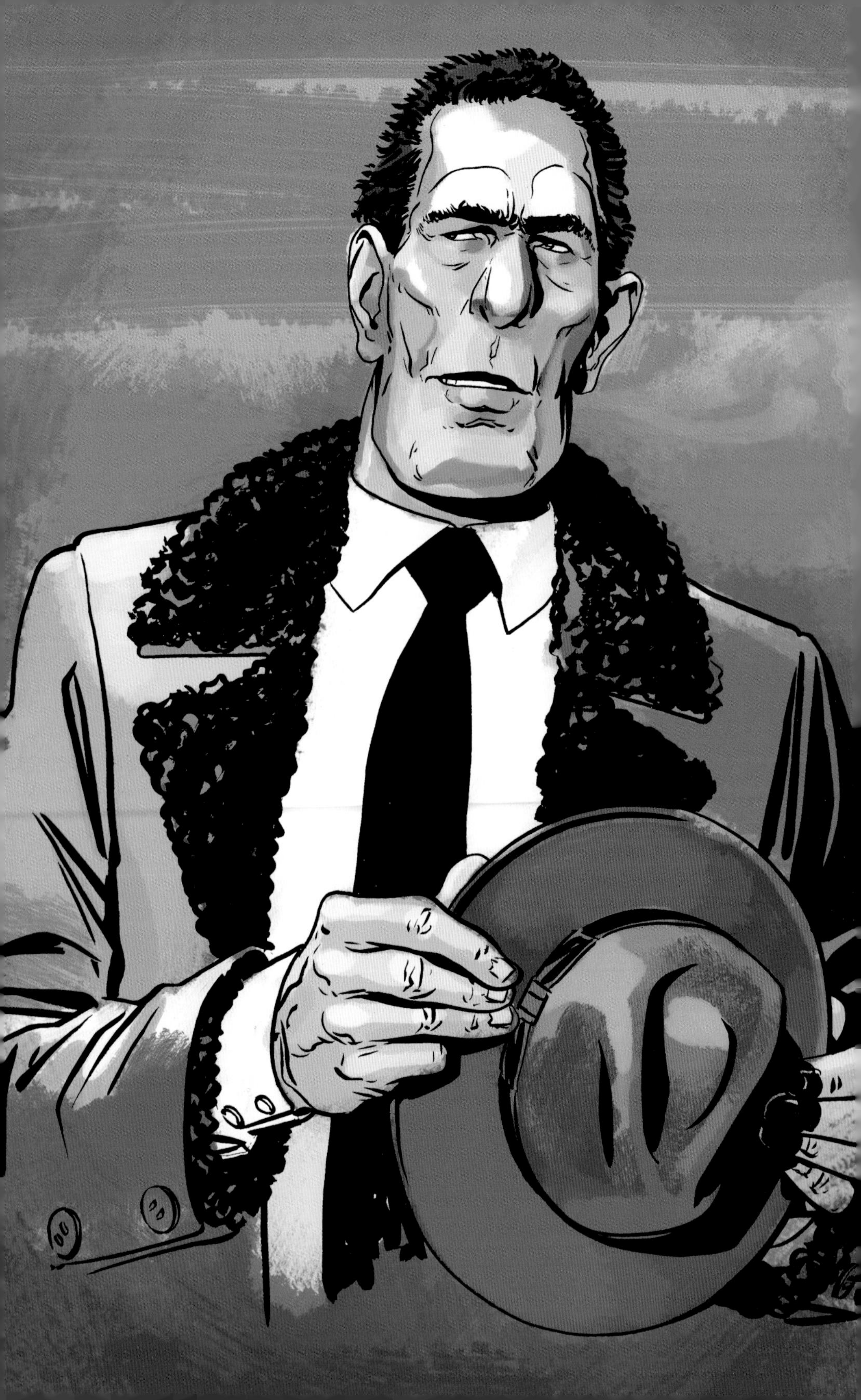

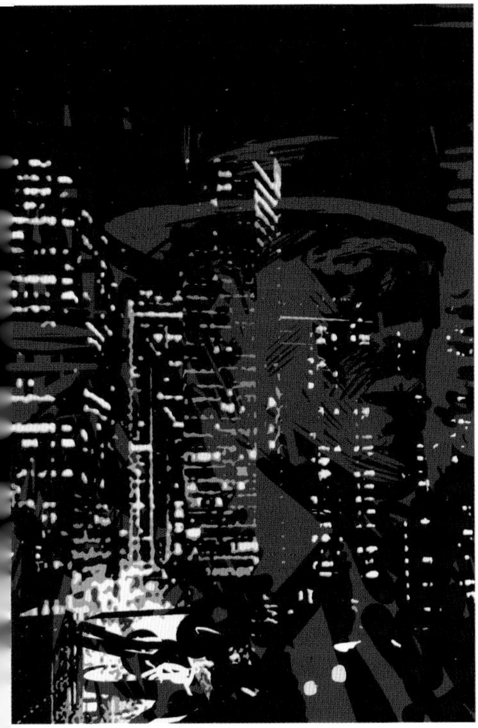

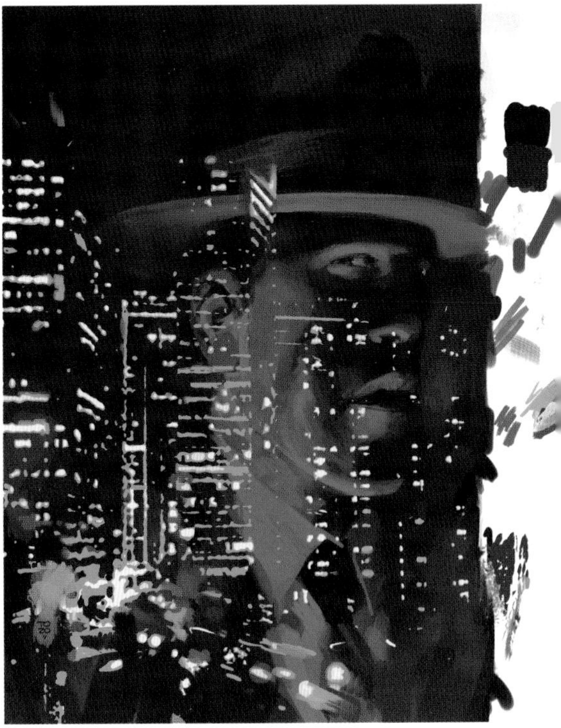

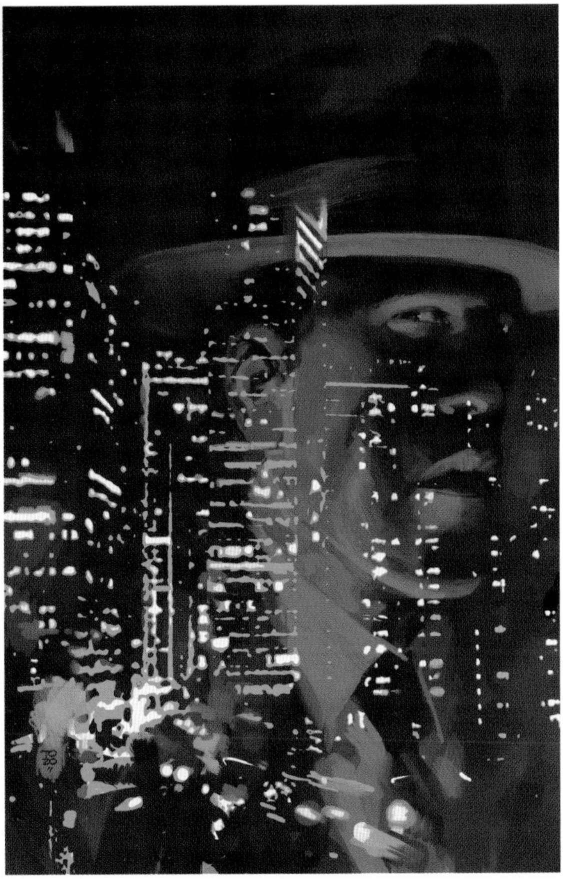

ARCUDI: Tonci Zonjic is amazing, and getting him (along with Frank Miller, Mike Mignola, and Ryan Sook) to do a cover for us was a great stroke of luck. As you can see here, he really fine-tuned this cover (for *Dark Horse Presents* #11) until he nailed it. Actually, he gave us several cover ideas, all great, but we had to reject one simply because it gave too much away for the *DHP* chapters. That idea later became the cover for this collection.

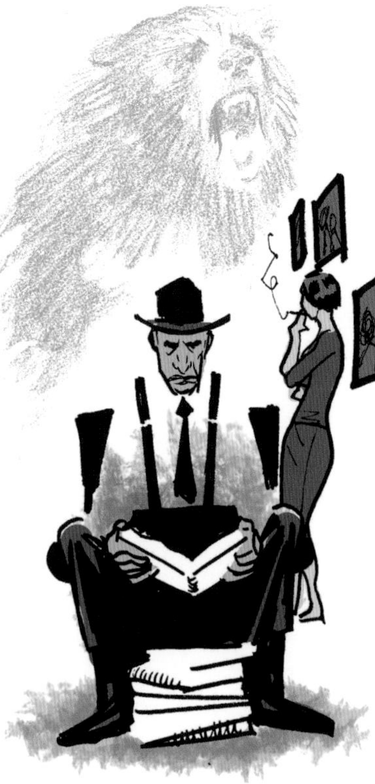

ARCUDI: Ryan Sook was another guest cover artist who gave us his all. He went through several different ideas, some pretty imaginative, until he arrived at the killer, killer "Oxel on the staircase" bit!! Moody as can be, the image at the lower right was his marker prelim—which I almost prefer to the final cover.

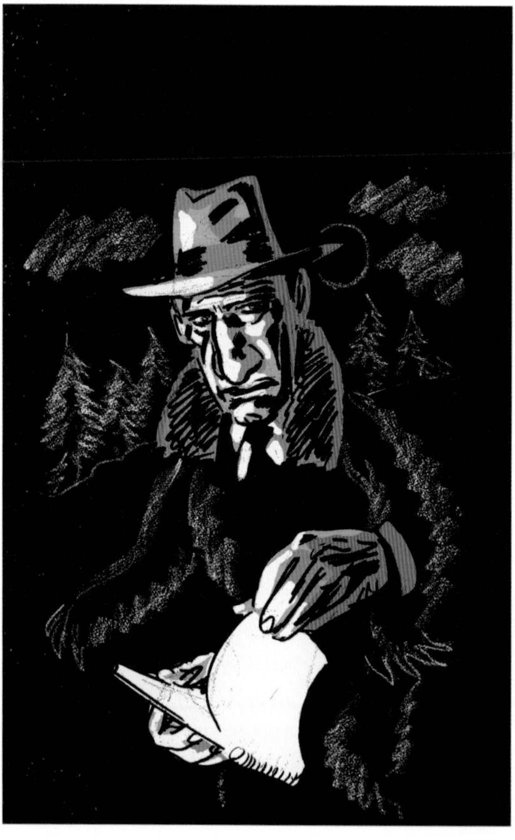

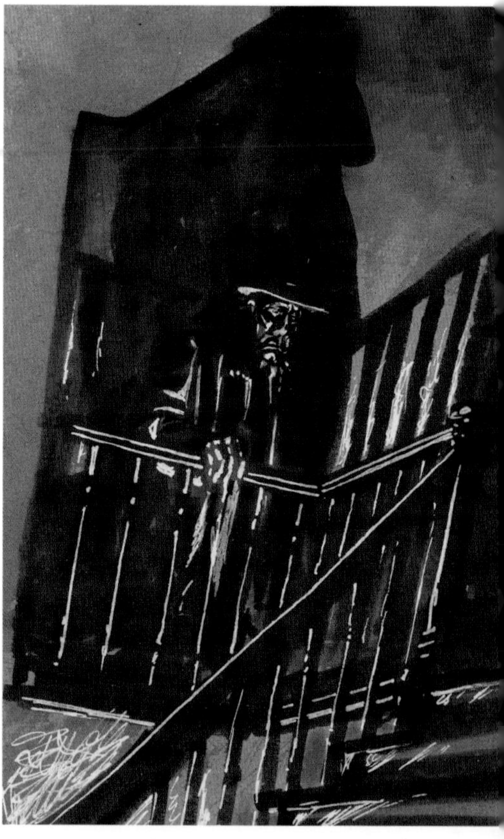

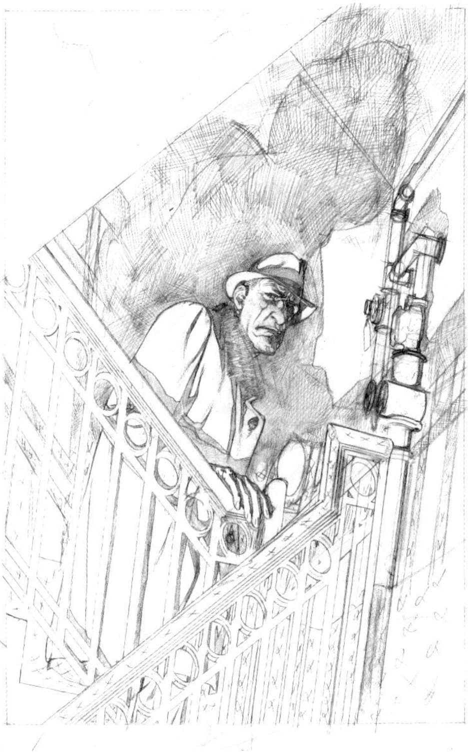

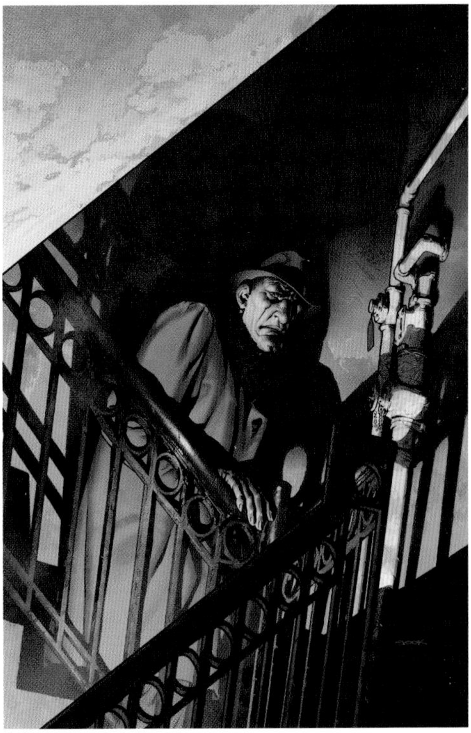

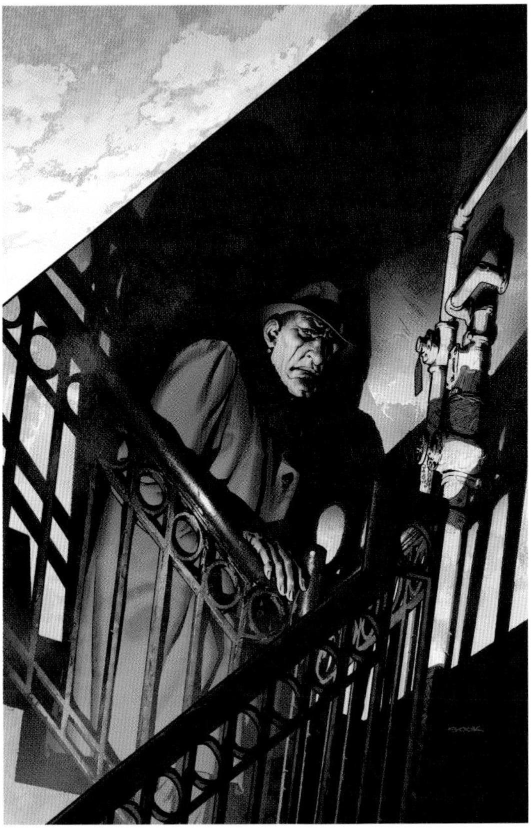

ARCUDI: Almost, because look at this! Ryan also did the colors.

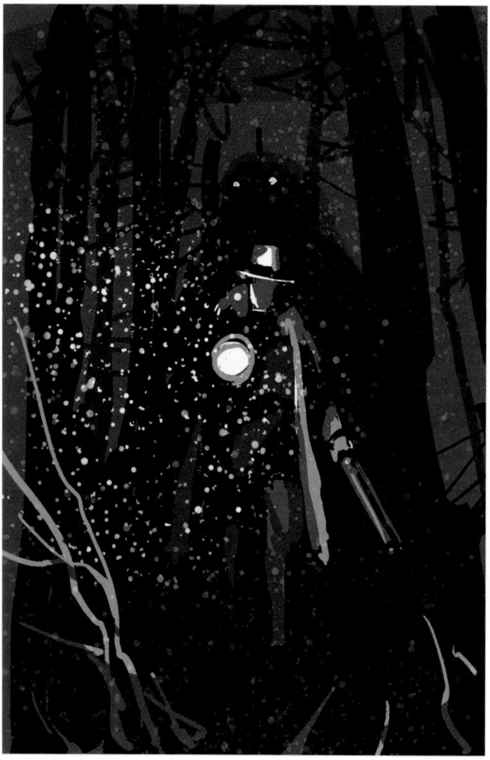

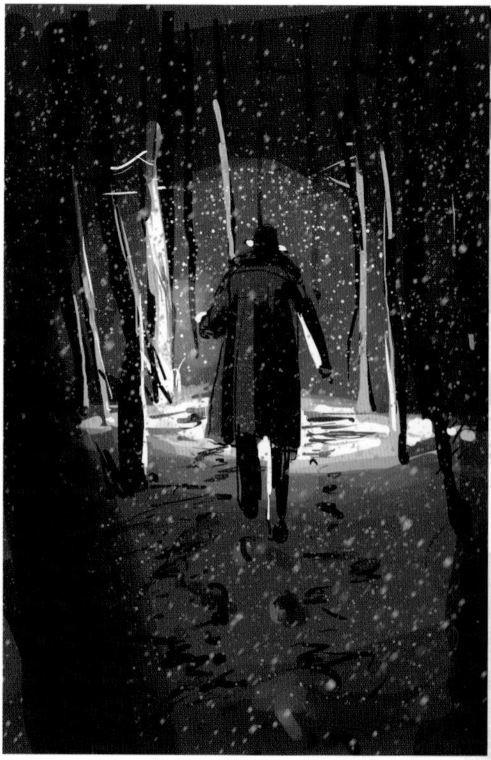

ARCUDI: You know, looking at these cover designs by Tonci Zonjic, I have to wonder why we didn't go with that first one. Hmmmm . . .

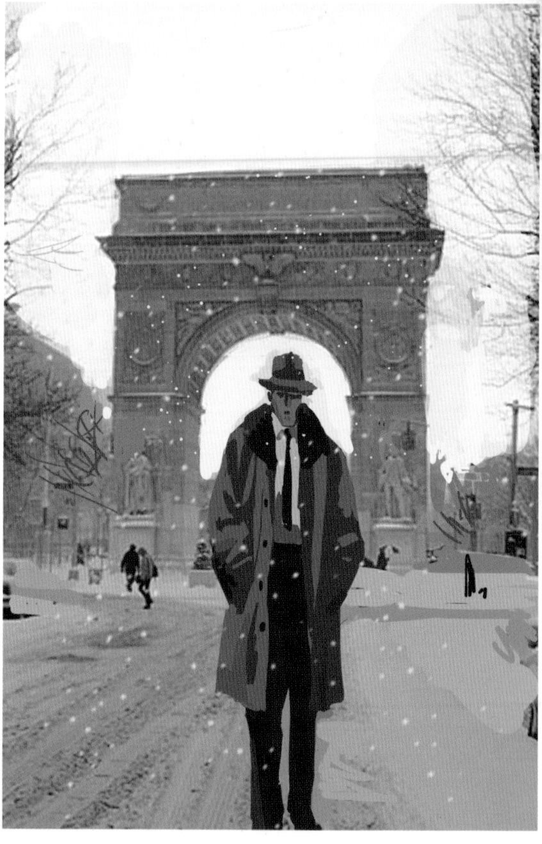

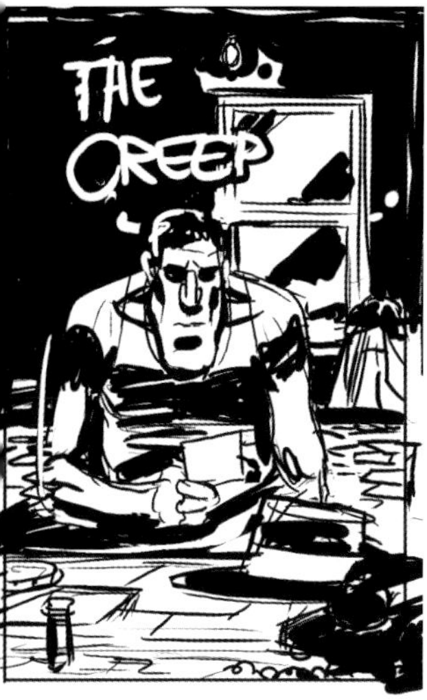
THE
CREEP

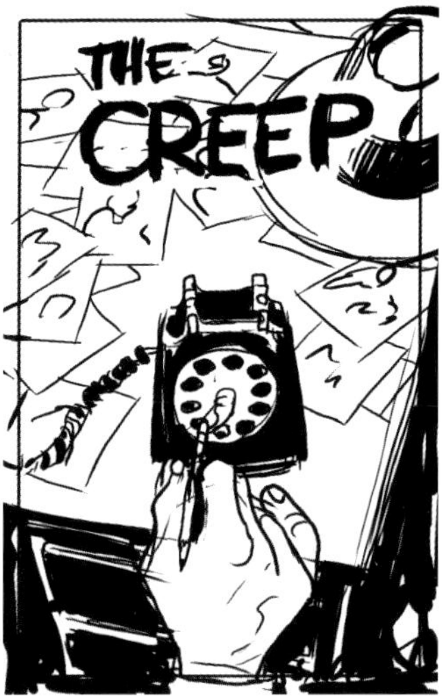
THE
CREEP

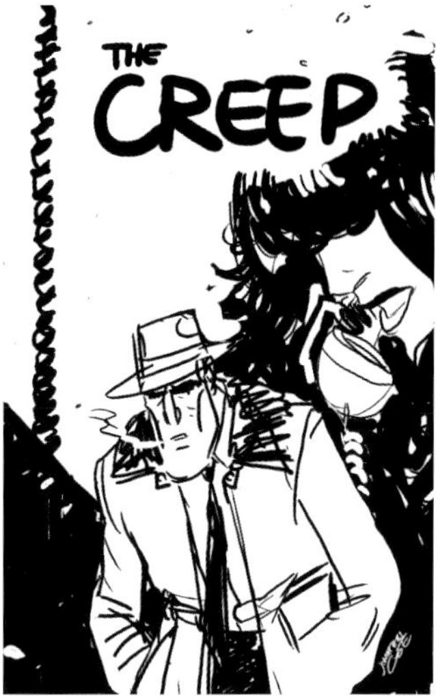
THE
CREEP

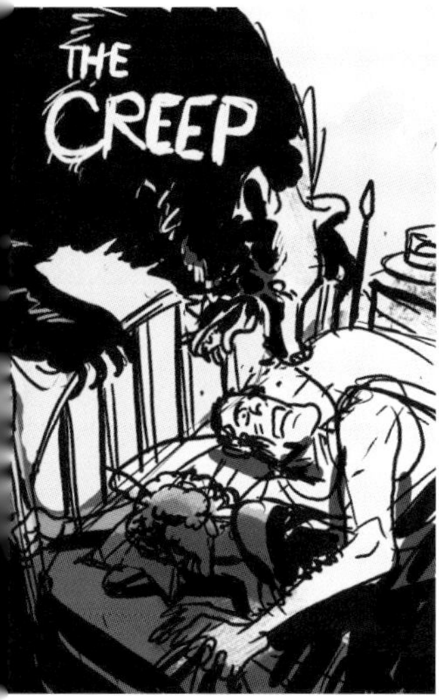
THE
CREEP

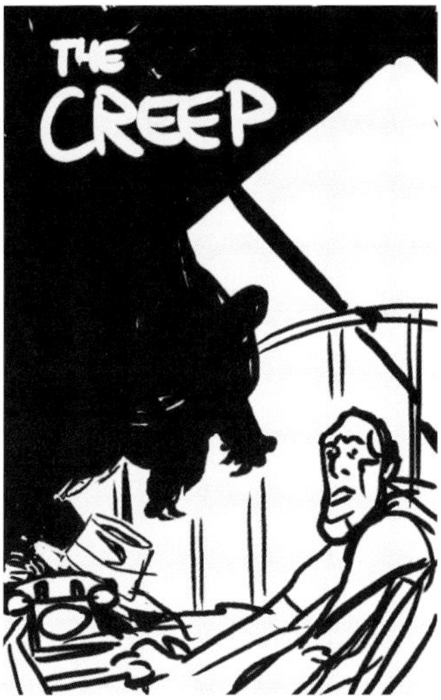
THE
CREEP

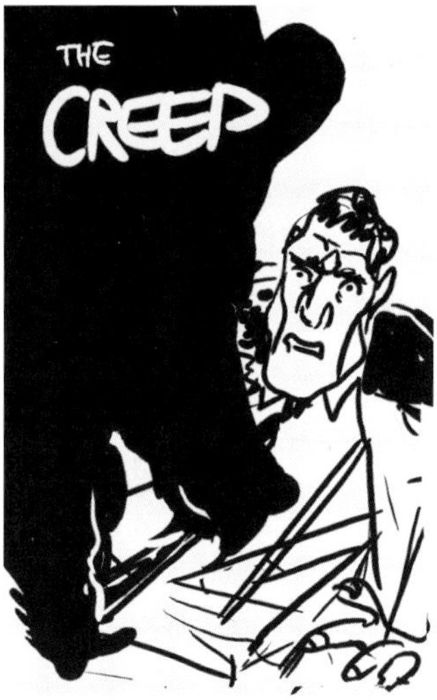
THE
CREEP

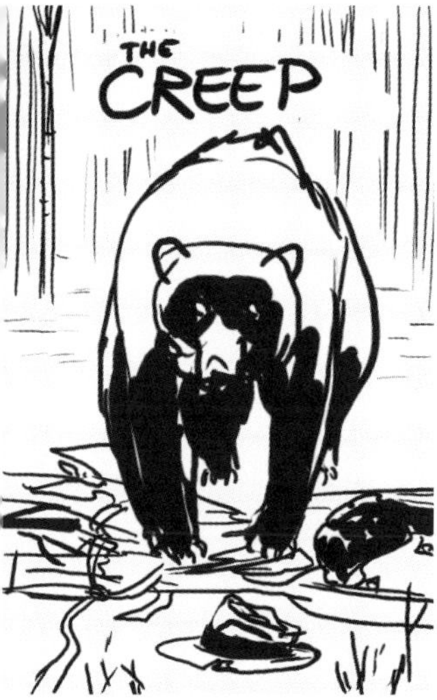
THE
CREEP

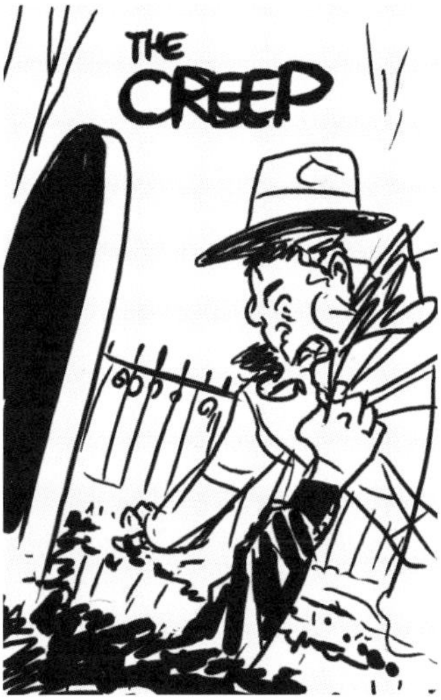
THE
CREEP

CASE: I thought I'd give our last issue the typical sleuthing guy and a dame cover, à la #3 here. I enjoyed drawing the phone conversations, and thought something incorporating that would be nice. It was time for something a little more active, though, so after many iterations, we settled on the grave take.

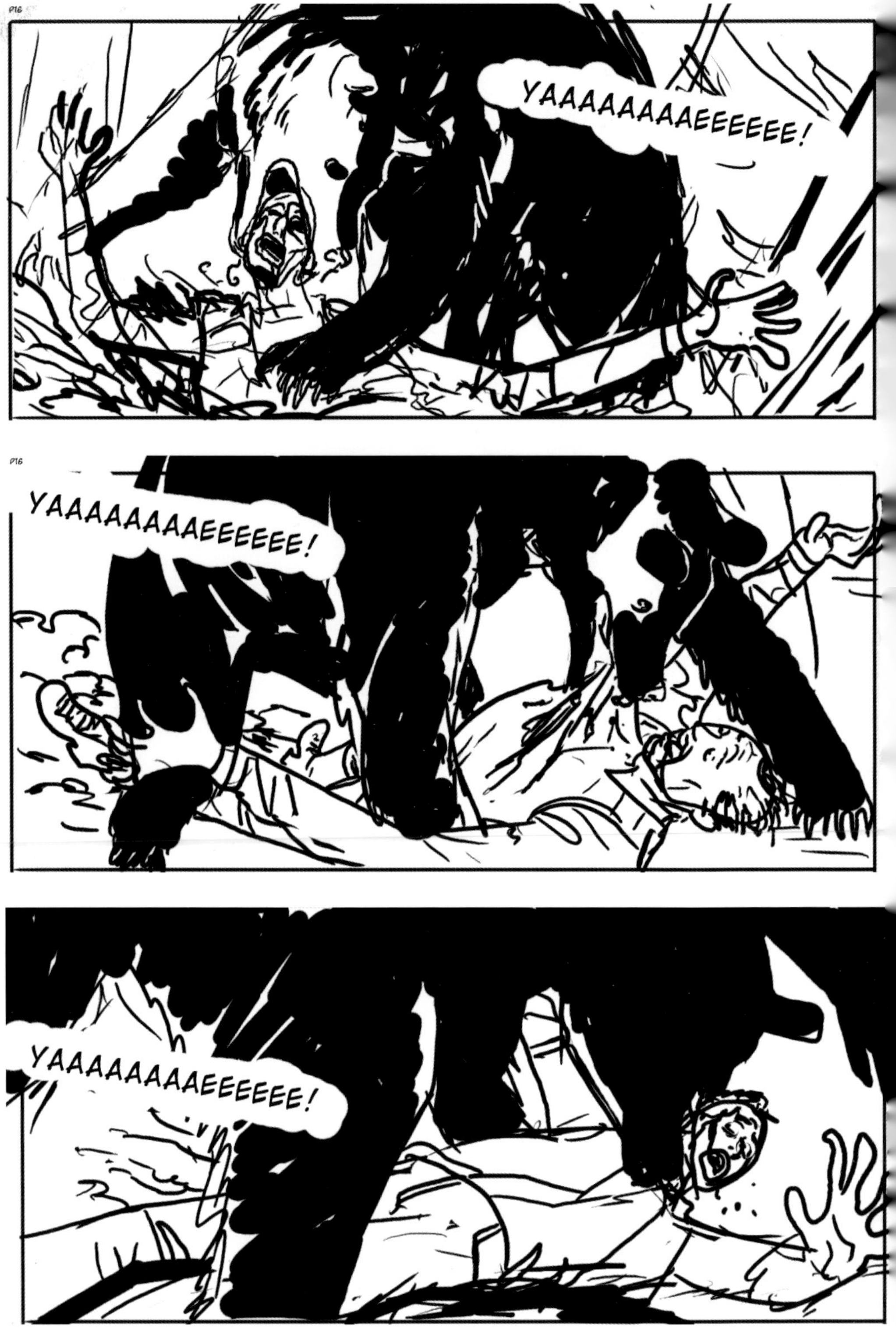
YAAAAAAAAEEEEEE!
YAAAAAAAAEEEEEE!
YAAAAAAAAEEEEEE!

CASE: How many ways can a guy get eaten by a bear? A lot, it turns out. I think we tried upwards of a dozen takes on this panel. Thank goodness for wisecracking studiomates at Periscope!

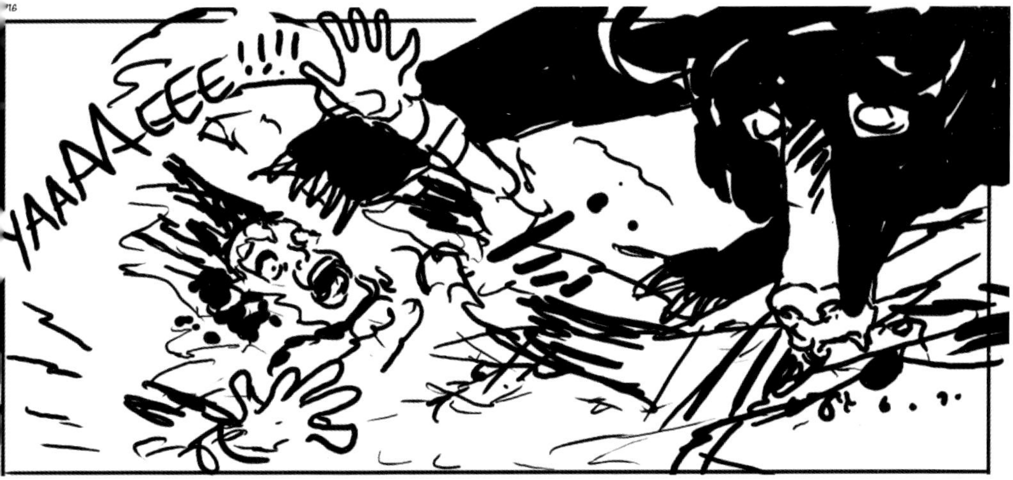
YAAAAEEE!!!!

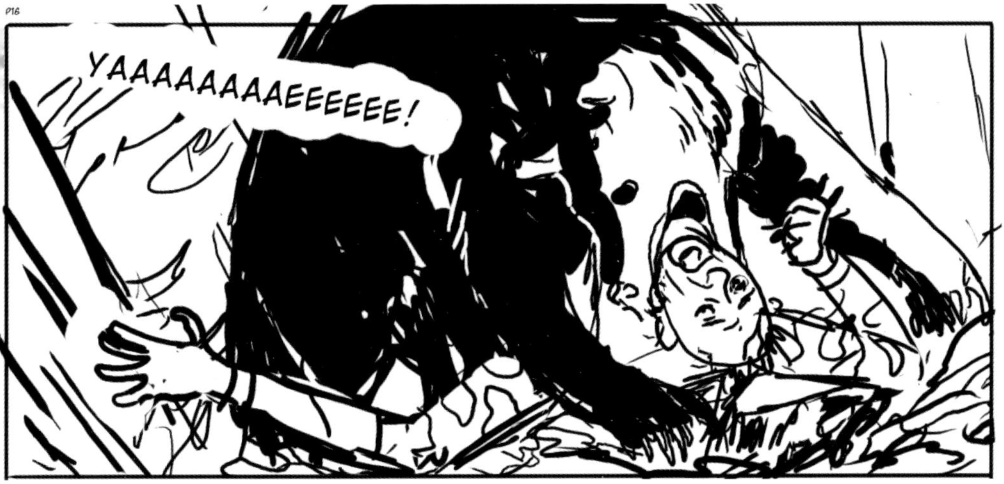
YAAAAAAAAAEEEEEE!

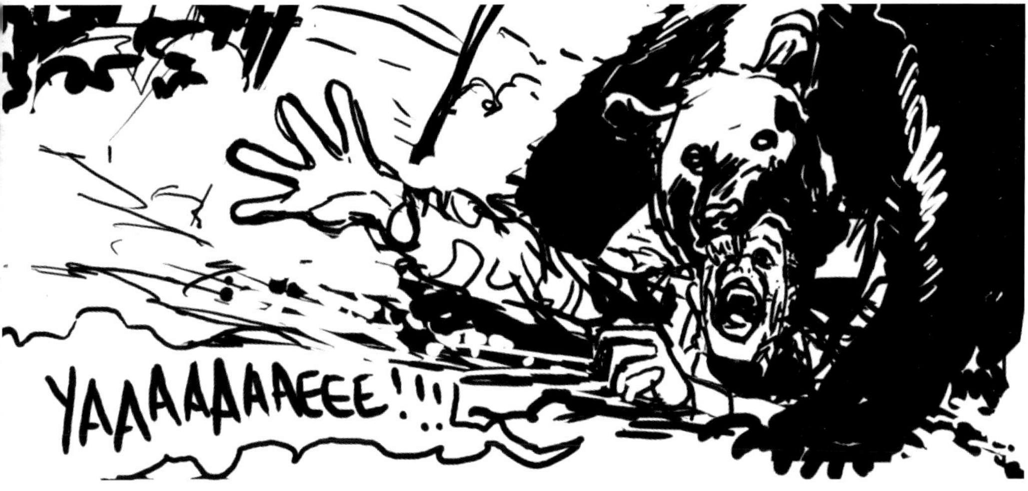
YAAAAAAAEEEE!!!

ARCUDI: I'm sure I drove Jonathan crazy with this scene. Sorry, JC.

ALSO BY JOHN ARCUDI AND JONATHAN CASE

THE COMPLETE MAJOR BUMMER SUPER SLACKTACULAR!
John Arcudi, Doug Mahnke

Lou Martin's just gained incredible superpowers! Too bad all he wants to do is stay firmly planted on the couch. But an alien got *Louis Martin*, slacker extraordinaire, and *Martin Lewis*, promising young lawyer, confused and sent an Extreme Enhancement Module to the wrong guy, and now Lou's got superheroes trying to get him to . . . *ugh* . . . *contribute to society*—and outlandish supervillains, monsters, and aliens are out to take him down!

$29.99 | 978-1-59582-534-6

B.P.R.D.: PLAGUE OF FROGS VOLUME 3
Mike Mignola, John Arcudi, Guy Davis, Dave Stewart

Following the Bureau's catastrophic encounter with the monster-god Katha-Hem, Kate heads to France with hopes of bringing Roger back to life, and Daimio reveals the truth about his death in the jungles of Bolivia. The coming frog apocalypse heats up as Abe meets a secret society of Victorian cyborgs with ties to his origins, and Liz's visions grow increasingly dire! From *Hollow Earth* to *King of Fear*—the entire war on frogs in four volumes!

$34.99 | 978-1-59582-860-6

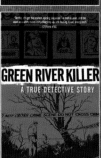

GREEN RIVER KILLER: A TRUE DETECTIVE STORY
Jeff Jensen, Jonathan Case

Throughout the 1980s, the highest priority of Seattle-area police was the apprehension of the Green River Killer, the man responsible for the murders of dozens of women. In 1990, with the body count numbering at least forty-eight, the case was put in the hands of a single detective, Tom Jensen. After twenty years, when the killer was finally captured with the help of DNA technology, Jensen spent 180 days interviewing Gary Leon Ridgway in an effort to learn his most closely held secrets—an epic confrontation with evil that proved as disturbing and surreal as can be imagined.

$24.99 | 978-1-59582-560-5

WITCHFINDER VOLUME 2: LOST AND GONE FOREVER
Mike Mignola, John Arcudi, John Severin, Dave Stewart

In the hellish frontiers of the American Wild West, nineteenth-century occult investigator Edward Grey finds himself caught in a showdown with an evil witch, bloodthirsty criminals, and zombie cowboys!

$17.99 | 978-1-59582-794-5

AVAILABLE AT YOUR LOCAL COMICS SHOP OR BOOKSTORE
To find a comics shop in your area, call 1-888-266-4226. For more information or to order direct, visit DarkHorse.com or call 1-800-862-0052 • Mon.–Fri. 9 a.m. to 5 p.m. Pacific Time. Prices and availability subject to change without notice.

Text and illustrations of *B.P.R.D.*™ and *Witchfinder*™ © Mike Mignola. *The Complete Major Bummer Super Slacktacular!* text, illustrations and logo are ™ and © John Arcudi and Doug Mahnke. "Captain Slackass," "Major Bummer," and all prominent characters and their distinctive likenesses are trademarks of John Arcudi and Doug Mahnke. Text and illustrations of *Green River Killer*™ © Jeff Jensen.